MONMOUTH COUNTY NEW JERSEY

~ DEEDS ~

Books A, B, C and D

Richard S. Hutchinson

HERITAGE BOOKS
2006

HERITAGE BOOKS
AN IMPRINT OF HERITAGE BOOKS, INC.

Books, CDs, and more—Worldwide

For our listing of thousands of titles see our website
at
www.HeritageBooks.com

Published 2006 by
HERITAGE BOOKS, INC.
Publishing Division
65 East Main Street
Westminster, Maryland 21157-5026

Copyright © 2000 Richard S. Hutchinson

Other books by the author:
Abstracts of the Council of Safety Minutes, State of New Jersey, 1777-1778
Burlington County, New Jersey Deed Abstracts: Books A, B and C
Middlesex County, New Jersey Deed Abstracts: Book 1
Abstracts of the Deaths and Marriages in the Hightstown Gazette, 18 April 1861-28 December 1871
Abstracts of the Deaths and Marriages in the Hightstown Gazette, 4 January 1872-27 December 1877
Abstracts of the Deaths and Marriages in the Hightstown Gazette, 3 January 1878-29 December 1881
Abstracts of the Deaths and Marriages in the Hightstown Gazette, 5 January 1882-31 December 1885
Abstracts of the Deaths and Marriages in the Hightstown Gazette, 7 January 1886-26 December 1889
The Mercer County Genealogical Quarterly, Volumes 1-6
CD: Mercer County Genealogical Quarterly [New Jersey], Volumes 1-6

All rights reserved. No part of this book may be reproduced or transmitted in any form or by any means, electronic or mechanical, including photocopying, recording or by any information storage and retrieval system without written permission from the author, except for the inclusion of brief quotations in a review.

International Standard Book Number: 0-7884-1479-8

Table of Contents

Introduction v

Book "A" (1669-c1680) 1

Book "B" (c1685-1690) 27

Book "C" (c1691-1696) 69

Book "D" (1697-1714) 103

Index 139

MONMOUTH COUNTY, NEW JERSEY
DEED ABSTRACTS - BOOK "A"

Monmouth County, New Jersey, one of the state's original counties, was formed in East Jersey in 1683. Some of the first settlers to this area came from Long Island and Barbados in the mid to late 1660s, while others originated from the New England colonies of Rhode Island and Massachusetts.

On the 7th of April in 1665, the second purchase of land was made from the Indians and is known as the Monmouth Patent. In it, twelve men were granted land in this new area that would become Monmouth County - William Goulding, Samuel Spicer, Richard Gibbons, Richard Stout, James Grover, John Boun [Bowne], John Tilton, Nathaniel Sylvester, William Reape, Walter Clarke, Nicholas Davis, and Obadiah Holmes. Many of the early settlers in this land were persecuted Quakers.

The present boundaries of the county place it in the east-central part of the state bounded on the northwest by present day Mercer County and Middlesex County, on the southwest by Burlington County, on the south by Ocean County, on the north by Raritan Bay, and on the east by the Atlantic Ocean. Its county seat is situated in the town of Freehold, New Jersey.

These abstracts were derived from the county clerk's copies of the recorded deeds maintained at the Monmouth County Court House, in Freehold, New Jersey.

MONMOUTH COUNTY DEEDS - BOOK "A"

The early deed books of Monmouth County, New Jersey, are made up of many types of recordings . They show the formation of the "government" in this new land while recording for us the names of those early settlers of this original county in New Jersey.

The records in deed Book "A" run from 1669 to ca. 1680, in Book "B" from ca. 1685 to 1690, in Book "C" from ca. 1691 to 1696, and in Book "D" from 1697-1714. Some of the early recordings are from the minutes and orders resulting from the first "Assembly". These records list the names of first inhabitants in these settlements and the number of lots they had purchased. They also deal with the day to day problems in the area that is today known as Middletown and Shrewsbury. These abstracts are from the recordings of the various "clerks" attending these meetings. They record appointments, elections, court cases, grand juries, and other items of interest. These early county deed books also recorded the day to day business dealings, land sales, marriages, notes, ear marks and many other types of records of the above communities. Eventually, these books were used primarily for the recording of deeds. The first names for the towns or sections in this area of Monmouth County, were known as and recorded, using the Native American names of Newasink, Narumsunk, and Pootapeck.

These early deed books reveal that many of the early inhabitants of Monmouth County, New Jersey came by boat from Long Island, New York and from the colonies of New England. Individuals doing research on families from these areas, but specifically from the state of Rhode Island, must look to the records in these early Monmouth County deed books. Many times, here in these books, they made and recorded their Rhode Island records.

MONMOUTH COUNTY DEED ABSTRACTS - BOOK "A"

[p 5]   "... inhabitants off Shrewsbury one Narumounk Neck ... Officers chosen by the inhabitants off Midltown ... [Richard Gibbins, Constable; Jonathan Holmes and Wm Lawrence, Overseers; Steven Arnold an James Ashton, Deputies. Henry Percy, Richard Richardson, and James Bowne.

Officers for Shrewsbury on Narumsunk - [Petter Parker, Constable; Christopher Alling, Edward Pattison, Eliakim Wardill, Barth° West; Overseers and Deputies.]

[p 6]   General Assembly ... "whereas certain Inhabittants off road Island or elsewhere have bin ingaged to have performed thare pt in the settl^{mt} off this land upon a day next, whareby thare former priviledges off free purchase with others is forfeited or last by thos neglect or remise dealings. It is hereby determined that all such persons aforsd which may happen to arrive hear between this and the next spring tide with intent to settell hear according to thare former grant ... The selling off strong

MONMOUTH COUNTY DEEDS - BOOK "A"

liquors to Indians is likewise by vertue off this act forbidden ... The admittance off townsmen is allowed soe far as to make up the Noumber off one hundred ... The money received for each township to remain in the seaver men's hands, viz: Wm Goulding, John Bowne, John Tilton, James Grover, Richard Stoutt, Samuel Spicer, Richard Gibbins ... Portland Poynt to bee reduced into ten pts, Divisions or Lotts ..."

Further Orders and / or Minutes

[p 13] APPRENTICESHIP OF MATHEW HOWARD

26 May 1669 - Henery Percy off Portland Point on Newasink Neck ... [and] ... Hester Howard ... for behalf of her son named Mathew Howard ... Hester doth ... agree with ... Henery Percy & Kathern his wife, that they ... from the day off the date hearoff take into thare ... custody the above named Mathew Howard aged seven years or thereabouts ... as a servant or apprentice for the ... tearm off fourteen years ... the above named Henery ... to teach & instruct hin the said Mathew in the ... trade off a blacksmith ... in case of mortalitie [and] Henery should die ... ye said Mathew is to be left in the custody ... Kathern Percy his wife ...; [Dated - 25 May 1669; Signed by Hester Howard; Attested to by John Tilton and R^d Richardson.]

[p 14] OATH OF OFFICE

26 May 1669 - I, underwriten ... promise ... to perform ye place & office off a constable ... in the towne of Shrewsbury ...; [Signed - Eliakim Wardell.]

The same ingadgment verbatum ... was subscribed to by James Ashton, constable off Midltowne ...; [Witness - Rd. Richardson.]

[p 14] 26 May 1669 - We underwriten doe hearby in our own behalf ... by order from Wm Goulding Pattentee give full power and liberty unto the rest of the Pattentees, Inhabitants of Midltown, to elect unto themselves three off the ablest & honestest Men to agitate and act with them as Pattentees ...; [Signed - John Tilton, Samuel Spicer; Attested to by Rd. Richardson.]

[p 15] 27th May - Order that Richard Richardson as recorder in general is to attend during the time of Court sitting ... [and to be paid 5 shillings] ... for one year from the day of date hereof.

[p 15] 27 May 1669 - Order - [that the Constable of Shrewsbury to notify inhabitants to meet & chose three to act as overseers and to go to the house of Richard Richardson and the constable is to report those] ... "found averse to ye peaceable settlement ..." Portland Point - 26 May 1669; by - John Tilton, Richard Stoutt, Samuel Spicer, Ja. Groves, Jo. Bowne, Rd. Gibbons, Edward Smith, Ja. Ashton, Jonathan Hulmes, Rd. Lipincot, Jo. Hance, James Bowne.

MONMOUTH COUNTY DEEDS - BOOK "A"

[Further Orders and / or Minutes]

[p 17] ZACHARY GANT to ARMIAS GANT

30 June 1669 - This deed ... I Zachary Gant off road Island have sould ...   my whole share off lands ... off that tract of wch Newasink in New Jersey is a part and off wch John Tilton off Gravesend & Walter Clarke of road Island are two of the Pattentees ... I have fully sould .. from or by me forever to my Brother Armias Gant ... off Saundisch ... [Sandwich] ...; [Dated - 10th of Mounth 1668; Witnesses - John Easton, Isaroll Gant.]

[The purchase of a share off land ... by Zachary Gant abovesaid was witnessed ... by Thomas Potter & Tho. Winterton; Proved - 30 June 1669; Rd Richardson.]

[p 18] JOHN THROCKMORTON, JUNIOR - POWER OF ATTORNEY

... I John Throckmorton, junior, off the towne of Midltown ... N. Jersey, doe hearby give full power ... and ordain my well beloved father Mr. John Throckmorton, of ye towne, off Providence in New England, my true & lawful attourney ... [of things] ... whatsoever wch shall be found to be in the hands off Richard Beeres off Watter town or in Judah Beeres, his   daughter, ... off my late deceased brother Freegiffte Throckmorton dying intestate ...; [Dated - 6 November 1669.]

[p 18] ... Jonathan Hullmes, son of Obidiah Hullmes off road Island ... Edward Smith, son to Mr. Edward Smith of road Island, being ... officers ... in the towne of Midletown; [Recorded - Rd Richardson.]

[p 19] 2 November 1669 - At a Court held ... at the house off Randall Huet ye elder on Portland Point - Present - James Ashton - Constable; Richard Stout, James Grover, W^{m}Bowne, James Bowne - Pattentees; Jonathan Hullmes, Edward Smith - Deputies.

Wm Bowne and James Bowne of ... Midltown on Newasink neck are appointed ... as Pattentees in the room of John Tilton & Samuel Spicer of Gravesand ... [per record of 26th May.]

[Further Orders and / or Minutes]

28 December 1669 - At a Court held a Portland Point - Present: John Bowne, James Grover, Richard Gibbins, Richard Stoutt, Wm Bowne, John Ruskman [Ruckman written above in pencil] - Pattenties; James Bowne, Jonathan Hullmes, Edward Smith, Richard Lipincott, Jahn Hance - Dep^{ties} & Overseers; James Ashton - Constable.

[p 20] Ordered ... granted unto John Hance off Shrewsbury ... two lotts ... near Cootapeck, and ... ye said John shall hould the said two lotts, for ... James Heard and Edward Wharton purchasseers ...

MONMOUTH COUNTY DEEDS - BOOK "A"

[Orders re: "Collonoll Richard Nichols, late Governor off New York..."; against the killing off unmark'd swine running wild or in ye woods ...]

[Further Orders and / or Minutes]

[p 22] JOHN JENKINS to GEORGE ALLEN

I, John Jenkins off the towne of Sandwich in ye collony off New Plymouth in New England widowed ... [for 12 pounds ?] ... paid by George Allen off ye towne off Sandwich in the colony afforesaid planter ... all my lands in ye county or colony off New Jersey ... containing one whole share ... bought off Willm Reap off Newport, upon Road Island, merchant, as may appear by a letter under the hand of Walter Clark off Newport upon Road Island, Clark for ye company off purchassess bearing date ... [17 November 1667] ..., and also by a receipt ... of Henery Bull of the same Island ... [dated 13 April 1665] ... which share ... [was purchased from the Indians] ... which lands listh in three necks ... called Newasink, Narumsink, & Pootapeck ... [Dated - 2 June 1670; Witnesses - Richard Handey, John Jening.]

[p 23] SAMUEL GOULD to GEORGE ALLEN

I, Samuel Gould off Newport on Road Island haveing half a share off land in ... New Jersey ... commonly called and Known by the Indian names off Newasink, Narumsunk, and Pootapeck ... [sold to] ... George Allen off Sandwich in the Colony of Plymouth in New England ...; [Dated - 14 April 1670; Witnesses - Wm Richardson, Walter Clark.]

[p 23] POWER OF ATTORNEY

I, Joshua Coggshell off Portsmouth on Road Island doe ... allow George Allen of Sandwich to ... dispose off my half share off land ... off New Jersey; [Dated 14 April 1670; Witnesses - Daniell Gould, Nicholas Easton, Junior.]

[p 24] 5 July 1670 - Court - Portland Point - Present - John Bowne, James Grover, James Bowne, Wm Goulding, Richard Gibbons, Richard Stoutt - Pattentees; John Hance, Eliakim Wardell, James Bowne - Dep^{ties}; Peter Tilton, William Shaddock, Eliakim Wardell & Richard Lippincott were established as overseers for the towne of Shrewsbury . " ...Willm Reap off road Island merchant being present ..."; [Reported - 4 May 1670 by John Willson towne deputy.]

[p 25] 15 February 1670 - [Notice of a meeting re: "Nominated Associates" at the house of James Grover's "at the mill".]

MONMOUTH COUNTY DEEDS - BOOK "A"

Nominated Associates - To Mr. Christopher Allmey, Eliakim Wardell, Jno Hance, Rd Lippincott, Wm Shaddock, Edward Pattison, Barth^o West, Nich^o Brown, Tho. Winterton.

"This Noat was directed to John Hance to communicate the contents ... [to the above persons] ... By Richard Hartshorne, John Bowne, Richard Gibins, Richard Stoutt"; [Attested to by Rd Richardson.]

[p 27] [The following are names found in a recorded "account of Disbursements of Wm Reape, dated 5 July 1670.]

- John Tilton
- To the sachim off ye gift land & to Randall Huet
- To a sloop hire ... upon a voyage wth the Pattentees to Pootapeck Neck
- To the charge of three men sent from road Island
- To the use of Dirrick Smith's sloope

Pattentees Signed - Will Goulding, James Grover, John Bowne, Richard Gibbins, Richard Stoutt [made his mark]. John Hance, Eliakim Wardell, James Bowne - Dp^s.; [Recorded by - Rd Richardson.]

[p 28] Newasink, Narumsunk, & Pootapeck is Dr. to the severall disburstments by James Grover, John Tillton, Wm Goulding & company [Below are listed some selected entries]:

- To Pappamora and his men at times in wine
- To severall men's wages for severall voyages made for the purchase off Newasink
- To recording the deed of sale in New York

[Below are listed some selected entries of "The account off the second Purchase"]:

- To expense on the Indians at New York
- To expense on them at Gravesend
- To our voyage in the purchase & marking out the 2 Necks Narumsunk & Pootapeck together with provisions ...
- To treat wht ye Jersey Governor
- To the Sachim
- To Christopher Alleny 50 gilders for himself & his boat at Narumsunk

[p 29] [Newasink, Narumsunk, & Pootapeck is Dr. to the severall disburstments by James Grover & company for the following persons]

Samuel Spicer, James Grover, Wm Goulding, Jno. Bowne, Richd Gibbons, Richd Stoutt, John Tillton, Nath^a Sillvester, Thomas Moor, John Cunklin, Walter Clarck, Petter Essin, Thomas Winterton, Richard Lippincott, Emmanuel Woolley, Wm Shaddock, Edwd Wharton, Richard Bordin, William

MONMOUTH COUNTY DEEDS - BOOK "A"

James, Robert Carr, Thomas Potter, George Webb, John Coggshell, William Coddington, Thomas Clifton, Henery Bull, Samuel Hollman, Nicholas Bowne, Richard Richardson, Christopher Allmy, Jonathan Hullmes, Jno. Clarke, Geo. Chutte, Mark Lucer, Obidiah Hullmes, Steven Arnold, Edward Smith, Nicholas Davis, Wm Shakerley, Roger Ellis & his son, Eliakim Wardell, Edward Tartt, Edward Pattisson, Barth° West, Robert West, John Horabin, James Bowne, John Willson, John Burkman, Thomas Cox, Edmund Laphitra, Francis Masters, Jno. Townsend, Henery Tippotts, Tobias Handson, John Hance, Zachary Gaunt, Francis Brindley, Ralph Gouldsmith, Walter Wall, Jno. Hall, Job. Allmey, Joseph Coleman, John Throckmorton, John Bowne of fl., Wm Bowne, Thomas Potter.

[p 30] [Newasink, Narumsunk, & Pootapeck is Dr. to the severall disburstments by Wm Reape for the following persons]

Edward Thurston, John Allen & Robert Taylor, Nathl Tomkins, Richard Lippincott, George Mount & Benjamin Bordin, Richard Bordin, John Jenkins, Daniell Gould, Joshua Coggshell, Richard Sissoll, John Wood, Gerard Bowne, Robert Story, William Shaddock, George Webb, Thomas Clifton, Robert Carr, Walter Clark.

[p 31] [... Debittor to William Reape as will particulary appear in folio 27 ... To John Tilton, James Grover, William Goulding & the rest of ye company as particulary appears in the 28th folio of this book ...]

[p 32] [1670 - By moneyes Payd to William Reape ... moneys Paid to John Tilton, James Grover & William Goulding & Company ... Examined off Shrewsbury & Middletown - [By John Hance, Eliakim Wardell, James Bowne - Debutye.]

[p 33] [A List off names of the names of the purchassers off Newasink, Narumsunk, & Pootapeck. The number behind each name indicates that number of shares each purchased.]
Samuel Spicer-1, James Grover-1, John Bowne-1, Richard Gibbons-1, Richard Stoutt-1, John Tilton-2, Nath^a Silvester-2, John Throckmorton-1, Walter Clarke-1, Peter Eassen-1, Tho. Winterton-1, Richard Lipencott-4, Emmanuel Woolley-1, Wm Shaddock-1, Edward Wharton-1, Richard Borden-3, Wm James-1, Robert Carr-1, Thomas Potter-1, George Webb-1, John Coggeshell-1, Wm Codington-1, Thomas Clifton-1, Henerey Bull-1, Samuel Holman-1, Nicholas Brown-1, Richard Richardson-1, Christopher Allmey-1, Jonathan Homes-1, John Cooke-1, Georg. Chute-1, Mark Lucor-1, Obadiah Hulmes-1, Steven Arnold-1, Edward Smith-1, Nich° Davis-2, Wm Shakerly-1, Roger Ellis & his son-2, Eliakim Wardell-1, Edward Tartt-1, Edward Pattison-1, Bartholomew West-1, Robert West-1, Thomas Whitlock-1, John Horabin-1, James Bowne-1, John Willson-1, John Ruskman [Ruckman written to the side]-1, John Townsend-1, Henery Tippites-1, Tobiah Handson-1, John Hance-1, Francis Brindley-1, Walter Wall-1, Job Allmey-1, Joseph Coleman-1, Wm Bowne-1, John Smith-1, Wm Reap-2, John Bown of fl.-1, Edward Thurston-1, Jno Allen-Rob't Taylor-1, Jno. Jenkins-1, Zachary Gant-1, Nathaniel Tonkins-1, Benjamin Speere-1, Joseph Beyer-1, Georg Mount-1, Ben Bordin-1, Richard Sissoll-1, Daniel Gould & Jos. Cogshell-1,

MONMOUTH COUNTY DEEDS - BOOK "A"

Gerard Bourne-1, Gideon Freeborne & Robert Hazard-1, Jno. Wood-1, Thomas Hart-1, Jno. Tomson-1, Edward Cole-1, Robert Story-2, Wm Gifford-1.

[p 34] [A List off names of the names of the purchassers off Newasink, Narumsunk, & Pootapeck. The number behind each name indicates that number of shares each purchased.]

James Leonard-1, Thomas Dungun-1, Jno. Hourdell-1, Marmaduke Ward-1, Richard Moor-1, Ralph Gouldsmith-1, James Ashton-1.

The Names of such who are entered as township men and the numbers of "townshippes" they had - Thomas Cox-1, Edmund Laphitra-1, Fra. Masters-1, John Hall-1, Bashan-1, James Grover, Junior-1, Richard Sadler-1, Daniell Estell-1, Wm Lawrence-1, Wm Cheesman-1, Anth^o Page-1, Wm Layton-1, Wm Goulding-1, John Stoutt-1, Henerey Percey-1, John Bird-1, Randall Huet Junr-1, Randall Huet Senr-1, Samuel Spicer-1, Barth^o Lippincott-1, Job Throckmorton-1.

[Page 35 Missing]

[p 36] 8 July 1670 - [List of names of Pattentees]

Wm. Bowne, Tho. Whittlock, John Willson, Jno. Ruskman, Walter Wall, Jno. Smith, Richard Richardson, Jno. Horabin, James Bowne, Janoathan Hulmes, Eliakim Wardell, Bartholomew West, Jno. Hance, James Ashton, Edward Pattison, Wm. Shaddock, Tho. Winterton, Edward Tartt, Benjamin Burden.

Those above named, were the abovesaid Pattentees have chossen to or selves to bee assosiates with us ... William Goulding, Rich. Gibbons, James Grover, John Bowne, Willia Reape, Richard Stoutt [made his mark]; [Attested to by Rd Richardson.]

[p 37] ["...the Noumber of associates whose names are inserted are not soe fuly completed...John Bowne, Will Goulding, James Grover, Rich Stoutt [made his mark], Richard Gibbins, Willia Reape ..."]

[Further Orders and / or Minutes]

[p 38] [8 July 1670 - That about Novoumber next the lotts of land remaining in common wanting of the full moumber of ... [118] ... are to bee layd out by James Grover ...]

[Further Orders and / or Minutes]

Ordered - That after debate concerning the two lotts of land at Pootapeck, in controversy between Wm Reape of road Island, Merchant & John Hance off the towne of Shrewsbury. It is hearby agreed upon by the major voat, that ... Wm Reape shall ... have the free possession off the ... lotts ... the

MONMOUTH COUNTY DEEDS - BOOK "A"

aforesaid Jno Hance hath not performed his promiss ... ye former order off court granted to ye afforesaid John Hance ...; [Dated - 28 December last.]

[Page 39 Out of Order]

[p 40] [15 May 1671 - At a meeting held the 15th ... Pattentees present ... John Bowne, Ja. Grover, Richard Stoutt, Richard Gibbins with the rest of the Inhabitants of Midltown & Shrowersbury ... Richard Richardson was appointed ... as Recorder for both townes ... Whareas Richard Lippincott & Nicholas Brown inhabittants of ... Shrewersbury ware formerly nominated for associates ... are likewise to bee addedd ..."]

[p 39] It was granted ... in July last 1670, that Margret Huet widdow relict off Randull the elder deceased, should have a part off the gift land ... formerly promised to him the late deceased Randall ... provided the said Margret shall redily contribute to ye cleering the same out of hands of ye Indians ...; [Witnessed - Rd. Richardson.]

[Minutes - Of a meeting of "sume Inhabbitants of Midltown & Shrewsbury May 15th 1672 at James Grover's houss ..."]

[Page 40 was Repeated]

[p 41] ROBERT STORY to JOHN JAY

16 May 1671 - Whearas ... Robert Story Merchant (formerly one of the purchassers, belonging to Newasink, Narumsunk & Pootapeck) ... [sold to] ... John Jay, planter, living ... in the Island of Barbadoes. And Whareas ... John Jay hath given full power ... unto John Burnyeatt and John Hance by vertue of a letter of Attorney ... [2 parts - (1) contains 6 acres; (2) contains about 45 acres] ... with all edifices and stock ...; [Witnesses - Rd. Richardson, James Bowne, John Horabin.]

[p 42] An Inventory of the cattell and other stock mentioned - [Two oxen, five cowes in all, ten cattell young & old; Foure Bredding sowes, In all twenty swine, young & old; One Breeding mare and other assorted items; Witnesses - John Buryeat, John Hance.]

[p 43] WILL OF RANDALL HUET THE ELDER

The Last Will and Testament of Randall Huet the elder of Portland Point in the province of New Jersey this 12th of January 1669 ... [mentions unnamed wife and children and gives half of land not yet layd out] ... to my wife and the other half I give unto my younger son Thomas] ... I give to my other two sons Randall and Joseph ... unto Ann Huet daughter to my son Randall ...; [Witnesses - James Bowne - Overseer, Henry Percey; Attested to Rd. Richardson.]

MONMOUTH COUNTY DEEDS - BOOK "A"

[p 44] WALTER CLARK to GEORGE ALLEN

[Record of Walter Clarck of Road Island ... to George Allen of Sandwicsh.]

12 January 1669 - I, Walter Clark of Newportt on Road Island ... [sold to] ... George Allen of Sandwich in the Collony of Plimouth in New England ... land ... in New Jersey, commonly called ... Newasink, Narumsunk & Pootapeck ...; [Witnesses - Robart Davis, Daniell Gould.]

[p 44] RANDALL HUET to DERICK TUNISON

[Record of Randall Huet ... to Derick Tunison - Octob 8th 1672.]

I Randall huet have sould unto Derick Tunison ... my house lott and houseing thereupon, containing eight accers ... on Portland Pt ... with two accers of meddow ... excepting sume certain fruit trees off apples and peaches ... In consideration wheareof the aforesaid Derick ... is to pay unto C'pher Allmy of Shrowersbury ... [5 pounds] ... as him the said Christopher shall except for accounts of him the said Randall ... at or before the 20 day of Octob next ...; [Witnesses - James Rylegh, Rd. Richardson.]

[p 45] THOMAS POTTER to EDWARD PATTERSON

[Record of Thomas Potter & Ann his waife ... unto Edward & Faith Pattisson this 8th of Octob. 1672.]

I Thomas Potter of Shrousbury have sould to Edward Pattisson of the same towne, my whole share off lands, except the mill lott ... In consideration whareof Edward Pattisson is to pay to Thomas Potter two cows, twenty bushells of Indian corn, seventeen shillings and six pence in pork and halfe a crown in silver ... Thomas Potter is to have use of the houses ... till Michael mass cume twelmunth and the said Thomas Potter is to deliver all his right and title of land in this purchase (only the Boards and door excepted) ...; [Witnesses - Thomas Winterton; Signed - Both Thomas and Ann Potter made their marks.]

Be it known ... Whereas, I Thomas Potter ... towne of Shrewersbury on Narumsunk Neck ... New Jersey did formerly make sale of one whole share of land excepting ... percells unto Edward Pattison late deceased ... [now sell above] ... unto Faith Patterson of the same towne abovesaid widdow (relict and executor unto him the above named Edward Patterson deceased ...; [Dated - 5 October 1672; Rd Richardson signum George Chute.]

[p 47] WILLIAM SHACKERLY to JOHN JAY

[Record of Wm Shackerly ... unto John Jay of Barbadoes ... 14 Octob. 1672.]

MONMOUTH COUNTY DEEDS - BOOK "A"

14 October 1672 - To all X' pian People ... I, William Shackerly of the Island of Barbadoes, marrine, ... [owned land ... called ... Newasank, Narumsunk & Pootapeck] ... [and sold for 3 pounds] ... paid by the Attourneys ... of John Jay of the aforesaid Island of Barbadoes planter (viz: John Hans and Peter Tillton who have acted herein in behalf of themselves and the rest) ... I have hearby unto set my hands ... at New York, the ... [26 September 1672] ...; [Witnesses - Peter Urys, John Clarcke.]

[p 48] **ROBART STORY to JOHN JAY**

[Record of Robart Story ... unto John Jay of Barbadoes ... 21 Octob. 1672.]

21 October 1672 - To all X'pian People ... I, Robart Story now resident in the Island afforesaid, merchant ... [sold for 60 pounds to ... John Jay of the Island aforesaid planter ... lands situate in the towne of Shrosbury ... County of New Jersey in New England ... [6 avcres including all buildings and stock] ... expressed in a list ... annexed ... [2 parcels of land with one being 40 or 50 acres] ... in the occupation of one Thomas Wright ...; [Dated - 18 March 1670; Witnesses - William Fuller, Rich Poore.]

[Barbadoes, 16 April 1672 - Richard Poor personally appeared before Chr. Codington re: the above deed; Recorded - 17 April 1672 by Richard Lake, Deputy Secretary.]

[Schedule or Inventory was annexed.]

[p 51] **WILLIAM ROGERS to WILLIAM SHADDOCK**

26 November 1672 - This showeth to home it may concern that I William Rogers have sould to William Shaddock my halfe share of land at Newasink ... 7th of March 1667; [Testis Rd. Richardson.]

[p 51] **ROBART CARR to GYLES SLOCUME**

[Record of Robart Carr of road Island ... unto Gyles Slocume of the same Island Novemb. 26th 1672.]

Be it known ... I Robart Carr of Newport on Rhoad Island in the Collony of Rhode Island ... New England ... lawfully purchased ... a whole & full share of land ... commonly called Newasunk ... Potapeck together with the sachims gift in New Jersey in Ammerica. Now ... [sell unto] ... Gyles Slocum of Portsmouth ... Rhode Island ...; [Dated - 23 May 1667; Witnesses - Samuel Hubard, Robert Taylor, Robart Williams; Signed - Robartt Carr.]

To wch said deed these lines were anexed. I have given to my son John Slocum my whole share of land above mentioned in the Deed; Witness my hand I say and his wife and there aires forever; [Signed - Gyles Slocum, Senior.]

MONMOUTH COUNTY DEEDS - BOOK "A"

[p 52] NICHOLAS DAVIS to THOMAS POTTER

[Record of Nicholas Davis his Deed to Thomas Potter for two shares of land November 27, 1672.]

I Nicholas Davis of road Isand Merchant doe acknowledge to have ... [sold to] ... Thomas Potter of Shrossbury or Potapeck ... two shares of land and meadow ... [26 December 1672] ...; [Witnesses - Thomas Taylor, Thurlagh Swyny.]

[p 53] KATHERN PERCY to CHRISTOPHER ALLMEY

[Record of Kathern Percy ... unto Christopher Allmy - 3 February 1672.]

To all X'pian people ... I Cathern Percy, widow, ... [sold unto] ... Mr. X'pher Allmey ... towne of Shrosbury ... province of New Jersey ... land ... in ... limits of Midltown or Portland point ... province of New Jersey ... [included land, buildings, and stock] ... I, the above named Kathern Percy of Portland point in the towne of Midletowne ... [sell for 30 pounds] ...; [Dated - 7 January 1672; Witnesses - James Bowne, Rd Richardson; Signed - Cathern Percy.]

[Inventory of the stock included "hoggs, Cattell & horss. The following are selected items from the inventory.]

Three Sowes, One Sow Shoat, One Barrow Shoat, One Boar ... Of Cow Kind four head of Cattell to bee divided between the said Kathern & Bernard Smith in halves ...; [Signed - Cathern Percy.]

[p 55] RANDALL HUETT to WILLIAM SMITH

[Record of Randall Huett his Deed of Gift to William Smith, Cooper recorded 10 February 1672.]

I Randall Huitt of Portland point ... Midltown ... promise ... to ... sett over unto William Smith Cooper of the same place ... halfe share of land lying in the same towne ... In consideration of which the said Wm Smith doth hearby ingadge to build a dwelling houss on the said land ... and to settle himself thareon, neare adjacent to the dwelling houss of the afforesaid Randall as a naighbour and in case the said Willliam Shall see cause to remove in 6time to cume, the said William is to make tender thareof ...; [Dated - 18 January 1672; Witnesses - Rd Richardson, Barnard Smith; Signed - Randall Huett, William Smith.]

[p 56] SAMUEL BORDIN to LEWIS MATTIX

[Record of Samuell Bordin of Portsmouth on rhoad Island, his Agreement with Lewis Mattix recorded 10 February 1672.]

MONMOUTH COUNTY DEEDS - BOOK "A"

Sam. Bordin of Portsmouth ... [sold unto] ... Lewis Mattis of the said Portsmouth ... That the sd. Samuel being the true owner ... of a share of land lying ... near New York in the necks of land called Newasink, Narumsunk & Potapeck ... [First] ... It is agreed that ... Lewis Mattix shall ... before the first of Apprill next ... remove himself & gor unto the said tract of land and shall thare take upp into his possession & allsoe settle ... so that ... Samuel Bordin may not cume to any damage ... for want of ... the said Lewis Mattix not settling and possessing the same ... [there are ten items of agreement where by they agree to do various things under] ... "a penall sume of forty pounds sterling each to other ...; [Dated - 12 February 1667; Witnesses - John Sanfford, Wm Smyton; Signed - Samuell Bordin, Lewis Mattix; Mattix made his mark when signing.]

[p 58] LEWIS MATTIX to SAMUEL BORDIN

Record of Lewis Mattix his acquittance to Samuel Bordin for the cow expressed in ye agreement ... This is to certify that Lewis Mattix doe acquitt and discharge Samuel Bordin from the within mentioned cow; [Dated - 7 August 1671; Witnesses - Peter Parker, John Hance; Mattix made his mark when signing.]

[p 58] LEWIS MATTIX to DERICK TUNMISON

[Record of the above Assignment ... by Lewis Mattix unto Derick Tunmison.]

I, Lewis Mattix, doe hearby ... set over all my right ... to mine the within mentioned fourth part of a share of land expres'd in this deed ... from Samuel Bordin of Rhoad Island ... [sett over] ... unto Derrick Timisson; [Dated - 7 February 1672; Witnesses - Rd Richardson, Wm Smith; Lewis Mattix made his mark when signing.]

[p 59] RANDALL HUETT to CHARLES HAYNES

[The agreement made and concluded on between Randall Huett ... and Charles Haynes ...]

The same Randall hath sould unto Charles Haynes one third of a certain boat or sloope, now in the possession of the sd. Randall, with one third of ye rigging cable, anchor & appertenunces to ye same boat ... for him ye sd. Charles ... to take into his possession ... the proffitts arrissing of wt is produced, of the the sloopes imployment is to bee shared & divided into three parts of wch ... Randall is to be ... [2/3rds and Charles the other 1/3rd] ... if he refuses the same Charles hath his liberty to ... [sell & pay Randall 17 pounds and 5 shillings] ... in goods or rate of goods at New Orrainia ...; [Dated - 12 April 1674; Witnesses - Rd Richardson, John Horabin; Signed - Randall huit, Charles haynes.]

MONMOUTH COUNTY DEEDS - BOOK "A"

[p 60] JURRATT BOURNE to CHRISTOPHER ALLMEY

[Record of Jurratt Bourne of Road Island ... to Christopher Allmey of Shrowsbury recorded 25 November 1674.]

2 November 1670 - I Jarratt Bourne of Portland Pt on Rhoad Island ... [sold for 10 pounds, 10 shillings] ... to Christopher Allmey of New Jersey ... [3/4 of a share of land at Newasink, Narumsunk, and Potapeck] ...; [Witnesses - Thomas Warte, Richard Bailey; Signed - Jarrad Bourne.]

[p 61] THOMAS MOORE to CHRISTOPHER ALLMEY

[Thomas Moore to Christopher Allmey Rec. 16 February 1674.]

I, Thomas Moore of Southhould, Senior, on Long Island ... sould ... to Chistopher Allmey, of Shrowsbury in New Jersey ... in a parcell of land ... commonly call Newasink, Narumsunk, and Pottapeck, and the other adjacent lands ... as to the Indians title of those lands, I being one of the first purchassers of the said lands ...; [Dated - 24 August 1674; Witnesses - Nathaniel Coddington, Anthony Walters.]

[p 61] CHRISTOPHER ALLMEY to JACOB COALE

[Christopher Allmey ... to Jacob Coale - 16 February 1674.]

I, Christopher Allmey of the towne of Shrowsbury ... New Jersey ... [sold to] ... Jacob Coale ... one share of land within the bounds of Potapeck or westward part of Narwasacum River, being a share of land wch I ... did buy of Thomas Moore, of South hould, Long Island ...; [Dated - 13 February 1674; Witnesses - Rd Richardson, Joseph Parker; Signed - Christph^r Allmey.]

[p 62] CHRISTOPHER ALLMEY to JOSEPH PARKER

[Christopher Allmey sold to Joseph Parker recorded 19 February 1674.]

I Chrstopher Allmey of Shrosbury ... [for 30 pounds sold] ... to Joseph Parker, of the towne ... [3/4 of a share of land] ... lying ... at Newasink, Narumsunk, & Potapeck ...; [Dated - 13 February 1674; Witnesses - Rd Richardson, Jacob Coale.]

[p 62] PETER TILLTON to ABRAHAM BROWNE

[Peter Tillton to Abraham Browne recorded 3 July 1675.]

MONMOUTH COUNTY DEEDS - BOOK "A"

I, Peter Tillton of the towne of Shrosbury in New Jersey ... [sold a purchassed share of land] ... to Abraham Browne of the same towne ... [for 25 pouinds] ... lying at Potapeck ...; Dated - 19 August 1670; Witnesses - Peter Parker, Sarah Parker; Signed - Peter Tillton.]

[Page 63 Missing]

[p 64] "Court of Sessions to be held in the Countie of Midltowne ... Sillence commanded ... call for the plantife, thus A.B. cume forth & preosecute they action against C.D. ... Court's proceeding & according to ye custome & manner of N.Y. govem't ... Richard Sadler of Midltowne appointed Cryer & County Marshall for the present year 1676 ..."

[p 65] "The place appointed for handling this court to be at Shrosbury at Fra. Bordin's house ... Richard Sadler swore & apointed County Marshall; [Dated - 21 August 1676.]

[They then established and put forth the form of an oath for a Jurate & Cryer or County Marshall, the form of oath for Clerk of Sessions, and the form of oath for a Witness.]

[p 66] 6 September 1676 - At a Court of Sessions held at Shrosbury ... Countie of Midltown ... Phillip Carterett Esq' Governor in the province of N. Jersey, Presentt - Mr. John Bowne, Mr. James Grover, Mr. Joseph Parker - Justices of ye Peace & Comm.

The Names of the Jury appointed, sworn & impaneled - Mr. James Ashton, John Willson, James Bowne, Thomas Cox, James Dorsett, John Stoutt - of Midltowne.

George Chute, George Hulett, Randall Huett, thomas Barnes, Thos Aplgate Senr, Henerey Sier - of Shrosby.

COURT ORDERS

Edmund Laphetra Pl'fe & Francis Masters def't ...

[p 67] At a Court of Sessions held at Shrosbury ... [7 September 1676] ... Henery Leonard pl. & Richard Sadler def't ...

Edmund Laphetra is action against Francis Masters ...

[They then established the form of a Verdict to be read in Court.]

MONMOUTH COUNTY DEEDS - BOOK "A"

" ... Thorlogh Swiney and Mary his wife upon a breach of the law for fornication before marriadge, as hath bin formerly evident, for the wch hee is fined ... [20 shillings] ... and his wife ... [20 shillings] ..., the one halfe to the Court & the other halfe to the towne.

COURT ORDER

[p 68] Record of an Atacthment for Thomas Applgate Senior November 20th 1676 ... To the Constable, ... to command you, to attach the cattell of Major John Fonicker, wch is in the hands of Thomas Applgate, Senior; [Dated - 29 October 1676; Signed - James Grover.]

To the Constable, ... to attach the estate of Nich° Davis in the hands of Thomas Potter to answer Edmund Gibbon by Richard Hartshorne his Attorney, in an action of debt, of ... [18 pounds] ... Midltowne; [Dated - 12 September 1676.]

[p 69] 21 November 1676 - Nathaniel Lippitt, plaintiff against Christopher Allmey def't in an action of the cass for breach of contract ... The names of the Jurymen impounded the day & year aboves'd - Mr Peter Parker, foreman, Jonathan Hulmes, Edmund Laphetra, Thomas Aplgate, Senr, Thomas Barnes, John Havens, George Mount, John Smith, Thomas Cox, James Dorsett, Richard Stout, John Stoutt.

[p 69] At a Court held in Midltowne ... [21 November 1676] ... Phillip Carteret, esq^r Governor - Present - Capt John Bowne, Mr James Grover, Mr Joseph Parker - Justices.

[p 70] The Verdict of the Jury ... between Mathaniel Lipitt plaint'f & Christopher Allmey defendant ... [Verdict was rendered].

[p 71] Upon the complanit of Richard Sadler Constable ... against Christopher Allmey for contemptuous demeanor towards him ... for detaining of certain writts ... by Mr James Grover & Joseph Parker, Justices.

Upon the County Marshall, his information ... of lawfull warning to Joseph Huitt, James Percey, & Derrick Tunnison ... [fined in contempt for not appearing].

[p 72] A Coppey of Att^{ch} Thomas Potter of Midtowne ... [9 October 1676].

"... to attach in the hands of Thomas Potter, of Shrosbury, all ye goods ... that hee ... hath in his hands of Nicholas Davis deceased ... for the payment of a debt dew from him the sd. Nicholas Davis unto

MONMOUTH COUNTY DEEDS - BOOK "A"

Mr. Samuel Shrimpton of Boston, Merch[t] for ... [the sum of 34 pounds, 18 shillings & a penny] ... By mee John Bowne to the County Marshall of Newasink".

Returned executed the 10th of Octob. 1676.

[p 72] Fra. Masters his action ag[t] Edmund Laphetra March 21st 1676.

[This was for a debt of 12 pounds, 12 shillings which was withdrawn before the Court's sitting.]

[p 72] March 13th 1676 - Christopher Allmey Plaintife Against Francis Masters deft.

[This was "an action of the case of Slander & Defamacon ..."]

[p 73] At a Countey Court of Sessions ... [27 & 28 March 1677] ... at Midltowne - Present - Mr John Bowne, James Grover, Joseph Parker - Justices.

The Jury impanelled ... Upon a full hearing of the business ... between Christop[r] Allmey plt & Francis Le Master def't.

In an action of Slander and defamation ... The action commenst by Francis Le Mester plaintif & Edmund Laphetra deft withdrawn ...

Thomas Applgate Plaintife ... called in Court but not appearing ... hee was nonsuited ...

Upon a full hearing of the business depending between Richard Hartshorne Att° of Edmund Gibbon & Mr. Samuel Moore, of Woodbridge in the behalfe of Mr. Samuel Shrimpton of Boston, Merch[t] concerning a debt dew from ye estate of Nich° Davis deceased to the said Edmund ... [and to] ... the said Mr. Shrimpton ... that what estate is to bee found in the hands of Thomas Potter of Shrosbury ...

[p 74] The oath of a Constable
Whearas you A. B. are chossen by to bee constable ... [the rest of the oath written but no identification given for A. B.].

[p 75] Thomas Huitt of Shrosbury sworne Constable ... [28 March 1677].

Actions entered against the next insueing Court to bee held ... [4 September 1677].

[p 75] 25 August 1677 - Thomas Applgate ye elder against John Fenwicke esq defend't ... Bartholomew and Thos. Applgate plaintifes in an action ... against the Inhabittants of the towne of Shrosbury deft ...

MONMOUTH COUNTY DEEDS - BOOK "A"

[p 75] 26 August 1677 - Nicholas Browne plaintife against Christopher Allmey deft ...

[p 76] Francis Le Mester, Plaintife against Edmund Lafetra, Defendant ... Whearas, hee the plaintife havening lodged the defend't one yeare in his house & washed his clothes and look't after his cattell ...

An Attachment

[p 76] To the Countie Marshall ... upon sight hereof ... to atach the cattell of John Fenwicke of New Sallem ... New Jersey ... being one paire of oxen ... & one black cow & calfe now running in the woodes near Shrosbury ... to answer Walter Woolley of the City of New Yorke ... or by his Attorney Richard Hartshorne in an action of debt of ... [20 pounds] ...; [Dated - 24 August 1677; by me John Bowne.]

This Attachment is served ... Richard Sadler.

Sumondes

[p 77] Midltowne August 16th 1677

To the Marshall of Midltowne ... require you to warne Benjamin Denall & Thomas Wright to appear at the Court held at Shrosbury ... to give thare evidence in the case ... betwixt Thomas Applgate Senior & the towne of Shrosbury - by mee John Bowne.

To the County Marshall ... require you to sumondes Thomas Cox ... at the next Court of Sessions ... for the County of the New sandes ... to give evidence, in a case ... between Thomas Applgate & Bartholomew Applgate & the inhabitants of the towne of Shrosbury ...; Dated - 25 August 1677; Signed - James Grover.]

[p 77] The names of the jurymen - James Ashton, Jo. Throckmorton, Jo. Stoutt, Randall Huitt, Richard Stoutt, George Bruiss, George Mount, John Smith, James Dorsett, Jonathan Hulmes, James Grover, Samuel Hutton, William Layton, Joseph Huitt.

Count Orders - 4 September 1677

[p 78] Present - Capt John Bowne, Mr. James Grover, Mr. Joseph Parker - Justices.

Orders - [Bartholomew & Thomas Applegate were "nonsuited" because of the failure of Bartholomew to appear before the Court. Also, "Thomas Applgate's ye elder attachment " was nonsuited as it was not legally executed against John Fenwickes Esqr. Thomas Applgate was allowed to reinstitute his suit against the inhabitants of Shrewsbury.]

MONMOUTH COUNTY DEEDS - BOOK "A"

[Action involving Richard Hartshorne was nonsuited.]

[p 79] Att a Court of Sessions held at Shrosbury ... Ordered ... between Nicholas Browne, plaintife & Christopher Allmey, deft ... [Allmey did not appear as required].

The Attachment served upon ye cattell of John Fenwickes esq^r ... for Walter Woolley of N Yorke is approved as legall & to to (sic) stand in full force untill ... further order upon request of Richard Hartshorne Att° ...

Ordered - ... between Francis Le Mester pltf and Edmund Lafetra deft ... Whareas it appears that thare is a certaine sum of money dew by bill unto Edmond Gibbon from ye estate of Nich° Davis deceased ... [which can be paid to Gibbon] by his lawful substitute at money priss ...

Tobacco at 2^d 1/2^d lb
Beefe at 30^s p. barrell
Butter at 5^d p = lb
Pork att 48^s = p = lb

... that ye said severall Specias as is here inserted is to bee prized according to ye present ... valluation, viz:

Pork at 3^{lb} p. barrill
Beefe att 40^s p barrill
butter att 6^d p lb
tobacco at 3^d p lb

Which is to be the prise for the payment of such debtes ... in th ehandes of any person ... being found to be of ye estate of Nicholas Davis, deceased dew to Mr. Shrimpton of Boston, Edmund Gibbon or others ...

[p 81] **ARREST WARRANT FOR X'PHER ALLMEY**

18 March 1677 - A Copy of ye wartt of arrest of X'pher Allmey; Whereas, I am informed that Christopher Allmey of the towne of Shrosbury in the County of Newasink hath unlawfully seized into his hands & converted to his own use a certain wrack o fsea being a vessel loaden with logwood & other comodities without giving accounpt thareod according to Law.

To the Marshall of ye County aforesaid or his lawful Deputy - These are therefore in his m^{ties} name to wills & require you on sight thereof to arrest ye body of the said Christopher Allmey & him safely keep in ye costody or convoy to the common geole there to bee held till he hath put in goo securitie to answer the action of William Sandford Att° for our Soveraign Lord ye King in an action upon the

MONMOUTH COUNTY DEEDS - BOOK "A"

Cass at the next Court to be houlden for the Countey aforesaid of five hundred pounds sterling & to stand the judgment of the said Courtt, hereof faile not at yor pirill, Given under my hands & seals at Elizabeth towne in the province afournamed, the 2^d day, of March An^o Dom 1677. [Signed - Ph. Carterett.]

[p 82] ACTIONS OF THE COURT OF MIDLETOWNE

18 March 1677 - Actions entered against this next insueing Court at Midletowne.

Philip Caterett Esqr Govener in the behalfe of Sr George Carterett lord proprietor of this province by Wm Sanford Attourney generall ... complainett ag't Christopher Allmey defendent in an action of the cass, damages, one hundred p^d sterling.

"... William Sandford Attourney plaintife Christopher Allmey def't ... pledges, ... [150 pounds] ... Sterling ... William Sandford in behalfe of ... the King plaintife & Christopher Allmey def't ... pledges Damag ... [500 pounds] ... Sterling.

[p 83] DECLARATIONS

Declaring that ye said Christopher Allmey contrary to law, seized upon, taken away, into his own possession & converted to his owne use, several wracks of Sea, viz: whale fishes wch being a Royaltie belonging to ye said Lord proprietor ... sayeth that, by the said illegal pledges ye said lord proprietor is damnified ... [100 pounds] ... for wch hee brings his actions ...

Declaring that hee the said Christopher Allmey did sumetime in August A^o 1673 seiz upon, take into his possession, and convert ... a certaine wrack of sea being a vessell loaden with logwood ...

[p 84] Declaring against ye said Allmey that hee hath made severall voyages to sea, & transported to other Collonies in a certaine vessell severell goods & comodities out of this province without a legall entery ... And notwithstanding the said vessell was arested in order to, atrail & not aqquited nor the seizure removed, but remaind till a fulll & due prosecution might bee made, the said Allmey having ingadged himself to bring the said vessell to Eliz^h towns, in order to a triall, hee ... not regarding his owne promise nor his M^{ties} lawes, went sondry voyages with the said vessell ... without paying ... also, a comdemnation of the said sloope, or vessell, accoring to law ...

[p 85] 18 February 1677 - [Allmey's arrest order was repeated in reference to his "departing with his slope loaden wth tobacco & other goods out of the port of Shrosbury aforesaid to road Island" and for his seizure & taking away certain wrakes & whale fishes, lying upon the shoar ...; Signed - John Bowne, William Pardon - Justices.]

MONMOUTH COUNTY DEEDS - BOOK "A"

[p 86] 21 March 1677 - Benjamin Devall his action and Declaration aginst John Whitlock.

Benjamin Devall plaintife against def't in an action of the cass & is for suspition of fellony declaring, that upon ye 20th day of this instant mounth, ye plaintife coming from his farme, goeing along the popler field by his owne fence, he saw two oxen eating without ye plaintifes sd. fence & going as ye place found the ye oxen was eating wheat in the straw, and then going to his stacke of wheat, found that thar had been wheat puled out thareof, then going homeward fetches John Stout & Jacob Brenewax to see the oxen eating of wheat, ... wch prooved to bee a paire of oxen in ye possession of William & John Whittlock, as ye plaintife can make appear, the said John Cuming & taking them away privately & unknowne to ye plaintife ...

23 March 1677 - James Grover senior, against ye estate of John Horabin, in an action of ye cass for debt & damage, of thirty pounds.

[p 87] Isack Cong Att° of Henerey Green plt agt Mary Barnes widow deft in an action of detinue for detaining of a cow calfe for the space of a year upwards for wch hee brings his action ...

A bill of costs drwan up in Court ... [March 28th] ... concerning whale fish Capt. Wm Sanford ... [4 pounds, 11 shillings,] ...

Also a bill of cost for the Marshall or his order to recover from John Champnis & others of 24 Shillings. This bill to Joseph Parker.

Allso, a bill of cost from Isack Conge, At° of H: Green of 23^s & is for court charge upon a nonsuit ...

Together with order ... to ye Marshall Richard Sadler to demand ... being for former Court Charges:

[Listed various court charges collected from X'pher Allmey March Court; Nich° Davis estat in ye hands of Eliakim Wardell; Francis Le Master; Thomas Applgate; Edmund Lafetra, Nich° Brown^e .]

[p 88] 28 March 1678 - A bill of cost was exhibits to this Court by Mr. Pardon in Mr Allmey's business of ... [7 pounds, 6 shillings] ... allowed thareon by order of Court, to Mr. Pardon againie.

[Repeated Orders re; Christopher Allmey & Isack Cong.]

Francis Jeferies an inhabitant of the Countie of Newasink, makes his declaration ... that hee ye pl'ff cuming from ye whale cast up, & having sume whale bone, Isack Bennet, Thomas Hers, John Chamness & Samuel White, tooke sume whale bone from ye sd. Francis whareby ye sd. plaintife pleaded damage by way of trespass to ye vallew of six pence ...

MONMOUTH COUNTY DEEDS - BOOK "A"

[p 89] 28 March 1678 - Midltowne

We whose names are underwritten having seriously ... considered ye matter ... [against Christopher Allmey] ... find according to evidence & ye best understanding in ye law ye defend't Allmey not guilty. March ye 26 the juries veredict for whale fish ... [Signed - James Ashton, Robert Hamblton, Henery Marsh, Willm White, Joseph Grover, Joseph Huitt, Thomas Cox, Richard Stout Senr, George Mount, James Dorsett, John Stout, Charles Eccles.]

[p 90] 3^d September 1678 - At a Court of Sessions held at Shrosbury

James Grover ye elder ... against John Horabin ... James Grover ... against Tho Applgate ... for debt ... withdrawn ... James Grover Senr ag't Daniell Applgate ... for debt ... withdrawn ... James Grover Senr ag't Randall Huitt ... for debt ... withdrawn ... James Grover Senr ag't Samuel Willcot ... for debt ... withdrawn ...

John Crawford of Midltowne is summoned ... to this Court, for disorders late past in his houses, notwithstanding warning given him by ye Constable John Jobes for selling drinks, whareby such disorders was begun ...

It is ordered that upon William Lawrence of ye towne of Midltowne his refusal of being invested into ye ofice & place of a Constable ... [after being voted for] ... that for such his refusal he is amenced by this Court to pay ... [5 pounds] ...

[p 91] 3 September 1678 - At a Court of Sessions held at Shrosbury at Francis Bodin's house.

Present - Capt. John Bowne, Leiut James Grover, Mr. Joseph Parker - Majestrates; Mr. Richard Gibbons and Mr. Jonathan Hulmes - Assistance.

[The following members of the jury were chosen - Peter Parker-Foreman, Thomas Cox, Richard Stout ye eld^r, James Grover Junior, John Stout, James Dorsett, Job Throckmorton, George Hulett, Nich^o Brown, Edmund Lafetra, John Worthley, Thomas Huit.]

The jury going forth upon the business between James Grover S^r ... & John Horabin ... the Verdict was ... Wee jurors doe find for ye, plaintife the goods of John Horabin, wch ye Marshall did attach in ye behalfe of James Grover ... [listing of certain items]; Dated - 4 September 1678 - Peter Parker, foreman.

[Juries verdict - plaintife James Grover is to "be possessed of what is found to bee ye proper estate of John Horabin.]

MONMOUTH COUNTY DEEDS - BOOK "A"

[p 92] Samuel Leonard, swore & appointed County Marshall ... Job Throckmorton, swore & appointed Constable of Midltowne.

18 March 1678 - Samuel Hutton plaintife against Samuell Cullver def' in an action of trespass for driving away his the said plaintife's boar away from waycake or thereabouts & leting him run at liberty ...

19 March - Thomas Snasself, By Richard Hartshorne In an action of debt - Isack Benett Deft Withdrawn.

Thomas Snowsell by Richard Hartshorne his Attorney is plaintife against Derick Tunisson ... for debt ...

[The Benett action was repeated.]

Walter Wall plaintife against John Crawford ... tresspass ...

[p 93] 26th & 27th March 1679 - At a Court of Sessions held at Midltowne at ye house of John Crawford ...

Capt. John Bowne and Mr. Joseph Parker - Majestriats or Justice of ye Peace; Mr. Richard Gibbons and Mr. Jonathan Homes - Assisstants.

[The following were named to the jury - John Havens, John Throckmorton, Richard Stoutt, Nicholas Brown, Edmund Lafetra, Peter Parker, James Ashton - Foreman, Thomas Cox, James Dorsett, Joseph Grover, John Smith, John Worthley.]

[p 93] 26th March - [Cases named were: ye busines of Samuell huton against Samuell Cullver; Thomas Snowsell against Derrick Tunisson; Walter Wall against john Crawford.]

[PAGE #93 WAS REPEATED IN THE BOOK]

[p 94] **VERDICTS**

[Verdicts were made in the Walter Wall case; Abraham Browne ... appeared in court and did acknowledge his debt of 15 pounds, 10 shillings, and 2 pence unto Thomas Snowsell]

[p 95] **ACCOUNTING OF COURT CHARGES - 6 SEPTEMBER 1676-28 MARCH 1679**

[The following names were mentioned in reference to court charges in the accounts during the above period - Edmund Lafetra, Fra. Le Mester, Richard Sadler, Henery Leonard, Richard Hartshorne, Edmund Gibbon, Eliakim Wardell, Samuel Moor, Mr. Shrimpton - m'cht of Boston, Nich° Davis estate, Thomas Applgate Senior, Major Fenwicke cattell, Nicholas Brown, Isack Ong, James Grover

MONMOUTH COUNTY DEEDS - BOOK "A"

Senior, Christopher Allmey, Samuel huton, Thomas Snawsell, Derick Tunison, John Crawford, Walter Wall.]

[p 96] **ACCOT'S OF COURT CHARGES AS FOLLOWITH DEW TO YE JURY**

[The following names were listed - Christopher Allmey in a triall of three actions in March 26,27 & 28 = 1678, Edmund Lafetra, Nicholas Browne, James Grover, Sam hutton, Thomas Snosell, John Crawford.]

DEW TO RICHARD SADLER FORMERLY COUNTY MARSHALL

[The following names were listed - Christop^r for Marshall's fees in an account produced & allowed of in Court amo^t to, Efiakim Wardell, fra. lemester, Thomas Applgate, Edmund lafetra, Nicholas Brown.]

DEW TO THE CLARK RICHARD RICHARDSON FROM CHRISTOP^R ALLMEY

Ditto in 2 actions triall in March 1678 moor

[The following names were listed - Eliakim Wardell, francis lemester, Tho. Applgate, Edmund lafetra, Nicholas Browne, James Grover senior, Isack Ong, Georg. Axton, Jacob Cole, Richard Sadler, John Champins & Comp^a, Samuell Willet, John Slocum, Ben Devall, John Crawford.]

[p 97] **COURT ACCOUNT OF CHARGES DUE RICHARD RICHARDSON CLARK**

[The following names were listed - Samuell hutton, Thomas Snosell, Isack Bennett on Sam. Leonards's acc't, Lewis Morris Junior, Eliakim Wardell, "to fra Bordin for diet & drink at Court time", John Crawford, Richard Sadler, Thomas Snosell.]

[p 99] Richard Sadler formerly County Marshall of ye County of Newasink ...

[The following names were listed - Christopher Allmey, Edward Lafetra.]

[p 100]   Richard Richardson, Clark

[p 102]   **4 AUGUST 1679 - OATH OF JAMES BOWNE, CLERK OF SESSIONS COURTS FOR MIDLETOWNE & SHROSBURY**

[p 106]   2 September 1679 - Actions entered against the next insuing Court to be held at Shrosbury

MONMOUTH COUNTY DEEDS - BOOK "A"

25 August 1679 - Thomas & bartholomew Apelgate, plaintife, in an action ... against the inhabitants of the towne of Shrosbury ... defendents for non-performance of a written agreement made by the towne Clarke in ye behalfe of the foresaid Inhabitants ...

John Henry of New York plantif ... against John Champnest of ye towne of Shrosbury in N. Jersey defendents for non-performance ... [re: not paying a bill in New York on 1 November 1677 of 56 gilders or more] ... 27 agust 1679.

[p 107]   [John Henry's action above against "John Champnis" was repeated and included the court's verdict. Also, the verdict of Sam Willit case.]

The judgement of ye Court upon John Higs is that hee shall for his living in fornication stand tyed to the whiping post with a bush of Roods tyed to his back halfe one ower and his wife by him ... [and was also fined 10 pounds for contempt].

[p 108]   [Verdict of Samuel Huton, who was fined and warned.]

PAGES #109 THROUGH #113 WERE MISSING - POSSIBLY BLANK, AS MANY IN THIS SECTION WERE, AND LEFT OUT INTENTIONALLY

[p 114]   March 1680 - Actions entered against the next County Court ... holden at Midletowne ... on the fourth or last Tuseday.

Benjamin Devel plaintife ... Thomas Williams defendents for not payment of ... [320 pounds] ... of tobaco ... withdrawn.

Derick Tonosson ... against francis Lemaster Defendent ... plaintif declare ... did in the year ... [1678] ... bulde an house for the defendent in length twenty foot in bredth sixteen foot about ten foot stud that is to say framed, the ... house calbords shingles mad doors, partitions, and ... the defendent doth refuse ... to pay ...

[p 115]   Derick Tonnison plantif against George Job ... for debt ... equivilant to boston money ... [defendent failed to pay for a house built].

Edman Lefatra ... against francis Lemaster ... for a debt ... from ... [Sept 1673].

[p 116]   William Ashton plaintif Richard Gardiner defendent ... action of salt & battery ... about ... [February 1679] ... at Tinton Manor in New Jersey made an assault and beat him ... withdrawne.

[p 117]   [A repeat of the above Ashton complaint which was withdrawn.]
John Chamnes plantif against John Henry ... for debt ... [re: 15 May 1677].

MONMOUTH COUNTY DEEDS - BOOK "A"
****

[p 118]   Samuell Lenard plantif against the estate of Isack bennit ... in the hands of Richard Sadler in the hands of John Crafford, and in the hands of Thomas Hueitt, and the rest of the whalle Company ... [about 26 March 1679 with the following names mentioned - Isack benett, Richard Hartshorne, attorney for Thomas Snozell.]

[p 119]   1680 - At a Court of Sessions held at Midletowne ... New Jersey.

Present - Mr. John bowne, Mr. James Grover, Mr. Joseph Parker, - Justices of the Peace; Mr. Jonathan Holmes - Asistant

Jurors for Midletowne - Mr. Charles Eccles - forman, James Dorset, John Stout, Thomas Cox, John Throckmorton, Job Throckmorton

Jurors for Shrosbury - Tho. Huit, John Havens, Abraham browne, Steven West, Edman Lefetra, John Wiliams.

[Court herd Derick Tonosson against francis Lemaster; Derick Tonason against George Job, Steven West fined 40 shillings for being absent as a juror from Court.]

[p 121]   3 May 1680 - Sr Edmund Andros Kn^t Lit^t and Governor Genl, & Vice Admirall under his Royall Highness James, Duke of York and Albany and of New York ... appoint ... Apt. John Bowne and Mr. Thomas Snozell to be Justices of the Peace for Midletowne and Shrosbury ...; [Signed - E. Andross; Mathias Nicolls secr.; A true copy ... James Bowne, Clark.]

[p 122]   **RECORDED EAR MARK**

11 February 1687 - Midletowne - John Browne his marke is two slitts on the right ear and one crop on the left ear which was formerly the mark of Joseph Hance; [Signed - Robt. Hamilton, Clarke].

[p 123]   **INDEX TO THE BOOK [MODERN ?]**

[p 124]   **AFFIDAVIT OF THE ABOVE RECORDINGS BEING A TRUE COPY**

Joseph Mc Dermott - Clerk of Monmouth Co swore before the court that the foregoing was a true copy of "Book A" ... for the Towns of Middletown and Shrewsbury ... "of the original book as the same remains of Record in my office"; [Dated - 10 August 1903.]

MONMOUTH COUNTY DEEDS - BOOK "B"

[p 1]   At a Court held in Shrowsbury in the County of Monmouth in New East Jersey on the 26th day of June 1683 ... The Court consisting of: John Bowne - President; John Hance, Joseph Parker, Peter Tilton, John Throgmorton - Assistants.

... Isaac Oung was chosen Cryer of the said Court ...; [Dated - 26 June 1683; followed by his Oath of office; he made his mark when signing his Oath of office.]

[p 2]   The Clerke read over & publisht foure acts of Assembly ...

I. An Act for the more orderly keeping of swine.
II. An Act that all processes & writts for accons shall issue from the Clerke of the peace or County Court.
III. An Act for the due Reulacons of Executions.
IV. An Act against trading with Negroe Stands.

The Court adjourned to ye 25th 7m next.

[p 2]   **GABRIEL HICKEY ATTACHMENT**

New East Jersey: To the high Sheriff of the Countey of Monmouth or his Deputy

These are in his Maj^{ties} name to require you to attach the cattell of Gabriel Hickey now in the hands of William Simpson of Shrosbury in the Countey faorsd. being at the request of the said Wm Simpson; [Dated - 9 July 1683; Signed - R. Gardiner, Clk.]

[p 2]   **ORDER FOR GABRIEL HICKEY ATTACHMENT**

9 July 1683 - To the Hight Sheriff ... forthwith to attach the cattell of Gabriel Hickey being two coews & two calfes in the hands of William Simpson of Shrewsbury ... to answer the said William Simpson in an action of debt ...; [Signed - R. Gardiner, Clk.]

[p 3]   **HENRY BOWMAN ATTACHMENT**

24 July 1683 - ... to attach all the Estate of Henry Bowman of the County of New Deale on Delaware River, now in the hands of William Case of Shrewsbury in New East Jersey ... one mare and what more can be found of the said Bowman's Estate in the hands of John Slocum of Shrewsbury aforesd. to answer Nathaniell Slocum in an action of Debt ...; [Signed - Rich. Gardiner Clk.]

[p 3]   **ARREST OF BENJAMIN DEVALL**

25 August 1683 - ... to arrest the body of Benjamin Devall and him safely keep ... to answer Thomas

MONMOUTH COUNTY DEEDS - BOOK "B"

Snawsell by his Attorney Richard Hartshorne in an action of debt ...; [Signed - Richd Gardiner, Clk.]

[p 4]   **BENJAMIN DEVELL ACTION OF DEBT**

Thomas Snawsell by his Attorney Richard Hartshorne is pl^{tt} - Benjamin Devell, Def't.

In an action of Debt of Twenty pounds to be paid in Good Sheep's Wooll at nine pence p. pounds.

17 September 1683 - The Plaintiff ... declares ... in an action of Debt ... under the hands ... bearing ... [dated 6 December 1680] ... by which obligacon the said Def't did ... cause to be paid unto the Plaintife ... [10 pounds] ... in good merchantable Tobacco in cash at two pence p. pounds gross weight and to deliver the same to him ... at Wakick free of all charge, and in case the Def't should fall short of paying the sum of ... [10 pounds] ... in tobacco ... then ... by obligation further engage himself ... to pay what shall be unpaid in tobacco ... to pay in good merchantable sheep's Wooll at nine pence p. pound, unto the plt ... att his store house att Middletowne ...; [Dated - 17 September 1683.]

[p 4]   **ARREST WARRANT FOR JOHN LIMMING**

21 September 1683 - ... to arrest the body of John Limming of the said County to answer Lewis Morris in an action of detainer for detaining a mare belonging to said Morris ...; [Signed - Richd Gardiner Clerk.]

[p 4]   **ARREST WARRANT FOR JOHN LEONARD**

21 September 1683 - ...to arrest the Body of John Leonard of the same Countey ... to answer Lewis Morris of the same Countey in an action of Detainer for taking away and detaining a horse colt belonging to the said Morris ...; [Signed - Richd Gardiner Clerk.]

[p 6]   **SUMMONS**

22 September 1683 - ... Summonds Thomas Harbart, Willm Whitlock, William Compton, James Bowne, Henry Marsh & William Layton, all of Middletown ... to give evidence in the case ... betwixt Thomas Snawsell & Benjamin Devell ...; [Signed - Richd Gardiner Clerk.]

[p 6]   **[Fees Collected by the County Clerk]**

[p 7]   **ATT A COUNTEY COURTHELD AT MIDDLETOWN**

25 September 1683 - Members of the Court - Present - Capt. John Bowne, John Hance, Joseph Parker, John Throgmorton, Peter Tilton.

MONMOUTH COUNTY DEEDS - BOOK "B"

Jurymen apointed & engaged for the Court were: Shrewsbury - John Slocum, Judah Allen, Samuell Dennis, William Shaddock, Thomas Hewett, Edmund Lafetra.

Middletowne - Samuell Leonard, William Leeds, Safety Grover, John Craford, John Whitlock, Direck Tunisson.

[Oath of the Jurymen]

[p 7] Richd Hartshorne Attorney to Thomas Snawsell brings his accon agst Benj^m Devall and publishes his letter of Attorney ... The Def't for plea affirms that he hath pd. a hh^d & a p' cell of Tobacco ... paid p. Wm Whitlock.

[p 8] [Verdict rendered] ...; [Signed - John Slocum forman.]

[p 8] **LETTER OF ATTORNEY**

The Court Orders That a letter of Attorney from Cornelius Stoenwicke of New York to Samuel Leonard be recorded which was produced & read in Court.

[p 8] **LETTER OF ATTORNEY**

And another Letter of Attorney from Thomas Snawsell to Richard Hartshorne ...

[p 8] **APPOINTMENT AS CONSTABLE**

Joseph Grover establisht Constable and take Engagem't appointed in the Law ...

[Oath re: The engagement of an Evidence.]

[Bill of cost for Benj^a Devell]

[p 9] **ATTACHEMENT OF JOHN KING ESTATE**

4 October 1683 - ... These are in his Maj^{ties} name ... to attech the Estate of John King (late deceased) to the Vallue of five pounds in the hands of Peter Tilton to answer the said Tilton in an action of Debt ...; [Signed - Richd Gardiner Clk.]

Peter Tilton against the Estate of John King Deceas^d ...

[p 9] Nicho. Brown plan^{tf} against Christopher Almey Defend^{tt} in an accon of Detainer unlawfully detaining a mare with her increase for severall years past ... [Withdrawn ye 13th].

MONMOUTH COUNTY DEEDS - BOOK "B"

Ye 15th - Christopher Almey p'lt against Jacob Cole, Restore Lippincott, and Nathaniell Slocum Defendants in an action of trespass for unjustly taking away, killing & destroying a parcell of Neat cattell ...

Ye 15th - Christopher Almey Rplt. against Richard Sadler Deft. in an acton of trespass ... for taking away two cows and two calfs ...

[p 10] 18 December 1683 - Charistopher Almey Plt against Jacob Cole Def't in an Action of Debt & Damage ...

[p 10] 18 December 1683 - Lewis Morris Plt. against Caleb Shreive Def't in an action of Trespass ... for taking and disposing of a young horse which the plt. lost out of his stable ...

Ye 19th - Isaac Bryon Pl't against Jeremiah Hood Def't in an Action of assault & Battery for violently assaulting & Beating the plantive as he was rideing on the King's Highway ...

Ye 24th - Nicholas Brown hath withdrawne his Action against X'top^r Almey.

[p 10] ARREST WARRANT FOR JOHN LIMMING

4 December 1685 - A coppy of an execution against John Limming ... [Arrest warrant & to attach ... the goods & cattle of John Limming of Middletown re: judgement against him by Coll. Lewis Morris in court of 23 September 1684]; [Signed - Richd Gardiner Clk.]

[p 11] ATT A COUNTY COURT HELD AT SHREWSBURY

25 & 26 December 1683 -   Present - Capt. John Bowne, President; John Hance, Joseph Parker, Peter Tilton - Assistants.

Jury Impannelled - Present - Samuell Dennis foreman, John Williams, Abiah Edwards, Judah Allen, Thomas Cook, Thomas Leeds, Benjamin Borden, James Grover (Jr), Francis Harbert, Walter Harbert, George Hulett

[Court adjourned till the 26th]

[Jury was summonedand set but three were missing so three alternates were chosen.]

Samuel Dennis foreman, John Williams, William Lawrence, Jun., Judah Allen, Thomas Cook, William Leeds, Benjamin Borden, James Grover, Junr, John Morford, Francis Harbert, Joseph Grove, George Hulet.

MONMOUTH COUNTY DEEDS - BOOK "B"

Peter Tilton plt brings in his action against the Estate of John King deceased ... for debt ...

[The Court held plt didn't have administration, nor did anyone else, so action couldn't be brought.]

[p 12] 26 December 1683 - Christopher Almy plt against Jacob Cole, Postore Lippincott & Nath[ll] Slocum ... trespass ...

Christopher Almey plt against Richard Sadler ... Trespass ... [Verdict].

Lewis Morris pl[t] against Caleb Shreive def[t] ... trespass ... [Verdict].

Isaac Bryan plt against Jeremiah Hood deft ... Assault & Battery ...

[Court adjourned till March.]

[p 14] Warrants & Summonds granted out ...

12 March - To Hugh Dickman to arrest Abiah Edwards ...

13 March - To Nich[o] Brown agst Jospeph Parker for marking a mare

13 March - To Summonds for John Slocum, John Hance, Abraham Browne & Caleb Shreive to appear as evidence

14 March - To John Crafford agst Peter Tilton for detaining two hogsh[d] Tobacco

14 March - To Lewis Morris ...

15 March - Actions entred against March Court

15 February - Richard Sadler plt against Christopher Almey Deft ... trespass ...

[p 14] 13 March - Nicholas Brown, Plantif against Joseph Parker deft ... trespass in the case for brand marking a mare with the letters C.A. that belonged to the said Nicholas ...

14 March - John Crafford Pltf against Peter Tilton Def't in an action of Detainer for Detaining two hogsh[d] of tobacco ...

18 March - Hugh Dickman plt against Abiah Edwards Def't in an accon ... for Detainer, for detaining ... [7 pounds valued at] ... Boston money.

MONMOUTH COUNTY DEEDS - BOOK "B"

20 March - Lewis Morris plan[t] against Def't in an accon of Trespasse ...

[p 16] **Att a Court of Sessions held in Middletowne**

25 & 26 March 1684 - The Court consisting of John Hance presid[t], Joseph Parker, John Throgmorton, Peter Tilton.

Jurymen chosen ... James Ashton foreman, Job Throckmorton, William Ashton, William Lawrence Jun[r], Benjamin Borden, James Grover Jun[r], John Slocum, George Hulett, Samuell Dennis, Abraham Browne, Judah Allen, Thomas Cooke.

[Oath given to the Jury]

Nicholas Browne pltf against Joseph Parker def't in an accon of trepass for brand marking a mare ...

The def't for plea, desires to know in what capacity the plt sewes and how the property of Bartholomwe West's estate came to be alltered. The plt. repls on the plea that Bar[t] West being dead and he the nearest relation, the right is now vested in him.

[p 17] John Slocum ... sayth that the mare sewed for was a mare formerly called the difference mare and was accounted a stray and that when the mare was about to be branded Kathrine Browne forewarned the branding of her, but Christop[r] Almy told her lett the mare be branded Sister and she shall be never the farther of from you for I have sold a beast to John Wood in Rhoad Island and I goe there and find whither that beast hath the same eare marke that this mare hath; then if she hath tis mine otherwise not. And this evidence forthe saith that he did see Joseph Parke brand the mare. Caleb Shreive sayth to the same Effect with John Slocum ... [Abraham Browne and John Haven gave the same testimony.]

[p 17] Hugh Dickman plt against Abiah Edwards deft ... Defts Plea ... [he denied the accusation and said the money was stole from him].

[p 17] Abiah Edwards and Richard Hartshorne, Attonney for Hugh Dickman ... Abiah Edwards brought John Slocum & George Hulett to engage that he ... shall ... pay unto Edward Thurston on Rhoad Island ...

[Verdict of Nicholas Brown vs. Joseph Parker was rendered; signed - James Ashton foreman.]

[p 18] [John Crafford case vs. Peter Tilton was dismissed.]

[Verdict of Chistopher Almey vs Richard Sadler was rendered.]

MONMOUTH COUNTY DEEDS - BOOK "B"

[p 18] JOHN WILLSON CHOSEN CONSTABLE

John Willson having been legally chosen by ... Middletowne for Constable ... for ensuing year.

[p 18] FRANCIS JACKSON CHOSEN AS CRYER

Franicis Jackson was engaged Cryer of the Court of Sessions for this Countey of Monmouth.

[p 18] ENGAGEMENT FOR BUILDING A COUNTY GOAL

Ordered by this present Court that John Throgmorton and the High Sheriffe are the men appointed to agree with a carpenter for to build a Country Goale at Middletowne, and what agreement the said two men shall make with any such Carpenter, this Court engages to stand by.

[Court adjourned till June]

[p 19] Accons Entered against June Court

14 June - Hugh Snell plt Richard Greener deft in an accon of ... Debt ... [Withdrawn].

18th - Samuel Leonard plt Samuell Woollcott deft in an accon of debt ... [Withdrawn].

[p 20] Att a Court of Session ... held at Shrewsbury ... Monmouth

24 & 25 June 1684 - The Court consisting of : John Hance President, John Thockmorton, Peter Tilton - Assistants.

[Bill of Costs granted re: Nich° Brown vs. Joseph Parker.]

[p 20] BASTARDY CASE

Mary Ong single woman being questioned by the Court concerning her having a child, and being examined who was the father of the said child and her engagement given her did declare & affirm that John Slocum was the father of the sd. Child upon which she was delivered in to the Constable's hands & a letter sent from the Court to John Slocum requesting his appearance at Court too morrow morning at eight a clock.

[p 21] Charles Dennis being sent for & brought to Court was questioned concering his living in fornication with her, that is now his wife, severall months before they were married to which he alleadged that there was noe authority in the place that would marry them sooner, upon which the

MONMOUTH COUNTY DEEDS - BOOK "B"

Court thought fitt to comitt him into the Constables hands a prisoner till next Court, or further, order.

[Court adjouned till too morrow morning 8 a clock.]

[p 21] The Court sett againe ... The jury appointed ... Sam^{ll} Dennis forman, Willm Shattocke, Peter White, Nich^o Brown, Abrah. Browne, John Stout, Hugh Dickman, Tho. Renshall, Willm Aston, Judah Allen, Ephraim Allen, George Curlis.

[Oath given to the Jury.]

[p 21] BASTARDY CASE

Mary Ong being again called and examined who was the father of her [child], she againe declared John Slocum to be the father of it.

John Slocum being called & examined concerning the same strongly denied it and delivered a testimony from the midwife & some other women yt were at ye woman's travill which the cause was delivered to ye jury.

[p 22] BASTARDY CASE VERDICT

[Verdict - "Wee Jurors find John Slocum Guilty of ye fact laid to his charge by Mary Ong ..."]

That John Slocum shall pay to Isaac Ong in consideration of the charge & trouble he was at with his Daughter & her child th esum of ... [50 shillings & 10 shillings for Court costs to be paid by tomorrow] ... and to give sufficient security to be of the good behav^r for six months ... or to gor to the comon Goale ... for the space of ten weeks.

Mary Ong shall be had from this place to ye whipping place, and there to be stripped downe to the waist and to receive five lashes on the bare back with a Rod or whip and to give sufficient security to be of the good behavior for six months ... or to goe to the common Goale, there to remain for the space of ten weeks.

[p 22] BASTARDY CASE SENTENCE CARRIED OUT

Thursday - 26 June 1684 - [John Slocum paid to Isaac Ong 50 shillings, plus the Court costs, and gave Bond.] Mary Ong received five lashes on the bare back & Isaac Ong became bound for her good behavior.

[p 23] Francis Jackson Attorney for Christop^r Almey took out an Execution against Richard Sadler upon a Judgem't granted last March ...

MONMOUTH COUNTY DEEDS - BOOK "B"

[Court adjourned till 4th Tuesday in September next]

[p 23] **Accons Entered agst next Court**

Gawen Lawrie Govern^r of the P'vince Lidia Brown [Bowne pencilled over name], Richard Stout, Senr, James Grover, Senr & Richard Hartshorne, plan^{ts} against John Peirce deft ... trepass ... [Withdrawn on the 16th].

Thomas Snawsell plt against John Crafford deft in an accon of Debt ...

[p 23] **MARRIAGE CERTIFICATION**

14 July 1691 - These are to certifie all to whom it may concern that Mordecay Andrews & Mary his wife are lawfully joyned together in wedlock according to ye appointment ... this ye ... [14 July 1691].

[p 24] **Action Entered agains Sepr Court**

Coll^o Lewis Morris plan^t against Henry Leonard Senr deft ... Debt ...

Coll^o Morris plan^t against John Liming ... Debt ...

[Copy of a Sciere facias against John Crafford; Dated - 17 March 1692; signed - John Webley, Cr.]

[p 25] **At a Court of Sessions ... Middletown**

23 September 1684 - John Hance Presid^t, John Throgmorton and Peter Tilton - Assistants.

Jury men chosen ... James Ashton foreman, William Aston, Benj^a Borden, James Grover, Junr, Nich^o Brown, James Dorsett, Judah Allen, Thomas Cooke, Peter White, Ephraim Allen, George Axton, Caleb Shreive.

Coll^o Lewis Morris plan^t against Henry Leonard Senr ... deft ... debt ...

Coll^o Lewis Morris plan^t against John Liming ... deft ... debt ...

[p 26] **VERDICTS & ORDERS OF THE COURT**

Ordered that if any action hereafter be withdrawn within four days of the Court, they shall pay halfe charges and the same for a nonsuit.

MONMOUTH COUNTY DEEDS - BOOK "B"

Ordered that there be a rate made for building the Prison and that Remembrance Lippincott for Shrewb[y] and James Bowne for Middletowne are the men appointed to make the rate and that all persons give in an accott of their Estates to remembrance Lippincott for Shrewsby and to Thomas Renshall for Middletown ... [if anyone neglects to bring in the accounts of their estates they will be adjudged double as much as the rate makers Judge their estates ... to be brought unto John Thogmorton for Middletowne and to Eliakim Wardell for Shrewsbury ...]

[p 26] **TAVERN LICENSES**

Thomas Renshall & John Crafford appointed Ordinarie keepers for Middletown for one year following.

[Court adjourned to 4th Tuesday December.]

[p 27] **Att a Court of Session Shrewsbury**

23 December 1684 - John Hance, presid[t], John Throgmorton and Peter Tilton - Assistants.

Jury mens Names - Samuel Dennis foreman, William Shattock, Remembrance Lippincott, Judah Allen, Thomas Cooke, Peter White, William Aston, John Stout, Benj[a] Borden, James Dorsett, Joseph Grover, John Clarke.

...Thomas snawsell (by his Attorney Richard Hartshorne) plaintif against John Crafford def't ... Debt ...

... Thomas Snawsell plant (by his Attorney Richard Hartshorne) against John Crafford ... Debt ... [of New England silver].

[p 28] [Verdicts rendered in cases.]

[p 28] **TAVERN LICENSE**

Thomas Renshall licensed to keep Ordinary att Middletown and his Bond ... taken for keeping an orderly house.

[Court Adjourned to the fourth Tuesday in March.]

[p 28] **Accons entered against March Court**

Christian Marks pl[t] Richard Sadler def't ... debt ... [withdrawn March 14th.]

MONMOUTH COUNTY DEEDS - BOOK "B"

Nich° Brown pl' against Rich'd Sadler def't ... debt ...

[p 29] Att a Court of Sessions held in Middletowne ... Monmouth

24 March 1684/5 - John Hance, president, John Throckmorton and Peter Tilton, justices.

Jurymen Impannelled - James Ashton foreman, Judah Allen, William Lawrence, Jun', Nicholas Brown Edmund Lafetra, George Hulett, John Slocum, Will'm Whitlock, Gerrard Wall, James Dorsett, John Vaughn, Benjamin Devall.

Samuel Leonard informs againsat Safety Grover for taking, keeping and Branding of a horse ... And for evidence bringeth Benj'a Devall who sayeth. That he did see a horse uppon the Pointt hills which he supposes was the same horse y' he saw Safety Grover have since ...

John Slocum for evidence sayeth that Safety Grover, did tell him y' he had taken up a wild horse as his own and y' William Laytor (being then by) did say y' he knew Safety to have such a coull'd horse coult in the woods and Thomas Herbert did agree with him ...

[p 30] A CERTIFICATE FROM JAMES GROVER, SEN^R, JUSTICE

That Safety Grover brought a horse of a bay coull' before me sometime ye last Sumer and I being sattisified that the horse did belong to him ... did allow the horse should be marked. [Signed - James Grover, Sen'.]

[Richard Mount and Thomas Harbert testified and a verdict was rendered. The Court found that Safety Grover was guilty of law for ranging the woods; Signed - James Ashton, foreman.]

[p 30] COMPLAINT BY CHRISTIAN MARKES

Complaint being made ... by Christian Markes (widdow) That Whereas Rich'd Sadler & his wife did ... bind thenselves by an Obligation ... that they would provide for her and see yt shee should want for nothing ... during her life & theirs ... Now the said Christian complains that they ... refuse to perform the said obligation, upon which the Court orders ... [Sadler to pay Christian 5 pounds per year for the rest of her life] ... from the date of ye obligation ... [dated 7 November 1683].

[p 31] CONSTABLE APPOINTED

John Stout engaged Constable for Middletowne for the ensuing year.

MONMOUTH COUNTY DEEDS - BOOK "B"

[p 31] CRYER APPOINTED & TAVERN LICENSE GRANTED

John Crafford engaged Cryer of the Court, and licensed Ordinarie Keeper in Middletown for one year next.

[Court adjourned to the fourth Tuesday in June.]

[p 31] ACCON ENTERED AG^T JUNE COURT 1685

Robert Hamilton ags^t John Vaughn ... debt ... [Withdrawn on May 30th.]

William Hunt ag^t Thomas Chambers ... debt ... [Withdrawn on June 1st.]

9th - Nich° Brown ag't Richard Sadler ... debt ...

11th - Thomas Snawsell by his Att° Richd Hartshorne ag't Richd Grover ... debt ...

... Thomas Snawsell by his Att° Richd Hartshorne ag't Geo. Job ... debt ... [Withdrawn].

... Thomas Snawsell by his Att° Richd Hartshorne ag't Thomas Ingram ... debt ... [Withdrawn].

... Thomas Snawsell by his Att° Richd Hartshorne ag't John Whitlock ... debt ... [Withdrawn].

[p 32] Nich° Brown ags't Capt John Slocum ... debt ...

[p 32] ATT A COURT OF SESSIONS HELD IN SHREWSBURY ... MONMOUTH ...

23 June 1685 - Being present - John Hance president, John Throckmorton and Peter Tilton, Justices.

Jurymens names: Thomas Whitlock foreman, John Clarke, James Dorsett, Benj^a Devall, William Whitlock, Rostore Lippincott, Edmund Lafetra, Judah Allen, John Havens, William Leeds, Francis Jackson, John Lippincott.

Nich° Brown agst Richard Sadler ... debt ... The def't owned the debt, but said it was paid wither to Steenwyck or Winder at N. York ...

[p 33] The plt for proof brings Robert Ashley who evidenced that he saw the delivery of the good menconed ...

George Axton, John Crafford & Nich° Browne declared all to the same effect ...

Nich° Brown ag^st John Slocum in an accon of the case for debt uppon Assumpsit ... John Crafford who testifies that John Slocum told him that he had agreed with Nich° Browne about the horse called long neck, and that he was to give ... Browne our pounds ...

Verdicts on Nich° Browne plt Richard Sadler, deft ... Thomas Snawsell plt Richard Greever, deft ... Nich° Brown plt John Slocum deft ... Sam^{ll} Leonard informer and plt Safety Grover deft ...

[p 34] ACCONS ENTERED AGST SEP^T COURT

Thomas Leonard agst John Robinson ... Lewis Morris Att° for Edm° Gibbon agst Walter Harbert ... Coll° Lewis Morris agst John Crafford ... John Hance ... Francis Harbert ... Sam^{ll} White Adminsi^{tr} to the Estate of Thomas White dec^d ... Morgan Bryon ... Jeremiah Bennet agst Wm Whitlock Administ^r of ye estate of Richd Gibbons ...

[p 35] ATT A COURT OF SESSIONS HELD IN MIDDLETOWN ... 22TH SEPTEMBER 1685

... the Court consisting of John Hance, presid^t, John Throckmorton, Peter Tilton - Justices.

[Actions heard by the Court - Richard Sadler ... Nich° Browne ... Sadler "produced a Certificate from Margarett Steenwyck of N. York that John Job is charged in the Bookes of Mr. Steenwyck & Nich° Bayard ... Andreis Greevenzaat ... John Palmer ... Mr. Winders ... William Simpson of Shrewsbury being presented by Samuell Dennis Constable of the same Towne for selling strong liquors and keeping a disorderly house ...]

[p 36] [Actions heard by the Court - Derrick Tunissen ... Robert Hamilton ... William Hamilton ... Nicholas Browne against John Slocum ... Jeremiah Bennett plnt against William Whitlock ... Richard Sadler ... against Nicho Browne ... Collo Lewis Morris against John Liming ...]

AT A COUNTEY COURT HELD IN MIDDLETOWN

[p 37] Subscription of James Browne for commission to hold small Court.

[Browne then took the Oath of Office on 23 September 1685 before the above three Justices - John Hance, John Throckmorton, Peter Tilton.]

[Actions heard 4 December 1685 by the Court - Lewis Morris against ... John Liming.]

[p 38] Subscription of Benjamin Borden commisionated to hold small Court.

[Borden took the Oath of Office on 14 December 1685 before Gawen Lewis.]

[p 39] [Actions heard by the Court] - Nich° Browne against Richard Sadler ...

MONMOUTH COUNTY DEEDS - BOOK "B"

2/9 - Dirick Tunisson against Thomas Webley of New York ...

3/5 - Richd Hartshorne ... agst Thomas Shearman ... John Vaughn agst Peter Tilton ...

8th - John Slocum ... agst Thomas White ... John Slocum cheif Ranger plt agst Ephraim Potter ... Sam^{ll} Leon^d plt agst Saml White Execut^{rs} of Thomas White dec'd in an accon of the case of Debt of four pounds or thereabouts, being the remainder of Sixteen pounds for an Indian Girl.

[p 40] This day John Slocum appeared before me John Throckmorton and did engage to perfom the place of a Ranger ... between the propriet^{rs} and the Inhabitants of this Country ... [Dated - 3 March 1685/6.]

ATT A COURT OF SESSIONS HELD IN MIDDLETOWNE ... [23 MARCH 1685/6]

Being present - John Hance, John Throgmorton, Peter Tilton

The Court sett and the Jury impanelled were as followeth - Judah Allen foreman, Willm Leeds, Banj^a Devall, John Haven, James Grover, Francis Harbert, John Clarke, Willm Scott, John Peirce, Willm Hamilton, Nich^o Browne, Edmond Lafetra.

[Actions heard before the Court - Sam^{ll} Lenard ... against Sam^{ll} White ... Robt Hamilton agst Dirick Tunisson ...]

[p 42] ATT A COURT OF SESSIONS HELD IN SHREWSBURY JUNE YE 22TH 1686

Justices being present - John Hance, John Throckmorton, Peter Tilton.

[Actions heard - Samuell Leonard against Samuel White ...]

[p 43] ATT A COURT OF SESSIONS HELD IN MIDDLETOWN SEPT YE 1686

Justices being present - John Hance, John Throckmorton, Peter Tilton.

[Actions heard - ... Lewis Morris was called being arrested to appear ... by warrant ... to answer to what should be alleadged against him ... concerning an informacon brough in about the death of a Negro woman named Francke.]

ACCONS ENTRED AGAINST DECEMB^R COURT

[Actions heard - Richard Hartshorne ... against John Crafford ... Lewis Morris plt against James

MONMOUTH COUNTY DEEDS - BOOK "B"

Grover & Richard Gardiner Execut[rs] of ye last Will ... of James Grover, dec[d] ... John Buck ... ag't James Johnston ...]

[p 44] **ATT A COURT OF SESSIONS HELD IN SHREWSBURY DECEMB[R] 28TH & 29TH 1686**

Justices being present - John Hance, John Throgmorton, Peter Tilton.

[Actions heard - John Buck ... against John Johnston ...]

Jury impanelled as follows - Judadiah Allen foreman, Juda Allen, Thomas Eaton, Samuell Dennis, William Scott, John Hampton, John Stout, William Ashton, William Cheesman, William Leeds, Thomas Bowles.]

[Actions heard - Lewis Morris ... against James Grover & Richard Gardiner...Richard Hartshorne as Atto to Lewis Morris ... Samuel Winder Atto to Lewis Morris ...]

[p 45] **DECEMB[R] YE 30TH 1686**

[Actions heard - John Buck against ... James Johnston ...]

ACCONS ENTERED AGAINST MARCH COURT

[Actions heard - William Leeds against Francis Jeffries ... Daniell Estall ... ag[st] Henry Marsh ...]

[p 46] **ATT A COURT OF SESSIONS HELD IN MIDDLETOWN MARCH THE 22TH & 23TH 1686/7**

Justices being present - John Hance, John Throckmorton, Peter Tilton, Lewis Morris.

Jury men impanelled - Thomas Eaton foreman, Jedediah Allen, Judah Allen, Eliakim Wardell, Samuell Dennis, Thomas Eaton, Peter White, Thomas Hewitt, John Clarke, Nicholas Brown, Benjamin Devall, William Lawrence.

[Actions heard - William Leeds ... ag[st] Francis Jeffries ... Lewis Morris ag[st] Richard Gardiner & James Grover ... James Emott ... attorney ...]

[p 47] This Court Lewis Morris was Commissionated Justice of the Peace.

MONMOUTH COUNTY DEEDS - BOOK "B"

Robert Hamilton Comission for Major and for Clarke of the peace was read, and he engaged for Clerke of the Peace.

ACCONS ENTERED AGAINST JUNE COURT

[Action heard - Lewis Morris ... against George Job ... Richard Sadler ... against Gerrat Wall ... John Campble ... against Daniell Eastell ... John Bowne ... against Richard Richardson ... Heugh Snell ... agasint John Craford ...]

[p 48] **ATT A COURT OF SESSIONS HELD IN SHREWSBURY FOR THE COUNTEY OF MONMOUTH ON THE 28 & 29 JUNE 1787.**

Justices present - John Johnson presid^t, John Hance, John Throckmorton, Petter Tilton, Lewis Morris.

Jury men impanelled - Elliakim Wardell foreman, Benjamin Burding, Thomas Cooke, Petter White, Juda Allen, John Williams, Tho. Hewit, Will Lawrans, Jose Grover, George Corless, Benj, Devell.

[Actions heard - Lewis Morris ... agasint George Job ... Saml Lenord his Aturnay ... Richard Sadler ... against Gerrat Wall ... John Campble ... against Daniell Estall ... John Bowne ... Against Richard Richardson ...]

[p 49] Order of the Court - ... by this present Court of Sessions held at Shrewsbury that twelve pounds be levied on the goods and chattels of Richard Richardson of the Iyland of Barbadoes ... Heugh Snell ... against John Craford ... William Leeds ... against Francis Jeffries ...

[p 50] [Action heard - Richard Gardiner and James Grover defts ... of Lewis Morris Sen. ... George Job deft ... of Lewis Morris, Junno ... John Campble plt ... of Daniell Eastell Deft ... Garret Wall Deft ... of Richard Sadler ...]

Order of the Court - [The Grand Jury shall consist of 14 men at the next Court & a petty jury of 12 men.]

John Bowne fyne ... [six shillings] ... for neglect of returning the Jurys nemae which he hath payd.

[p 51] To the Corono^r - ... You are hearby required .... that you leavie of the goods and chattalls of Richard Richardson of the Iyland of Barbadoes which are now in the hands ... of Lewis Morris Junr of Shewsbury ... [and then engage two men to deliver those items] ... to John Bowne high Shreefe ... [Dated - 1 July 1786; signed - Robt Hamilton Clarke.

MONMOUTH COUNTY DEEDS - BOOK "B"

To the Corono^r - ... you atatch in the hands of Lewis Morris, Jun of Shrosbury ... the sum of twelfe pounds ... in good & chattels ... belonging to one Richard Richardson late of Midletowne ... now of the Iyland of Barbadoes ... for the use of John Bowne high Shreefe ... being so much dew to ye sd John Bowne from ... Richard Richardson ...; [Dated - 11 June 1687; Rob Hamilton, Clarke.]

[p 52] To the High Shreefe - ... to attach ... Richard Hartshorne of Midletown ... [25 pounds] ... as belonging to Thomas Snosell late of Middletown ... for the use of the sd. ... Hartshorne as being so much dew ... from the sd. Thomas Snosell ...; [Dated - 31 August 1786; signed - Rob. Hamilton, Clarke.]

ACTIONS ENTRED AGAINST SEPT. COURT

[Actions heard - Richard Hartshorne ... against Thomas Snosell ...]

[p 53] **ATT A COURT OF SESSIONS HELD IN MIDLETONE ... 27 SEPT 1687**

Justices present - John Johnson presd^t, John Hance, John Throckmorton, Peter Tilton.

Grand Jury men impannelled - William Leeds foreman, Abraham Brown, James Grover, Niccollis Brown, John Ruckman, Epheraham Allen, Thomas Rousle, Francis Burding, John Pearce, Job Throckmorton, Calleb Shreefe, John Willson Jun^{or}, Benj^a Devall, Richard Sadler.

[Actions heard - Richard Hartshorne ... against Thomas Snosell.]

[p 54] To the high Shreefe - ... to arrest ... John Lenord ... and him safely keep ... to answer John Slocum ...; [Dated - 27 September 1687.]

31 October 1687 - Execution granted to John Campble agannst the estate of Daniell Eastall ... attache the bod of Robt Holman of Middletown ... to answer Daniell Eastell of Middletown ... to attach the body of Sam^{ll} Lenord late of Colts Neck ... to answer Richard Stout, Jun^{or} of Middletown ... to attach the body of Richard Beast of Middletown ... to answer John Willson Jun^{or} of Middletown ...; [Dated - 24 November 1687.]

[p 56] ... to atach the body of Margaret Leads, widow of the Tho. Leads late of Shrosbury deceased and Executr to the last Will ... of the sd. Tho. Leads ... to answer William Leads ...; [Dated - 13 December 1687.]

... to summonde Gilbert Lunsdale and Jon Whit ... to give in the evidence ... betwixt ... the King and John Lenard ...; [Dated - 18 December 1687.]

MONMOUTH COUNTY DEEDS - BOOK "B"

[p 57] [Actions heard - John Johnson ... against John Lenord ... Daniell Eastall ... against Robt Hoolman ... Rich. Stout ... against Sam^{ll} Lenord ... John Willson Jun^{or} ... against Richd Beast ... Phillip Smith ... against ... John Craford ... Rich. Mount against Mr. John Johnson ... William Leads ... against Margrate Leads ... Benj^a Devell ... Aginst William Snead ...]

[p 58] ATT A COURT OF SESSIONS HELD ATT SHROSBURY ... ON 27, 28, 29 OF DECEMBER 1687

Justices present - John Hance presdt, John Throckmorton, Petter Tilton, Lewis Morris.

The Jury impannaled were - Sam^{ll} Denis foreman, Thomas Potter, Petter White, John Williams, John Woorthly, George Heulit, Thomas Cooke, John Craford, William Casse, Clame Masters, John Whitlock, John Lippingcoot.

[Jury was sworn; actions heard - John Johnson ... Against John Lenard ... Deft apoynted Sam^{ll} Lenord for his Aturney ... William Leads ... against Margaret Leads ... Rich. Hartshorne ... Richard Mount against John Johnston ... Great Wall for evidence payeth the mare as he soposeth to be the mare he gave to his sister Rebecca Richard Mount's wife was the same mare.]

Judgment ... that William Leads ... have execution upon the ... body of Margaret Leads ... the cost of the shuit was given by the members of the Court to the sd. Margaret Leads as gift ... Richard Mount ... have execution upon the ... body of John Johnston ... Benj^a Devell shall pay half charges for cost of shuit ...

[p 61] Order of the Court - [Fines were set for non-appearance; Constables were to be fined for non-appearance when the Court was in session; and the Court will be meeting on 16 January 1687 at the falles at Shrosbury and the Constable of Midletown to give notice to the inhabitants on the north side of hooper river & the Constable of Shrosbury to give notice to the inhabitants on the South syde of hooper river.]

[p 62] Ordered - Daniell Eastall shall pay unto John Campble ... for keeping his hourse ... then the sd. Daniell to have his horse returned ...

[31 January 1687 - And. Hamilton orders the John Johnson case to be heard at the next court.]

To the high Shreefe - to serve an Execution upon the Esate of Lewis Morris Junr ... to answer a judgment of Court ... against Lewis Morris by George Jobs ...; [Dated - 21 January 1687; signed - Rob Hamilton, Clarke.]

MONMOUTH COUNTY DEEDS - BOOK "B"

[p 64] ATT A COURT OF SESSIONS HELDE ATT MIDLETOWNE ... 27 MARCH 1688

Members of the Court were John Hance. All members of the Court not being present ... noe business done.

Complaint ... by James Dosset Constable of the sev^l abuses done upon the Sabbath day, Benj^a Devall in contempt to athority did give scurvie languadge to the Constable ...

Acctions entred against June Court - [Actions heard - Rob't Ashley ... against Abia Edwards ... Benj^a Devall ... against John Lenord ... Thomas White ... against Walter Pomfret ... John West ... against Tho. Webly ...]

[p 65] ATT A COURT OF SESSIONS HELD ATT SHROSBURY ... 26 JUNE 1688

Members of the Court - John Hance, president Petter Tilton, Lewis Morris.

The Jury impannalled were Samll Dennis foreman, Petter White, Ephraim Allen, John Williams, George Heulett, John Willson, Tho. Applegate, Tho. Heuet, John Tucker, Will Scott, Frances Iaxsone.

[Jury Sworn - Actions heard - John West ... against Thomas Webley ...]

[p 66] Thomas Webley of Shrosbury Gen^{ll} was attached to answer John West ... whereof he with forse & armes, one tract ... of land ... from the highway that passes from Shrosbury to the jyrme woorkes and to the swimming River bounded on the South by the high way, on the north with the said river, on the east by land of John Neumans ... on the west by a highway that divides him and Stephen West containing in all ...[50 acres] ... together with one dwelling house belonging thereunto which Joseph West of the foresd towne did promise for a tearme which is not yet past did enter & him the sd. John West from his farme aforsd. did eject & other hermes to him did ... that now is & thereupon the sd. John West by Sam^{ll} Leanord his Atturnay ... Whereas the Joseph West ... [on 10 March last] ... at Shrosbury, did demise to the sd. John West, the tenement aforesd. with the ... [50 acres] ... of land ... unto the end & tearme of five years ... Thomas Webley afterward ... [on 20 March last] ...

[p 67] [Actions heard - ... John West plt & Thomas Webley deft ... Richard Hartshorne Aturnay for William Neuman ... John Slockin for evidence sayeth that he was at the layeing out of that shaire of land that was twixt Robert West & Stephen West and first he layd out Rob't West's part & then he laid out Stephen West's part . Niccollos Brown for evidence sayeth to the same purpos ... Rob't Holman shall have all these goods that James Dorsatt being Constable did attach ...]

MONMOUTH COUNTY DEEDS - BOOK "B"

[PAGE 68 THROUGH 100 ARE BLANK. BEGINNING AT PAGE 101, THE PAGES HAVE BEEN RE-NUMBERED. IT IS AT THIS POINT THAT THE RECORDING OF THE COURT RECORDS IN THE DEED BOOKS BEGINS TO END WHILE THE RECORDING OF DEEDS BEGINS.

BEGINNING AT PAGE 101, THE PAGES HAVE BEEN RE-NUMBERED AND BEGIN WITH "1" THROUGH THE BALANCE OF DEED BOOK "B".]

[p 1]   **RECORD OF MORGAN BRYAN'S BILL OF SALE TO RICHARD GARDINER FOR A HORSE**

... I Morgan Bryan of Shrewsbury ... farmer ... [sold for 6 pounds to] ... Richd Gardnier ... one chessnutt coull^d horse aged four years ... with a starre in the forehead, one white foott, with a stilt in the near eare and a crop on the off eare ...; [Dated - 21 June 1683; signed - Morgan Bryan made his mark; witnesses - Nathaniell Leonard, Edward Williams made his mark; att. R. Gardiner, Clk; recorded - 25 June 1683.]

[p 2]   **THOMAS SNAWSELL HIS LETTER OF ATT'NEY TO RICHARD HARTSHORNE**

... I Thomas Snawsell the Elder of Middletowne ... New Jersey, Merchant, appoint my trusty & well beloved friend Richard Hartshorne of the ... [same place] ... to be my trew .... Attorney ...; [Dated - 9 September 1681; signed - Thos. Snawsell; witnesses - John Bowne, James Bowne; att. Rich Gardiner, Clk; recorded - 26 September 1683.]

[p 4]   **CORNELIUS STEENWICKE OF NEW YORK HIS LETTER OF ATTORNEY TO SAMUELL LEONARD**

... I Cornelius Steenwicke of the Citty of New York, Mch^{tt} ... appoint ... my trusty & beloved friend Samuell Leonard of Neversinke my ... Attorney ... & to recover ... from Thomas Snawsell, Richard Sadler, John Job & John Crafford now or late Inhabitants at the Neversink ...; [Dated & sealed in New York - 14 August 1683; signed - Corn. Steenwicke; witnesses - Antho. Brockholls, John West; att. Richd Gardiner, Clk; recorded - 27 September 1683.]

[p 6]   **RICHARD STOUT SEN^R & PENELOPE HIS WIFE, THEIR BILL OF SALE TO THOMAS SNAWSELL FOR A HOUSE & LAND**

... wee Richard Stout Senr of the Towne of Middletown ... East New Jersey planter and Penelope Wife of the said Richard ... [sold for 66 pounds, 5 shillings, 3 pence to] ... Thomas Snawsell Senr now Resident in the Towne of Middletowne ... Merchant ... a lott of up land lying in the Towne of Middletown ... with a dwelling house & barn ... with an orchard ... [16 acres in lenght and in breadth

MONMOUTH COUNTY DEEDS - BOOK "B"

4 chaynes] ... as the same is menconed ... in the Patent ... [dated 4 June 1677] ... bounded on the borth by the highway, west by John Smith, South by land ... East by the house lott formerly ... of Richard Gibbons and now in possession of John Crafford. Together with nine acres of upland in the Poplar field ... [adjacent land owners or names - Stephen Arnold, William Layton, Edward Smith] ... as allso nine acres of meadow ... [adjacent land owners or names - William Cheeseman, John Stout, a Creek which parts Wakick necke and Shoale Harbour Neck. Likewise Six acres of meadow at Wakick Creek or Necke ... [adjacent land owners or names - Edward Smith, Anthony Page] ... and for him the said Snawsell ... to ... possess the same as of the manner of East Greenwich in free & comon Soccage ...; [Signed - Both Richard and Penelope Stout made their marks when signing; witnesses - John Brown, Thomas Lawrence; att. Richd Gardiner, (Clk); recorded - 7 October 1684.]

[p 8] RECORD OF AN AGREEMENT BETWEEN PETER TILTON & JOSEPH GROVER ABOUT THEIR LAND

... Whereas, Peter Tilton late of New Shrewsbury and now of Marvell Hill ... New Jersey ... [did purchase] ... of Napeson, Checaucus, Cawsehoe, Meninvein & Awayeis five of the Indian Sachems and other Indians of the Towne Called Ramezing ab^r Ramezonk ... [dated] at Middletown ... the three & twentieth day of Aprill, the seventeenth day of July called the fifth month and the four & twentieth day of the same fifth month, all within the year ... [1675] ... And Whereas, Phillip Carterett, Esqr Govern^r ... did ... petition of James Grover, Senr ... to divide the said tract of Land between the said petition^r and him the said Peter Tilton who was to be reimbursed by the said James Grover, one full moyetie of what the said Sachems had recieved of him the said Peter Tilton ... which ... Peter Tilton refused to accept ... untill there was an agreem^t made by ... James Grover ... that the boundary ... line between them should be so fixed as that ... Peter Tilton should mot be prejudiciall so he was like to be ... as is menconed the ... severall Pattents ... [dated 30 June 1676] ... Now These presents ... James Grover ... endorsed ... his said Pattent ... & granted all the land, meadow & swamp therein ... unto his second son Joseph Grover ... by the said Pattent & Assignment at large ... [dated the even date with these presents] ... [and Peter Tilton and Joseph Grover had agreed upon and] ... Joseph Grover ... shall have ... all that ... land on which he now dwelleth ...; [19 February 1678; signed - Peter Tilton, Joseph Grover; witnesses - Fenwicke Thorlagh Swyny; Nathaniel Slocum signed on the instrument - 23 September 1684.]

[Both Tilton & Grover appeared before Justices - John Hance, John Throckmorton; att. Richd Gardiner, Clk; recorded - 7 October 1684.]

[p 11] MEMORANDUM

... on the back side of Richard & Penelope Stout's Bill of Sale ... [was the acknowledgement that they appeared before Justices - John Hance, John Throckmorton, Peter Tilton] ...; [Dated - 23 September 1684.]

MONMOUTH COUNTY DEEDS - BOOK "B"

[p 11] RECORD OF AN INDIAN BILL OF SALE TO RICHARD HARTSHORNE

... Powropa, Emoroas, Wawapa, cheif Sachems of Ramesing ... Greeting ... [they agree to sell land] ... for a valluable sum of money in Indian trading goods ... paid unto us ... by Richard Hartshorne of Middletowne ... New Jersey ... being three neckes of land called by the Indians, Wacake, Arowonoc, Coneskunk ... [adjacent land owners or names - Wakecake Creek, meadoww called Walter Walls meadow, the Indian path from Wakecake to the Indian towne called Seapeckamcke] ...; [Dated - 22 May 1676; signed - by the marks of Perropa, Wawapa, Emoras; witnesses - James Dorsett, Gerard Wall; att. Richd Gardiner, Clk.]

[Both Wall & Dorsett appeared before Justices - John Hance, John Throgmorton, Peter Tilton indicating that they witnessed the Indian Sachems sign the deed; recorded - 23 December 1684.]

[p 14] RECORD OF AN ACCO^{TT} OF WHAT JOSEPH GROVER EXECUTORS OF THE LAST WILL ... OF THORLAGH SWINY DEC^D

[The following items were selected from the Inventory of the Estate of Thorlagh Swiny: For a cofin - 5 shillings; For goeing to Eliz^d Towne to Record the will - 4 days - 10 shillings; For 3 daies for a man to thrash Indian corn - 7 shillings, 6 pence; For carting a parcell of wheat & a barr^l of porke to Wakick and for a boat hire to N. York - 8 shillings; For going to the Sectretaries Office - 3 daies - 7 shillings, 6 pence.]

[p 15] RECORD OF AN ACCO^{TT} OF DEBTS THAT WAS OWING BY THORLAGH SWINEY DECEASED, AND PAID BY HIS EXECUT^{OR} JOSEPH GROVER

[The following names were listed - Judah Allen, George Curlis, John Woolley, Restore Lippincott, William Leeds, Kathrine Browne, John Haven, Edmund Lafetra, Christopher Allmey, Richd Hartshorne, Jeremiah Bennett, Thomas Morford, John Crafford, Richd Hartshorne on acco^{tt} Tho. Snowsell, William Lawrence Junr, John Stout, William Layton, James Stout, James Bowne, Ruth Gibbons; Dated - 14 April 1684; recorded - Richd Gardiner, clk.]

[p 16] RECORD OF A MARRIAGE BETWEEN JOB THROGMORTON & SARAH LEONARD

These may sattisfie whom it may concerne that wee whose names are underwritten, are Witnesses that Job Throgmorton & Sarah Leonard have been lawfully married by Peter Tilton Justice of the Peace, as Witness our hands in Middletown this ... [2 February 1684] ...; [Signed - Peter Tilton; witnesses - Henry Leonard, William Hunt, Samuell Leonard, John Leonard, Mary Leonard, Rebecca Tilton, Anne Hunt.]

MONMOUTH COUNTY DEEDS - BOOK "B"

[p 16] RECORD OF AN INDIAN LEASE OF LAND TO WILLIAM LEADS & DANIEL APPLEGATE FOR 315 YEARS.

This Indenture made bewteen Iraseeke of Wickaton, Sachem ... [sold to] William Leeds & Daniel Applegate of Middletown ... land lying in Middletown or Chawcosette called by ye name of Amoskake and marked out by my uncle Seahoppa in ye p'sence of Nochtoha & powraas my brothers: To have & to hold ... from ye date hereof from one & twenty years to one & twenty years untill ye end & tearme of three hundred & fifteen years from hence ... paying therefore yearly & every year dureing ye said tearme unto ye said Iraseeke ... four yards of Duffield or equivalent in rum at or uppon ye first day of November Known to ye English by ye name of the feast of all Saints or all holland tide, yearly & every year ... [adjoining land owners or names - On ye South ... bounded wth a tract of land that in a Pettent is called premy corne quick, Benjamin Borden, Wiliam Lawrence, hop River, Thomas Applegate's mill, a place sometimes called plain dealeing, Joseph Grover] ... And further that & if at any time wth in ye tearme ... Iraseeke shall come unto ye houses of ye sd. Leeds & Appleg^t ... shall lend him or them a gun ... [and they shall pay for any damages to it and were required to bring it back within 48 hours or the person who lent the gun was to receive half of what] ... ye sd. borrowed killeth wth ye s^d gun ... Provided the said Leeds & Appleg^t shall ... have in hand paid ... nine quarts of rum, with a caske bearing it, and three Blankeets or match coats or six yards of Duffield and two good new shirts and two more good new shirts ... it is to be understood that the four yeard of Duffield aforesd. is meant two blanketts or trucking cloathes such as Indians now weare uppon their backs and that Leeds & Applegate are to be at their choice either to pay Duffield or rum ...; [Dated - 16 July 1684; signed - Iraseeke made his mark; witnesses - William Scott, Jeremiah Bennett.]

[24 March 1684 - Scott and Bennett appeared before Justices John Hance, John Throckmorton, & Peter Tilton and stated they saw Iraseeke sign the Deed; att. R. Gardiner, Clk.]

[p 22] SAMUELL MOORE to JOHN CRAFFORD

... I Samuell Moore of Woodbridge ... East New Jersey Yeoman, Attorney to Mr Anthony Cheekley of Boston in New England Merchant ... [for 120 pounds of Boston silver] ... [sold unto] ... John Crafford of Middletown ... Yeoman ... land ... in Middletown ... [20 acres] ... allso ... [9 acres] ... of upland at a place known by the name of the Poplar field, and ... [15 acres] ... of Marsh or meadow ... oppon Wakicke Creek, all which parcells of land, I recovered by law from Thomas Snawsell ... and was delivered to me by the Marshall ... [dated 10 July 1682] ...; [Dated - 11 July 1682; signed - Sam^{ll} Moore; witnesses - Rob. Hamilton, John Stout.]

[24 March 1684 - Hamilton & Stout appeared before Justices John Hance, John Throckmorton, and Peter Tilton and stated that they saw Samuell Moore sign the deed.]

MONMOUTH COUNTY DEEDS - BOOK "B"

[p 23] JUDGEMENT OBTAINED BY ANTHONY CHEEKLEY AGAINST THOMAS SNAWSELL

... I, Samuell Moore of the town of Woodbridge ... East New Jersey, Provost Marshall, ... to me given ... an execution ... [dated - 23 May 1682] ... obtained by M[r] Anthony Cheekely of Boston Merchant plt against M[r] Thomas Snawsell of Middletowne ... East New Jersey deft have delivered unto Samuell Moore of Woodbridge ... Attorney to the above named Anthony Cheekley ...; [Dated -10 July 1682; signed - Sam[ll] Moore; witnesses - Robert Hamilton, John Stout.]

[24 March 1684/5 - Both Hamilton and Stout appeared before Justices - John Hance, John Throckmorton, Peter Tilton and stated that they saw Moore sign the deed; att. R. Gardiner, Clk.]

[p 24] RICHARD HARTSHORNE to JOHN CRAFFORD

... Richard Hartshorne of Middletowne in New Jersey ... [sold for 28 pounds] ... [15 acres] ... of upland ... at a place called poplar field within the bounds of Middletowne ... [9 acres] ... [adjacent land owners or names - William Lawrence Jun[r], Richard Sadler] ... [and 6 acres] ... [adjacent land owners or names - William Lawrence Jun[r], Richard Sadler, Stephen Arnold] ... by Patent ... [dated 5 December 1678] ... granted to Richard Hartshorne ... by these presents granted unto ... John Crafford ... [for half a penny] pr acre for every one of the fifteen acres yearly ... to be holden as of the mannour of East Greenwich in free and comon Soccage the first payment to begin ... [25 March 1679] ...; [Dated - 20 April 1680; signed - Richard Hartshorne; witnesses - John Richardson, Ian Iansen; att. R. Gardiner, Clk.]

[p 26] POWER OF ATTORNEY

... I, Lewis Morris, commonly called Coll[o] Lewis Morris of New Yorke ... does put & constitute my loveing freind Thomas Webley of Tinton in the New East Jersey to be my true & lawfull Attorney ...; [Dated - 15 June 1685; signed - Lewis Morris; witnesses - Chr. Smith, Edward Squire, W[m] Bickley.]

[20 June 1685 - Both Smith & Bickley testified before Justice John Hance that they saw Coll[o] Lewis Morris sign the above deed; att. R. Gardiner, Clk.]

[p 27] TESTIMONY

23 June 1685 - ... George Axton aged about forty years did declare upon his engagement that he did heare Joseph Parker deceased about 3 or 4 months before he dyed say: that he had sold Thomas Hearce a peece of land lying on the East side of the Alewife brooke ... [adjoining land owners or names - John Hance] ... And further sayeth yt the sd. Joseph Parker did further say that he had received from the said Hearce one horse, and one cow & calfe in full sattisfaction for the said land.

(50)

MONMOUTH COUNTY DEEDS - BOOK "B"

Att the same time appeared John Slocum aged about 36 years and did declare that Joseph Parker told him he had sold Thomas Hearce a small piece of land lying beyond the Alewife brooke ... he thinks he told him it was all the land he had on that side the Brooke, and further that said Parker did declare he had received satisfaction for the same by a horse and some money and further sayeth not.

[p 28] RECORD OF SAMUELL SHATTOCK'S LETTER OF ATTORNEY TO JOHN HANCE

... wee, Samuel Shattock Senr and Samuel Shattock, Junr the true and lawfull Attorneys of George Wharton of London & brother & Administrat^r of Edward Wharton late of Salem have ... and in our stead & place by these presents putt ... our trusty well beloved friend John Hance of Shrewsbury in ... New Jersey to be our true & lawful Attorney under us in the name & to the use of the said George Wharton ...; [Dated - 29 October 1681; signed - Sam^{ll} Shattock Senr, Sam^{ll} Shattock Junr; witnesses - Edward Marole, John Attwater.]

[1 November 1681 - both Shattocks appeared before William Bowne assistant; recorded - 22 September 1685 at a Court of Sessions in Middltowne before John Throckmorton & Peter Tilton; recorded by R. Gardiner, Clk.]

[p 30] POWER OF ATTORNEY

... I, Lewis Morris comonly called Coll^o Lewis Morris of New Yorke in America, have ... put ... my loveing freind Richard Hartshorne of Portland point to be my ... Attorney for me ...; [Dated - 18 April 1685; signed - Lewis Morris; witnesses - Edward Squire, Tho. Webley, Wm Bickley.]

[16 September 1685 - Both Webley and Bickley appeared before Justice John Hance and tesitifed that they saw Coll^o Lewis Morris sign the above item; recorded - R. Gardiner, Clk.]

[p 31] POWER OF ATTORNEY

... I, Phillip Smith of Newport on Rhoade Island and providence plantacons doe hereby assign ... appoint ... my loveing freind John Bowne of Middletown ... East New Jersey to be my true and lawfull Attorney ... that now are or hereafter ... due ... unto my brother Edward Smith deceased in ... East New Jersey ...; [Dated - 22 April 1686; signed - Phillip Smith; witnesses - James Bowne, Obadiah Bowne basically notorized the signature of Phillip Smith before him on the above date.]

[Both James and Obadiah Bowne appeared in open Court before John Hance, John Throckmorton, and Peter Tilton regarding the above; recorded - R. Gardiner, Clk.]

MONMOUTH COUNTY DEEDS - BOOK "B"

[p 33] INDIAN DEED to JOHN BOWNE

Know all men ... that wee the cheif Sachems of Wromasung & Machayis, vis^{tt} Porruppo, Irasecott, Pemhoose & propriet^{ors} of a certain tract of land ... [agree to sell the land for] ... Sundry species of trading goods ... to be full & ample satisfaction for the said tract of land ... unto John Bowne of Middletown, Yeoman ... New Jersey A ... trackt of land beginning at Wropockotong ... [adjacent land owners or names - hop river, between Memcokomuk and tangan awamess, Richard Stout's land, a small run called Moharhes, Memcokomek path, a branch of Changaroras river, Connescone, Richard Hartshorne's former purchase, untill it falls into the bay] ...; [Dated at Middletown - 29 September 1676; witnesses - John Smith, James Dorsett, Henry Marsh, Edward Smith; signed by the marks of Peruppo, Penhoose, Myawicke, Irasecott.]

[22 June 1686 - Both James Dorsett & Henry Marsh appeared in Court before Justices John Hance, John Throckmorton, and Peter Tilton and testified that they saw the above Sachems sign the deed.]

[p 35] INDIAN DEED to JOHN BOWNE

Know all men ... That wee the chiefe Sachems of Wickatong viz ^{tt} Quahicke, Jonathan, Perorack, Shenatapo & Pandam, cheife Sachems ... of a certain meadow, Know by the of Goanocken hereafter ... [sold] ... in consideration of Sundry species of trading goods ... [to] ... John Bowne of Middletown ... New Jersey, yeoman ...; [Dated - 8 October 1679; witnesses - John Stout, James Bowne, Edward Smith; signed with the marks of Quahicke, Jonathan, Perorack, Shenotope, Pandam.]

22 June 1686 - Both John Stout and James Bowne appeared in Court before John Hance, John Throckmorton, and Peter Tilton and testified that they saw the Sachems sign the above deed; recorded - R. Gardiner, Clk.]

[p 37] JONATHAN HULMES LETT^R ATT^O TO RICH^D HARTSHORNE

... I Jonathan Hulmes of Newport on Rhoad Island in the Colony of Rhoad Island and Providence plantacon in New England & late of Middletown ... East Jersey ... have ... putt & constitute my trusty & well beloved freind Richard Hartshorne of Middletown ... my true & lawfull Attorney ...; [Dated - 27 October 1684; witnesses - Aaron Davis, Thomas Ward.]

[18 February 1685 - The above signature of Jonathan Hulmes was notorized before Justice John Throckmorton; recorded - R. Gardiner, Clk.]

[p 38] FREDERICK FLIPSON'S LETT^R OF ATTO^R TO RICH^D HARTSHORNE

... I Frederick Flipson of the City of New York, Merchant ... in regard of ... confidence ... to my loving freind Richard Hartshorne of Middletowne Gent, ... appointed ... [him] ... to be my true &

MONMOUTH COUNTY DEEDS - BOOK "B"

lawfull Attorney ...; [Dated - 24 December 1685; signed - Fredryck Flipson; witnesses - Rombout Phillipse, I.S. Swinton.]

[27 February 1685(sic) - Abiah Edwards testis - Abiah Edwards, Thomas Heirs appeared before Justice John Hance in reference to seeing Flison sign same; recorded - R. Gardiner, Clk.]

[p 40] INDIAN DEED to JOHN SMITH

... wee Indians being cheife Sachamachas or Sachems sometimes stild the Janatan, Irasecutt & Wamatam at present inhabiting at Wiquatung by us so called within East New Jersey alias New Cesaria ... in consideration of Sundry Species of trading goods ... by estimacon ... the sum of ... [25 pounds] ... to us ... paid ... by John Smith Batchelor and late school master of Middletown ... [sell] ... A certain tract of land ... within the County of the said Middletowne ... [adjacent land owners or names - foot path leading South from Jonathan Hulmes, the West side of William Lawrence Senr land bought of the Indians] ... known by the Indians by the name of Mengache, but from henceforth ... to be known & called amongst our English by the name of Smith feild & now in the possession of the foresaid Sachmachas ...; [Dated - 22 June 1678; witnesses - John Bowne, Jonathan Hullmes, Sohoppo, Henry Marsh; signed by the marks of Chococus, Jonatan, Irasecut, Wamuton.]

[22 June 1686 - Henry Marsh appeared in Court and testified that he saw the Indians sign the above document.]

16 March 1686/7 - Wamuton appeared before Justice John Throckmorton and acknowledged that he and the rest of the Indians signed the above document; recorded - R. Gardiner, Clk.]

[p 43] BILL OF SAILE FRANCES URSINTONE

... Rob. Hamilton of Middletone in the County of Monmouth ... New East Jarsey ... yoman ... [sold for 19 pounds] ... to Frances Ursintone of Statton Iyland ... New Yorke ... two towne lotts of land joyning together lying in Middleton ... [adjoining land owners or names - Job. Throckmorton, Richard Sadler, John Stout] ... [and 6 acres of meadown] ... [adjoining land owners or names - Stephen Arnold, John Bonne] ... [sold by] ... Jacob Treuax of Midleton ... as of the manor of East Greenwich ...; [Dated at Middletowne - 4 May 1687; signed - Rob. Hamilton; witnesses - Thomas Rousell, Dericke Tunison, William Scott who made his mark.]

[7 May 1687 - a paragraph was added to the above before the same witnesses.]

[29 June 1687 - Rob. Hamilton appeared in Court before Justice John Johnson, John Throckmorton, Peter Tilton; recorded - Rob. Hamilton, Clk.]

MONMOUTH COUNTY DEEDS - BOOK "B"

[p 45] DEED THOMAS STATHAM to LEWIS MORRIS

... Thomas Statham now of the Tonneshipe of West Chester ... [sells to] ... Lewis Morris of Shrosbury ... the within menconed Blackstone horsse for a vallowable consideration ...; [Dated - 3 August 1685; signed - Thomas Stratham; witnesses - Daniell Mallson, John Marlon.]

[29 June 1687 - John Marlin appeared in Court before Justice John Throckmorton & Peter Tilton; recorded - Rob. Hamilton, Clk.]

[AT THIS POINT, THE PAGES ARE AGAIN RENUMBERED BEGINNING WITH PAGE 43 (a).]

[p 43a] JOHN CRAFFOORD HIS BILL OF SAILE TO PETTER TILTON

... John Crafford of Middletowne ... East Jarsey have a housse, land, orchard, meadow, which I formerly bought of Sam^{ll} Moore of Woodbridge Atturney to Anthony Chedly of Boston Mass ...[for 60 pounds] ... to me at the signing ... payed by Petter Tilton of Midletowne ... have by these presents ... sell ... from me ... unto Petter Tilton ... [all that I bought of Moore Attorney to Chedly] ... as by the bill of saile ... [dated 11 July 1682] ... the home lott being in Middletown ... [adjoining land owners or names - John Smith, John Carfford] ... [20 acres] ... and in the poplar feild ... [9 acres] and 5 acres meadow] ... uppon Weacocke Creike ...; [Dated - 16 April 1685; signed at Middletown - John Crafoord; witnesses - John Throckmorton, Robt Hamilton.]

[16 April 1685 - Crafoord acknowledged receipt of the 60 pounds before John Throckmorton and John Stout.]

[27 September 1687 - The deed of saile ... is proven before us ... John Johnson, John Hance; recorded 19 November 1687 - Rob. Hamilton.]

[p 44b] PETTER TILTON to RICHARD HARTSHORNE

... Peter Tilton of Marvill Hill in Middletown ... County of Monmouth ... East New Jersey ... whereas Phillip Cartrett Governor ... did give ... unto Richard Stout Senyo^r ... [40 acres] ... of upland and meadow ... and the sd. Richard Stout did sell the same unto Thomas Snosnell and the sd. Snosnell did by his Atturney sell the same unto John Crafoord ... and the sd. Crafoord did by deed sell the sd. land and meadow unto me Petter Tilton. Now these presents ... [Tilton sells for 54 pounds to Richard Hartshorne of Portland point land] ... lying in Middletown ... [adjoining land owners or names - John Smith, Richard Hartshorne, home lott formerly of Richard Gibone] ... and ... [9 acres] ... in the poplar field and ... [9 acres] ... of meadow and ... [6 acres] ... of meadow lying in Middletowne meadows ...; [Dated - 27 September 1687; signed - Petter Tilton; witnesses- John Johnston, John Hance, John Throckmorton; recorded - 19 November 1687; Rob. Hamilton, Clk.]

MONMOUTH COUNTY DEEDS - BOOK "B"

[p 44c] **THE INDIANS BILL OF SAILE TO JONATHAN HOLMES OF MIDDLETOWN**

... we the Cheefe Sachem of Wromanasung viz: Jonatan, Pororo, Caheck, Mosehoppe, Shenolape, and remote proprietors in Cheefe of a certain tract of land ... [sell fo] ... Sundry Spations of trading goods ... unto Jonathan Holmes of Middletown yoman ... New East Jarsey ... land ... betweene the two hoope Rivers, on the East side: Bounded by the river knowne by the Indian name Wromanasung or the eastern hoope river ... to a brook ... called by the Indian name Redquapiaqneck ... till it fall in to the West hoope river or by the Indian name Mongomhonnick ... till the two rivers come to meet ...; [Dated - 12 August 1677; witnesses - John Bowne, John Smith, John Dorsete; signed by the marks of Jonatan, Porore, Qahick, Misehoppe, Shenotape, Waymoto.]

NOTE - [The above written instroment is entred on Record in the 105 padge in the book of law evidence No [3] belonging to ye towne of Newport on Rhod Iyland; signed - Weston, Clarke.]

[17 February 1685 - James Dorset appeared before Justice John Throckmorton and stated that he say the deed signed by the Indians.]

[27 February 1687 - the above deed was proved in open Court before John Johnston, John Throckmorton, and John Hance; recorded - 19 November 1687; Rob' Hamilton, Clarke.]

[p 47] **JOHN CRAFFORD to PETER TILTON**

... I, John Crafoord of Midletowne ... County of Monmouth ... East Jarsey ... yeoman ... Whereas Richard Stout of Middletown ... on ehouse loot in Midletown ... [16 acres] ... and [9 acres] ... in the poplar feild & ... [9 acres] ... of meadow in one parcell and ... [6 acres] ... in another ,,, in Midletowne meadows as by pattent ... by Governor Carterett ... and ... Richard Stout and Penelope his wife ... sell the above ... [40 acres] ... unto Thomas Snosell of Middletown ... [dated 26 February 1679] ... [and Snowsell by his Attorney Richard Hartshorne sold it by deed dated 10 April 1682] ... Now know ye that I the aforesd. John Crafoord of Middletown ... East Jarsey ... [sell it for 60 pounds] ... to Petter Tilton of Middletown ...; [Dated - 10 April 1682; signed - John Crafoord; witnesses - Thomas Cooke, Peter White.]

[29 December 1687/8 - Thomas Cooke and Peter White and John Crafoord appeared before Justice John Hance and John Throckmorton; recorded - Rob. Hamilton, Clarke.]

[p 49] **HENRY MARSSH to JOSEPH THROCKMORTON**

... whereas Phillip Cartret Governor ... did give ... unto John Rachan of Midletowne ... Monmouth ... East Jarsey ... [126 acres of upland by patent dated 10 January 1676] ... and the said John Rachan

MONMOUTH COUNTY DEEDS - BOOK "B"

... [sold it to Henry Marssh of the same place afores'd ... Now know yee that I the foresd. Henry Marssh planter ... [for 16 pounds] ... payd by Joseph Trokmorton of Middletown ... Mariner ... [adjoining land owners or names - Richard Gibons, a small brooke called the porrasy river] ... [sold by deed from Rachan to Marssh on 30 March 1688] ; ... [Dated - 6 April 1688; signed - Henry Marssh; witnesses - Rob' Hamilton, clarke and Petter Tilton, Justice.]

[10 April 1688 - Henry Marssh acknowledged that Throkmorton paid him 16 pounds before Justice Peter Tilton and Rob. Hamilton Clarke; recorded - Rob. Hamilton, Clarke.]

[26 June 1688 - Petter Tilton and Robert Hamilton stated before Justice John Hance that Marssh signed the deed.]

[p 52] LETER OF ATURNAY THOMAS CLIFTON AND PATIENCE BEERE TO JOHN HANCE

... we Thomas Clifton & Patiance Beere both of the tonne of Newport on Rhode Iyland & providence plantations in New England ... doe nominate our trusty & well beloved friend John Hance of the towne of Shrewsbury ... Monmouth ... New Jarsey our ... lawfull Autrnay for us ...[regarding] ... Abraham Bowne now or late inhabitant in the aforesd. tonne of Shrosbury ...; [Dated - 14 April 1675; signed - Thomas Clifton, Patience Beere; witnesses - William Coddington Go^v, John Easton.]

[The seal of the Collony affixed as atested - John Sanfoord, Recorder.]

[26 June 1688 - The Court orderit it to be recorded; signed - Justices Peter Tilton & Leiws Morris.]

[p 53] SAMUELL DENNIS HIS REVOCATION OF A SHARE OF LAND

Whereas I formally gave William Leeds an order to dispose of the share of land that I and ... William Leeds bought of John Bonne of Flushing in Long Iyland provided the said order was not cancelled these are to signifie ... that I doe by these presents firmly ... revoke the sd. order and all other writtings ... concerning the disposeing of the sd. share of land ...; [Dated - 26 June 1688; signed - Sam^{ll} Dennis.]

[26 June 1688 - It was ordered to be recorded; signed - Justices John Hance, Petter Tilton, Lewis Morris.]

[p 54] RICHARD HARTSHORNE to HENERY MARSSH

... Now know yee that whereas Phillip Cartright governor of East Jarsey ... did ... grant unto Richard Stoutt Senio^r ... [9 acres of upland] ... [and Stout sold it to Thomas Snosell, and by his Aturnay to John Crafoord, and Crafoors to Petter Tilton, and from Tilton to Richard Hartshorne] ... Now these

MONMOUTH COUNTY DEEDS - BOOK "B"

presents ... I the sd. Richard Hartshorne ... of Portland point ... Monmouth ... East Jarsey ... [for 5 pounds sold to] ... Henry Marssh of Midletown ... yeoman ... [9 acres in the place called poplar field] ... [adjoining land owners or names - Stephen Arnold, William Layton, Edward Smith] ...; [Dated - 25 September 1688; signed - Richard Hartshorne; witnesses - John Hance, Lewis Morris; recorded - 2 Oct 1688, Rob. Hamilton Clarke.]

[p 55] JOHN VAUHAN to HENERY MARSSH

... I, John Vauhan of Midletown ... Monmouth ... East Jarsey, carpenter, ... [for 15 pounds sold to] ... Henry Marssh planter of the same place ... [126 acres] ... of upland lying ... in Midletown ... [adjoining land owners or names - Richard Gibons, a small brook called porisy rune] ... [the same land was granted to Vauhan by Patent from the Governor of New Jersey dated 10 January 1676] ...; [Dated - 30 March 1688; signed - John Vauhan; witnesses - Rob. Hamilton Clarke, Petter Tilton Justice.]

[31 March 1688 - John Vauhan acknowledged that he received the 15 pounds for the 126 acres; witnesses - Rob' Hamilton, Clarke and Petter Tilton, Justice; recorded - Rob' Hamilton, Clark.]

[25 September 1688 - John Vauhan appeared before Justices John Hance & Lewis Morris.]

[p 57] RECEIPT - RICHARD HARTSHORNE TO JOSEPH THROKMORTON OF FIVE POUNDS IN FULL SATTISFACTION FORE EIGHT HUNDRED ACRES OF LAND

30 March 1688 - ... Witnesseth that I Richard Hartshorne ... [received from] ... Joseph Throkmorton ... [5 pounds] ... by order of Sam'' Spicer which five pounds is in full satisfaction for about ... [800 acres] ... of land that is to say, for the Indain purchase that Sam'' Spicer hath pattented and bought and now sould to Joseph Throckmorton , which land lyes on the South side of Middletown, and land that I, underwritten bought three parts of the Indians, and doe by these for me ... and it is to be understood the ... 120 acres] ... that John Vachan pattented is contained in the aforesaid ... [800 acres] ...; [Signed - Richard Hartshorne; witnesses - Robt Hamilton Clarke, Petter Tilton, Justice; recorded - 23 November1688, Rob' Hamilton, Clarke.]

[p 58] ESTABLISHED ACTS

28 November 1688 - An act for establishing Courts of Indicature and public Justice; ... Several laws made by the Governor and Council to be in force within the lat Collony of Conetticott now anexed to this Government ...; laws made by the Governor & Councill to be in force within the late province of New York, and East and West Jersey now anexed to this Government ...

MONMOUTH COUNTY DEEDS - BOOK "B"

[p 58] MARRIAGE

13 December 1691 - Shrowsbury - William Beedell Junior of Burlington ... & Lydia Wardell of ye towne ... wery joyned together in Marriage ...; [Signed - Lewis Morris.]

[p 59] ATT A COURT OF SESSIONS HELD AT MIDDLETOWN

25 December 1688 - John Johnston, President; Peter Tilton, John Hance, Lewis Morris - Justices.

[p 59] ATT A COURT OF COMMON PLEAS HELD AT MIDDLETOWN

25 December 1688 - Andrew Hamilton, Judge; John Johnston, Peter Tilton, John Hance, Lewis Morris.

... Judge Hamilton ... to be Judg of the Court of Common Pleas of the four Counteys of East Jersey viz: Essex, Middlesex, Bergen & Monmouth ...

[p 60] AN INVENTORY OF YE GOOD & CHATTELLS OF HENERY CHAMBERLIN OF MANUSQUAN, LATELY DECEASED

[Most of the Inventory dealt with 32 different types of animals. Other items were a silkgrass bed, furniture, a weaver's loome & harness, one gun and one carbine, clothing, etc. Total of Inventory was 42 pounds, 17 shillings. The estate was appraised by Nicholas Browne, who made his mark when signing and Edward Williams who made his mark when signing. There was no date.] Thomas Webley, Clk.

[p 61] FRANCES LAFETRA to JOHN WEST

25 January 1688 - To All Christian People ... I, Frances Lafetra, late wife of Edmond Lafetra, deceased of the town of Shrosbury ... Monmouth ... New East Jersey, in New England send Greeting: ... I ... Frances Lafetra for and in consideration of ye naturall affection and motherly Love, which I have & beare unto my well beloved son John West of ye place aforesaid ... have given ... unto ... John West all those tracts of land I have ... at or near Manasquan River ... Monmouth being ... [100 acres] viz: one half on ye South side of Manusquan river ... [39 acres] ... bounded East by the sea, West by land unsurveyed, North by land of Richard Hartshorne, South by lands of Tobias Hanson. As allso another tract ... on the North side of Mannasquan river ... [60 acres] ... bounded Southeast by the river, Northwest by land unsurveyed, Northeast by land of John Williams & William Woolley, Southwest by land of Ephraim Allen. Also one acre of upland by the south side of the river ... along the river ... bounded easterly by Richard Hartshorne, Westerly by Tobias Hanson, their acre lotts ... to John West [and his heirs] ... and for want of such heirs to fall to my daughter Sarah Lafetra ...;

MONMOUTH COUNTY DEEDS - BOOK "B"

[Signed - Frances made her mark when signing; witnesses - Nicholas Browne made his mark, William Kilmister; Thomas Webley, Clk.]

[p 62] **ACCONS ENTERED AGAINST MARCH COURT**

Capt Andrew Bown against John Craford ... withdrawn; Coll° Lewis Morris against John Crawford ... withdrawn; John Barclay against Samuel Leonard; The proprietors of East New Jersey against Thomas Iukrain ...

[p 63] **A RECORD OF BOND GIVEN BY CAPT. JOHN SLOCUM TO SUSANAH WRIGHT**

... I John Slucum of the towne of Shrosbury ... Monmouth ... Yeoman do ow & stand duly indebted unto Susanah Wright, of the place aforesaid ...; [Dated - 25 March 1690; Signed - John Slocum; witnesses - William Scott, Tho. Webley, Clk; before Peter Tilton.]

[p 64] **ELIAKIM WARDELL to EPHRAIM ALLEN**

... Eliakim Wardell of Shrowsbury ... Monmouth ... New East Jersey yeoman ... [for a certain sum paid] by Ephraim Allen, yeoman inhabitant of ye sd. Towne ... [sold] ... land ... being upon Romsonts North within ye bounds of ye to Town ... [290 acres] ... bounded on ye North by Neversinck river, East by John Hance, West by Francis Borden, South by his own meadow ... [230 acres with allowance for swamps, highways, etc with one exception] ... a small piece of upland known by ye name of Great Meadow Island, lying at Shrowsbury river ... [7 acres] ... bounded by ye S. By ye sd. River, on ye E. & W. By two by the mouth of two creeks & N. By ye meadows of Thomas Huett, Robert Leacock & Abraham Brown ... [and the above 7 acres being in two parcels bounded] ... on ye East by John Hance, W. By Francis Borden, S. & S.E. by William Shattock & Shrowesbury river and N. By his owne upland ...; [Dted - 22 day of the 3 Mo. 1684; Signed- Eliakim Wardell, Lydia Wardell; witnesses - Joseph Parker, John Starke made his mark.]

[22 June 1686 - Eliakim Wardell acknowledged the deed in open court before John Throckmorton, Peter Tilton, and John Hance.]

[p 67] **ROBERT HAMILTON to RICHARD HARTSHORNE**

23 February 1685 - ... Robert Hamilton of Midletown ... Monmouth ... East New Jersey ... [sold for 8 pounds to] ... Richard Hartshorne ... [40 acres] ... of upland ... on ye South side of Middletown ... record in the Secretary's office lying between John Job & John Crawford ... Bounded on the North by John Crawford, South by John Job , West by land unsurveyed, East by a highway ...; [Signed - Robt. Hamilton; witnesses - David Brown; John White made his mark; acknowledged before John Throckmorton - Justice.]

MONMOUTH COUNTY DEEDS - BOOK "B"

[p 69] ATT A COURT OF SESSIONS ... SHROWSBURY

26 March 1689 - ... Mr. John Johnston shall be paid ... for the dyett of John White ... he being sick and ill of an ulcer ... Uppon application of Nathaniell Cammock that a warrant be immediately granted to the Constable of Middletown ... that he repair to the house of William Leeds of the said town and there take into his custody Jonathan Leeds his son and deliver him to his said Master Nathaniell Cammock to serve him as an apprentice the remaining part of his time according to an Indenture here in Court produced.

[p 70] AN INVENTORY OF THE ESTATE OF JOSEPH GROVER TAKEN 25 MARCH 1689

[The Inventory consisted of several animals, four beds & bedding, brass powler potts & other household goods, farm implements, one cart & veheecles and "One Negro at 16 pds." Inventory was taken by Peter Tilton, William Scott, and Samuell Forman.]

[p 71] ATT A COURT OF COMMON PLEAS

26 March 1689 - Lewis Morris of passage point against Morgan Bergen; Nathaniell Cammock against William Leeds for trepass; The King against Benjamin Devall; Daniel Applegate against William Leeds, Junior; John Throckmorton against Benjamin Devall; Benjamin Devall against Abiah Edwards; Samuell Leonard against Derrick Tunnison.

[p 72] ATT A COURT OF SESIONS ... MIDDLETOWNE

[25 June 1689 - The Grand Jury call ... John Slocum & John Baker [both fined for not appearing]

Jury - Jedeiah Allen, Thomas Potter, John Williams, Georg Curliss, Francis Borden, William Scott, Mordacay Gibbons, Jonathan Stout, William Lawrence Jr, William Lord, Thomas Roberts, Garret Wall, Joseph West.

[The Grand Jury fined] ... Ephraim Potter, Benjamin Stick, Stephen Cooke, Richard Brnes, Joseph Hick, Thomas Heart ... for horss raceing, playing at nyne pinns on ye Sabath day, also Nicholas Brown was presented for selling of run to ye Indians ... Also ye Court ordered that ye daughter of Tommason Sarah Hall tendered to his father-in-law and for shee to give him, provided he will, allow her sufficient maintenance, if not it was ordered ... that Peter Tilton, John Hance & Lewis Morris shall have ... authority to bind the said maid to what master or mistress the said Justices shall see fitt ... untill she be eighteen years of age ...

MONMOUTH COUNTY DEEDS - BOOK "B"

[p 73] INFORMATION

25 June 1689 - An information was given in by Benjamin Kick ... [to John Hance] ... against John Jennings, John West, Edward Williams, Lewis Morris, Calieb Shrive, Clemment Masters, John Lippincott Junior, William Hulett, Peter Parker, Edon the Indian, Thomas Wainwright, for running of races, playing at nyn pinns on the Sabath day ...

[p 73] ATT A COURT OF COMMON PLEAS ... MIDDLETOWN

25 June 1689 - Coll. Andrew Hamilton, Judg; John Johnston, Peter Tilton, John Hance, Lewis Morris - Justices.

Jury - Judah Allen, John Barchley, Nicholas Brown, Ephraim Allen, Calieb Shrive, Jeremiah Bennett, John Crawford, Richard Davis, Job Throckmorton, George Jobes, Enoch Hill, John Willson Junior.

[Court heard cases of: Nathaniell Cammock against William Leeds; The King against Benjamin Devall by his attorney James Emott re: the forfeiture of a bond which was for the maintenance of a bastard child; Devall's attorney was Samuell Leonard. The Jury called John Worthley and upon his evidence ... Obiah Edwards [blank] for the maintenance of the child of Mary Sutton.]

Joseph Hick did declare ... that Obiah Edwards did send to ye house of ... Worthley for ye said child by them the said Joseph, Ephraim Potter & Richard James, they did demand ye child from John Worthley, the said John Worthley's wiffe would not let it go because the mother of the said child was not at home.

[p 75] POWER OF ATTORNEY

24 October 1687 - ... George Wharton ... town of London yeoman, Executor of ye will ... of Edward Wharton his late brother late of Salem in New England, glazier, deceased, and John Harwood of London, merchant doe send: Greeting: Whereas ... Edward Wharton ... by his wrighting ... [dated 31 November 1669] ... did ...confirm unto ... John Harwood ... the moyety or half part of a certain parcell of land called Newison ... being New York & Dellaware Bay in New England ... Whereas ... [the above is property vested to George Wharton by the will] ... Now Know ye that wee ... George Wharton & John Harwood ... constitute our trusty & Loveing friend John Hance of Newison near Dellaway our ... attorney ... [regarding the above lands] ...; Signed - George Wharton, Jon. Harwood; witnesses - John Wilde, John Hoy; Boston in New England, 10 July 1688.]

[The above instrument was acknowledged by the witnesses in Court before F. Randolph of the Councill; recorded in Court before John Johnston, Peter Tilton, Lewis Morris.]

MONMOUTH COUNTY DEEDS - BOOK "B"

[p 78] JOHN CRAFFORD to JOHN WILLIAMSON

25 June 1689 - ... John Crafford of Middletown ... Monmouth ... New East Jersey yeoman, sends greeting: Now know ... whereas Andrew Hamilton Governor of New East Jersey ... did ... grant unto John Craffors ... [200 acres] ... of upland within ... Middletown as by patent ... [dated 2 December 1787] ... Now these presents ... [Crafford sold for 20 pounds to] ... John Williamson of Middletown ... yeoman ... [130 acres from out of the 200 acres] ... [adjacent land owners or names - Swiming river, Richard Gibons] ...; [Signed - John Crafford; witnesses - Robert Hamilton, John Barclay.]

[p 80] RICHARD HARTSHORNE to JOHN CLAYTON

22 September 1681 - Richard Hartshorne ... of Middletown ... [for 5 pounds].. paid by John Clayton of Wakeich ... [sells to him] ... several small pieces of meadow ... [adjacent land owners or names - pine necke, Wacaick neck, fresh brook] ... [amounting to 16 acres] ... [by virtue of a patent to Hartshorne on 5 December 1678] ...; [Signed - Richard Hartshorne; witnesses John Hance, Peter Tilton, Robert Hamilton.]

[25 June 1689 - Hartshorne acknowledged same when he appeared in Court before John Johnson, Lewis Morris.]

[p 82] RICHARD HARTSHORNE to JOHN CLAYTON

25 October 1686 - Richard Hartshorne of Middletown ... [sold for 110 pounds to] ... John Clayton of Wakayeck ... one neck of land commonly called Wakeake Neck ... [adjacent land owners or names - on SW side of Middletown harbour, pine neck, Wakeck neck] ... [215 acres] ... by patent ... [dated 28 June 1678] ... from Phillip Cartteritt to Hartshorne ...; [Signed - Richard Hartshorne; witnesses John Hanse, Peter Tilton, Robert Hamilton.]

[25 June 1689 - Hartshorne appeared and acknowledged the deed before John Johnston, Lewis Morris.]

[p 84] GEORGE MOUNT to JOHN THROCKMORTON

20 June 1689 - ... I George Mount of Middletown ... Smith, ... [for 20 pounds] ... paid by John Throckmorton of the same place ... [sell to him] ... [500 acres of upland & meadow ... at a place commonly known & called by the name of Cohanzy in West Jersey ... [adjacent land owners or names - Mount's Creek, Cohanzy River, Benjamin Burden] ...; [Signed - George Mount made his mark when signing; witnesses - John Bowne, John Stout, Thos. Webley.]

MONMOUTH COUNTY DEEDS - BOOK "B"

[p 86] ATT A COURT OF SESSIONS AT SHROWSBURY

24 September 1689 - John Johnston, President; Peter Tilton, John Hance, Lewis Morris, Justices.

Grand Jury - Frances Jackson, Thomas Potter, John Stout, John Read, Abraham Brown, George Curlis, Thomas Vicars, James Stout, Ephraim Allen, John Hart, Elisha Lawrence, Joseph West, Samuell Applegate.

The Servant of John Read was brought to Court to be Judged of his age and what time he should serve his said Master. John Anderson the servant of John Read was Judged to be sixteen years of age and that he shall serve five years from ye day ...

The Grand Jury came into Court againe and did present thomas Wainwright, Ephraim John West (sic), Clement Masters, for playing at nyne pinnes on ye first day, also did present Morgan Bryan for fighting ...

[p 87] AT A COURT OF COMMON PLEAS ... SHROWSBURY

24 September 1689 - Coll Andrew Hamilton, Judge; John Hance, John Johnston, Peter Tilton, Lewis Morris, Justices.

[p 87] MARRIAGE

28 March 1690 - William Hullett and Mary Sutton appeared before me and the abovesaid ... [both took each other] ... to be ... wedded ... till death part them; [Signed - Peter Tilton.]

[p 88] PETER EASTON to JOHN TUCKER

14 June 1687 - ...I, Peter Easton of Newport on Rhoade Island ... [for 20 pounds sold to] ... John Tucker of East Jersey ... all my ... lands, and meadows ... in the County of Monmouth ...; [Signed - Peter Easton; witness - James Clarke, West Clarke; attested to by Walter Clarke one of ye Councill of New England.]

[PAGE 89 WAS SKIPPED.]

[p 90] ACCONS ENTERED ... COURT

George Woolley against Thomas Wainewright; Robert Coale against Benjamin Devill.

MONMOUTH COUNTY DEEDS - BOOK "B"

****

[p 90] ATT A COURT OF SESSIONS ... MIDDLETOWN

23 December 1689 - John Johnston, President; Peter tilton, John Hance, Lewis Morris, Justices.

Jury - Jedediah Allen, William Ashton, Ephraim Allen, Francis Jackson, John Willson Senior, John Pearce, Samuell Culver, Henery Marsh, William Layton, Samuell Willett, Mathias Mount, Daniell Aplegate, Thomas Warn.

[Richard Hartshorne & John Throckmorton were appointed "overseers of ye poore" for Middletown Township.]

[p 91] ATT A COURT OF COMMON PLEAS ... MIDDLETOWN

24 December 1689 - Coll. Andrew Hamilton - Judge; John Johnston, Peter Tilton, John Hance, Lewis Morris - Justices.

Robert Coale against Benjamin Devell; Abraham Smith Against Thomas Warn that he had not ye promises performed as his Indenture specified ... Thomas Warne is to put ... Smith to a sound trade ... to be aught to read & wright according to his Indenture ... or sett him free ...

[p 92] ARRAMASOAK to SAMUELL LEONARD

24 June 1689 - Arramasoak, Hougham, Wayanocan of Mannusquan ... [sold to] ... Samuell Leonard of Coults Neck ... [for match Coates & rum] ... All that tract of land ... at Mannusquan ... [adjacent land owners or names - Squancum, Mannusquan river, William Worth] ...; [Signed - The Indians signed by making their various marks; witnesses - Robt. Coale, Tho. Webley, Edward Williams.]

[p 93] SAMUELL LEONARD to RICHARD STOUT

19 December 1689 - This Indenture ... between Samuell Leonard of Colts Neck ... Monmouth ... New Jersey yeoman ... [sold to] ... Richard Stout of Manusquan ... [for 3 pounds] ... all the tract of land which this within wrighten Deed doth specifie ... [however, nothing was specified] ...; [Signed - Samuell Leonard; witnesses - Rob. Coale, Thos. Webley.]

[p 94] ATT A COURT OF SESSIONS ... SHROWSBURY

25 March 1690 - Jury - Samuell Dennis foreman, Francis Jackson, Ephraim Allen, Abraham Brown, William Ashton, William Layton, John Barckley, Calieb Shreive, John Baker, William Scott, John Williams, Daniell Aplegate, Hanaiah Gifford.

MONMOUTH COUNTY DEEDS - BOOK "B"

Thomas Warne of Middletowne did complain ... against his servants Thomas Hankinson & Peter Hankinson, that the said servants had absented themselves severall times from his service ... [The court judged Thomas Hankinson to be 18 years of age & should serve 3 years more and 6 months more to the court's trouble and if he does it again he is to be taken to the whipping post.] ... Peter Hankinson ... was called & judged by the Court to be ... [16 years of age and he was to serve until he was 21 years plus an additional 6 months for the Court's trouble and also a warning in reference to the whipping post for the next infraction.]

[p 95] GUARDIANSHIP

Susannah Wright, daughter of Thomas Wright deceased did come into Court and did chuse Capt. John Slocum to be her Gardern.

Thomas Warne doe also complain against his Servant Abraham Smith ... [re: Smith running away for 1 month & 5 days...].

[p 95] ATT A COURT OF SESSIONS ... MIDDLETOWN

24 June 1670 - John Johnston, Judge; Peter tilton, John Hance, Lewis Morris, Justices.

[p 96] JOHN SMITH to RICHARD HARTSHORNE

12 December 1687 - I, John Smith & Mary, my wife, of Middletown ... Monmouth ... New Jersey ... Whereas ... [Smith was granted a house lott of 16 acres] ... [adjacent land owners or names - Richard Stout, Walter Wall] ... by a patent ... [dated - 1 December 1676] ... [now sells it for 40 pounds to] ... Richard Hartshorne of Portland point ...; [Signed - John Smith, Mary Smith; witnesses - Joseph Throckmorton, William Barnes.]

[p 97] JOHN CRAFFORD to JEREMY BENNETT

19 September 1685 - ... John Crafford of Middletown ... Monmouth ... New East Jersey ... [sold for 40 pounds to] ... Jeremy Bennett ... [of the same place] ... [130 acres] ... by Neversinks river, within ... Middletown ... [adjacent land owners or names - Richard Hartshorne, Samuell Culver, Neversink river] ...; [Signed - John Crafford; witnesses - John Stoutt, Henery Marsh.]

[p 98] LEWIS MATTIX to RICHARD HARTSHORNE

22 February 1688 - I Lewis Mattix of Shrowsbury ... Monmouth East New Jersey planter ... [sold for 4 pounds to] Richard Hartshorne of Portland Point in Middletown ... all those tracts of upland

MONMOUTH COUNTY DEEDS - BOOK "B"

& meadow ... [in Monmouth] ... [19 acres] ...; [Signed - Lewis Mattix made his mark when signing; witnesses - Walter Harbert, Tho. Webley.]

[p 100]   **JOSEPH WEST to JOSEPH WEST ET AL**

2 April 1688 - ...I, Joseph West ... [planter] ... of Shrosbury ...Monmouth ... East New Jersey ... [having a grant for several tracts of land in the right of Eliakim Wardell on the Southside of Manasquan river] ... [150 acres] ... [sells ½ share of land in Shrosbury to Joseph West and Also sells to Robert West ... [100 acres] ... [adjacent land owners or names - Rembrance Lippincott, Richard Hartshorne, Judah Allen, John Williams, William Woolley] ... [one Indenture dated 13 July 1686] ...; [Signed - Joseph West; witnesses - George Axton, Thomas Wainewright.]

[There was a mark of a William Leeds with "Victor" behind the name associated with this item.]

[p 102]   **NICHOLAS BROWN to WILLIAM WOOLLEY**

20 June 1690 - ... I Nicholas Brown of Shrowsbury ... Monmouth ... East New Jersey planter ... [for 6 pounds sold to] ... William Woolley of the same place ... All that ... upland & meadow ... at a place commonly known as Shark River ... [adjacent land owners or names - Thomas Hearts, Shark River or brooke, Thomas Hearce] ... [owned by a patent dated 5 May 1688] ...; [Signed - Nicholas Brown made his mark when signing; witnesses - Richard Hartshorne, John West.]

[p 104]   **JAMES JOHNSTON to LEWIS MORRIS**

23 March 1690 - James Johnston ... Middletown ... Monmouth ... East New Jersey Gent: ... [sold to] ... Lewis Morris of Tintam Iron Works ... [Monmouth County, New Jersey] ... [for 8 pounds] ... land in Monmouth ... [adjacent land owners or names - Mine bogg, saw mill brooke] ... [100 acres] ...; [Signed - James Johnston; witnesses - William Bickley, Roger Barton.]

[p 106]   **NATHANIELL WOOLLCOTT to EDWARD WILLIAMS**

12 March 1691 - Nathaniell Woollcott ... Shrosbury ... Monmouth ... East New Jersey carpenter ... [sold to] ... Edward Williams ... [of the same place for 14 pounds] ... one share of land ... in ... Shrowsbury ... now in ye possession of ... Edward Williams ... [160 acres] ... [adjacent land owners or names - Stephen West, Neversink river, Coll. Morris formerly Samuell Leonard's] ... also ... [6 acres of meadow] ... [adjacent land owners or names - John Hance, Edmond Lafetra] ... also ... [4 acres on Rackoone Island ... [adjacent land owners or names - Gideon Freehorn, Narawaticonk river, Shrowsbury River] ...; [Signed - Nathaniell Woollcott made his mark when signing; witnesses - Samuell Leonard, William West, Tho. Webley]

[28 June 1692 - Webley and Leonard acknowledged the deed in Court.]

MONMOUTH COUNTY DEEDS - BOOK "B"

[p 108]   **NATHANIELL WOLLCOTT to EDWARD WILLIAMS**

10 May 1690 - Nathaniell Wollcott ... Shrowsbury ... Monmouth ... East New Jersey, Carpenter ... [sold to] ... Edward Williams ... [of the same place for 14 pounds] ... one moyety or half part of a share ... which formerly did belong unto Samuell Woollcott deceased ... in Shrowsbury ... now in possession of Edward Williams ... [adjacent land owners or names - Coll. Lewis Morris, road to Long Branch, Veversink river, Stephen West] ...; [Signed - Nathaniell Wollcott made his mark when signing; witnesses - William W. Havens, Audrey Webley, Thos. Webley.]

[23 September 1690 - Thomas Webley acknowledged the deed before Peter Tilton and Lewis Morris.]

[Pages 110 through 112 were the accountings of the Court for various years.]

[END OF BOOK "B"]

I, Joseph Mc Dermott, Clerk of the County of Monmouth, certify the foregoing copy of "BOOK B" to be a true copy of the original Book in my office ... [Ordered to be done because of the bad condition of the original on 9 February 1900] ...; Signed - Joseph McDermott, 10 August 1903.]

MONMOUTH COUNTY DEEDS - BOOK "C"

[p 1] **RECORDS OF YE HIGH WAYS IN YE COUNTIE OF MONMOUTH**

2 March 1687 - [Laid out on this date] - From Shrowsbury falls to swining river bridge as the lyeth to two girdled trees on ye South side of ye at John Rutmans hill ... along ye King's highway ... through Middletown street as ye road now lyeth at the bridg a little Easterly from John Stout's house ... following the old way through ye poplar field and out by James Grover to thee ... of the lott that was Jonathan Holmes ... to ... ye lott that belonged to James Ashton ... by James Grover to ye most easterly side of Stephen Arnolds poplar lott ... to William Laytons ... up the hill ... that goes towards portland point ... to poore mans plain ... over ye stoney run ... to Richard Davis's ... [page not further copied in book] ... And beginning at the way by William Laytons as lyeth to James Grover's mill & mill brook and bog at the front of Stephen Arnold's lott ... to ye head of the cold spring and line that parts James Ashton's land & Job Throckmorton ... to Thomas H path ... to ye bay side ... at ye pond by Richard Gardiner's meadow the way to Thomas Harbert's path & thence as ye way goes to Benj. Devall's house ... till it comes in the way in poore plain to ye grave. And beging att Thomas Morford's on Navesink's river ... as the way now goes Middletown road by John Stouts bridg and begining the Kings highway in Middletown ... lying betwixt Richard Hartshornes lott & said Reap's ... to William Cumptons, And a Kings highway James Grovers to the mouth of Waykick Creek ... Thomas Whitlocks ... to the Kings way in Middletown and a passage for people ... to cart their hay ... And beginning at Kings highway in Middletown by the prisson on the West by Robert Hamiltons lott and Mary Pedlors or Thomas Cox's lott ... to Swiming river bridge ... [page not further copied in book] ... And it is to be noted that these three highways are not to be fenced in. First ... lying betwixt Richard Hartshorne & Sarah Reap ... the Second ... bounded west by Robert Hamilton's lott & east by Thomas Coxes lying from ye prisson south ... the third ... bounded west by Robert Hamilton and east by Samuell Spicer's ... over against the prisson North ... east of Leonard's saw mill ... to Peter Tilton's cart way to hop river ... westward of William Leads new house ... into the Kings highway and Burlington path ... from Crosswicks Creek by George Keiths plantation to John Hampton's plantation the path ... now goeth to hop river at the usuall crossing Westerly of William Lawrence field ... through John Bray's land & Elizar Cottrell ... by mnarked tress to goe betwixt Elizar Cottrell and Jonathan Holmes ... to the brook of Cheesman ... crossing the brook at the usuall place ... betwixt Cheesman's & Morford's land ... to an old path to Middletown ... by the side of John Ruckman's hill ... to the widow Bowne's ... to the head of Cheesquake's and thence to the ferry over against Perth Amboy.

And a way is to go from Shrowsbury falls ... to Richard Stout the Younger, his plantation, And from the crossing hop river at Burlington path a way is to goe ... to John Reid's ... by Burlington path on the East side betwixt John Hampton's & hopp river ... to the East side of Baker's fence at Wickatoung ... to John Reid's way that goeth to the landing place at Mattawan Creek on the South side.

MONMOUTH COUNTY DEEDS - BOOK "C"

[p 5] NICHOLAS BROWN to WILLIAM WOOLLEY

7 October 1691 - Nicholas Brown ... of Shrowsbury ... Monmouth ... East New Jersey yeoman ... [sold to] ... William Woolley of Shark River ... [of the same place] ... [for 5 pounds] ... a certain peece ... of land and meadow ... being on Barnigatt beach ... by the bay ... by land of ... Nicholas Brown ... by land of Edward Woolley ...; [Signed - Nicholas Brown made his mark when signing; witnesses - Walter Pumphrey, William West, Tho. Webley.]

[28 X'ber 1692 - The deed was acknowledged by Brown before Andr. Hamilton.]

[PAGES 7 THROUGH 14 WERE LEFT BLANK]

[p 15] EDWARD WOOLLEY to WILLIAM WOOLLEY

27 October 1692 - Edward Woolley of Manusquan river ... Monmouth ... East New Jersey Hatter ... [sold to] ... William Woolley of Shark river ... [for 5 pounds] ... a certain piece ... of land & meadow ... att barnigatt beach ... by the sea ... by the bay ... by the land of Nicholas Brown & North by land of ... Edward Woolley ...; [Signed - Edward Woolley; witnesses - Walter Pumphrey, William West, Tho. Webley.]

[p 17] THOMAS HEARSE to THOMAS WEBLEY

23 January 1691 - Thomas Hearse ... Town of Shrowsbury ... Monmouth ... East New Jersey, Yeoman ... [sold to] ... Thomas Webley ... [of the same place] yeoman ... [for 40 pounds] ... a certain tract ... being at Shark river ... [adjacent land owners or names - Shark river, to Nicholas Brown's Indian purchase upon the river, William Woolley, John West] ...; [Signed - Thomas Hearse made his mark when signing; witnesses - John Hance, William West, Edward Williams made his mark.]

[p 19] STEPHEN WEST to THOMAS WEBLEY

18 December 1691 - William West ... town of Shrowsbury ... Monmouth ... East New Jersey, carpenter, now Attorney for Stephen West of Mackataugh Island in New England ... [sold on behalf of Stephen West to] ... Thomas Webley of ... Shrowsbury ... [for 21 pounds] ... a tract of land lying on Ransont Neck ... [adjacent land owners or names - highway to Long Branch, Samuell Woollcott, Naversink river, Iron Mills] ... Also ... [3.5 acres] ... of meadow lying at Narawaticouck ... [adjacent land owners or names - Roberts West, Mrs. Katherine Brown] ... also ... [2 acres] ... of upland lying on Goose Neck ... [adjacent land owners or names - Sarah Reape, Mistress Katherine Brown, John Chambers, Shrowsbury river] ...the ... tracts of upland & meadow ... [66 acres] ...; [Signed - William West; witnesses - George Luett, Katherine Brown made her mark when signing, Edward Williams made his mark when signing.]

MONMOUTH COUNTY DEEDS - BOOK "C"

[p 21] NICHOLAS BROWN to THOMAS WEBLEY

23 September 1692 - Nicholas Brown of ... Shrowsbury ... Monmouth ... East New Jersey, Yeoman ... [sold to] ... Thomas Webley ... [of the same place] ... Yeoman ... [for 4 pounds] ... A certain tract ... of upland & meadow ... being upon a certain place cal'd ... Barnigatt beach ... [adjacent land owners or names - [by the sea, Nicholas Brown, William Woolley] ...; [Signed - Nicholas Brown made his mark when signing; witnesses - Lewis Morris, George Hulett, George Curliss.]

[p 23] LEWIS MORRIS to THOMAS WEBLEY

26 December 1692 - Lewis Morris of Tinton Mannor ... Monmouth ... East New Jersey ... [sold to] ... Thomas Webley ... Shrowsbury ... [for 90 pounds] ... tract of land ... near the Leonards saw mill ... [adjacent land owners or names - Swiming river, the saw mill brook, Lewis Morris, John Leonards] ...; [Signed - L. Morris, Isabella Morris; witnesses - Ja. Fullertone, Richard Lesley.]

[p 25] THOMAS POTTER to SAMUELL DENNIS

1 November 1688 - Thomas Potter of ... Shrowsbury ... Monmouth ... East New Jersey Yeoman ... [for 150 acres of land lying in Shrowsbury bounded as in the patent dated 15 January 1679, sold for 17 pounds to] ... Samuell Dennis of ... Shrowsbury ... all those tracts ... with all ye housing, orchards & fencing ... I formerly bought of John Woolley ... [9 October 1688] ... that is to say one house lott ... [of 7 acres] ... [adjacent land owners or names - Joseph Parker, John Worthley, Shrowsbury river] ... also a tract of land and a house lott formerly belonging to Francis Lemaster ... [on Shrowsbury river of 86 acres] ... [adjacent land owners or names - John Worthley] ... with a piece of meadow and a bitt of upland ... [3 acres] ... [adjacent land owners or names - Judah Allen, Peter Parker] ... also ... [2 acres] ... of Meadow ... [adjacent land owners or names - Shrosbury river, Nicholas Brown, Judah Allen] ... ye whole to remain for ... [92 acres] ...; [Signed - Thomas Potter made his mark when signing; witnesses - Thomas Cooke, Peter White, Thomas White.]

[11 February 1692/3 - Thomas Potter acknowledged the above deed before L. Morris, Justice of Peace.]

[p 27] RECEIPT

1692/3 - Received of Samuell Dennis of Shrowsbury ... Monmouth ... East New Jersey ... [150 acres] ... of upland and meadow ... and ... [15 pounds] ... I say received by me. [Signed - Thomas Potter made his mark when signing; witnesses - Thomas Cooke, Ephraim Allen.]

MONMOUTH COUNTY DEEDS - BOOK "C"

[p 27] RECEIPT

9 February 1688 - Recieved then of Samuell Dennis of Shrowsbury ... Monmouth ... East New Jersey ... [1 pound, 10 shillings] ... being the remaining part of seventeen pounds that ... Samuell Dennis agredd to give more then ... [150 acres] ... I say receaved the sum aforesaid by me; [Signed - Thomas Potter made his mark when signing; witnesses - Peter White, Abraham Brown.]

[1692/3 - The above receipt was acknowledged before L. Morris.]

[p 28] MARRIAGE

31th the 5th 94 - EAST NEW JERSEY - This may certifie whom it may concern that on the day & yeare above wrighten was Thomas Alfree and Elizabeth Brown, the daughter of Abraham Brown was lawfully joyned in the bond of Marriage by me. [Signed - John Hance; witnesses - Thomas Cooke, Mary Brown, Samuell Forman, Samuell Thropp, Elizabeth Cooke. Signed - Thomas Alfree, Elizabeth Alfree.]

[p 29] JOHN TUCKER to THOMAS HILBOURNE

18 August 1687 - I, John Tucker of Deale ... Monmouth ... East New Jersey ... Whereas Peter Eason of Rhoad Island ... of New England did by a deed ... [dated 14 June 1687] ... sell all his right of lands & meadows in East Jersey unto ... [me] ... I, John Tucker ... [sell for 20 pounds to] ... Thomas Hilbourne of Shrowsbury ... all the lands & meadows ... I bought of Peter Eason ...; [Signed - John Tucker; witnesses - Sam^{ll} Dennis, John Williams, Thomas White.]

[28 March 1693 - The above deed was acknowledged before Andrew Brown, Lewis Morris, John Hance. The name Brown was pencilled over with "BOWN".]

[p 31] EDWARD WOOLLEY to JOHN BOWN

5 March 1690 - Edward Woolley of Manusquan ... Shrowsbury ... Monmouth ... East New Jersey, Hatter ... [sold to] ... John Bown of Middletown ... Yeoman ... [15 pounds] ... All that tract of land ... in the County of Monmouth ... within ye Indian purchase called passequanequa ... [adjacent land owners or names - Rostere Lippincott, George Keeth] ... [96.5 acres] ... also ... [3.5 acres] ... of meadow ... [by John Burdon, John Worthley] ... [100 acres by the patent for same] ...; [Signed - Edward Woolley; witnesses - John Williams, George Allen.]

[p 32] JOHN BOWN to THOMAS LAYTON

28 March 1693 - John Bown, Yeoman, of Middletown ...Monmouth ... East New Jersey ... [sold to]

MONMOUTH COUNTY DEEDS - BOOK "C"

... Thomas Layton planter of the same place ... [for 15 pounds] ... all that tract of land ... within the Indian purchase called Posaquanequa ... [adjacent land owners or names - Restere Lippincott, George Keith] ... [96.5 acres] ... [This is the same deed as recorded above] ... [Signed - John Bown; witnesses - Sam^{ll} Dennis, Tho. Webley.]

[p 33] THOMAS WHITELOCK to JOHN WHITELOCK

12 February 1691 - Thomas Whitelock of Middletown ... Monmouth ... East New Jersey, Senir ... [for 11 pounds] ... payed by John Whitelock of the same place my son ... All that tract of land ... [adjacent land owners or names - Mahorn brook, Garrett's bridge, William Whitelock, Garrett Wall, John Whitelock] ... [90 acres] ... as the same were granted ... to me amongst other tracts by pattent from the propriators ... [on 10 March 1676] ...; [Signed - Thomas Whitelock made his mark when signing; witnesses - John Reid, Robt. Johnes, Walter Wright, William Whitelock.]

[29 March 1693 - The above deed was acknowledged by Andrew Brown before Lewis Morris and John Hance. Penciled over the name Brown was "Bown".]

[p 34] HUGH DICKMAN to FRANCIS JACKSON

14 September 1692 - Hugh Dickman ... of Shrowsbury ... Monmouth ... East New Jersey Yeoman ... [sold to] ... Francis Jackson ... [of the same place] ... Carpenter ... Whereas ... Hugh Dickman on ... [17 June 1675] ... by a deed ... conveyed to him ... from Edward Thurston of Phode Island for a ... tract ... of land ... being in ... [Shrowsbury] ... Now know ye that ... [Dickman sell for 15 pounds to] ... Francis Jackson ... the moyety or half part of the ... tract ... [adjacent land owners or names - Thomas Huett] ...; [Signed - Hugh Dickman; witnesses - Samuell Child, Jessie Carton, William Woodmansy, Tho. Webley.]

[25 April 1693 - The above deed was acknowledged by Samuell Child & Thomas Webley before Lewis Morris, John Hance, Lewis Morris.]

[p 36] JOHN CRAFFORD, SR to JOHN CRAFFORD, JR

3 August 1691 - I, John Crafford of Middletown ... Monmouth ... East New Jersey for & in consideration of the natural affection and fatherly Love, which I have & do beare to my well beloved son John Crafford of the said Town ... [and by valuable consideration received from his son] ... [sells to] ... John Crafford my son all that plantation and tract of land at Wacaek ... [280 acres] ... [adjacent land owners or names - Richard Hartshorne, Robert Hamilton, Whitelock] ... Also, ... [6 acres] ... at Waycake ... [adjacent land owners or names - Stephen Arnold] ... Also the moiety or one half of my nine acres of meadown at Waycack ... The said ... [280 acres to me by patent dated 12 March 1687] ... and the ... [6 acres by sale] ... from Richard Hartshorne ... [4 August 1689] ... and the said meadow

MONMOUTH COUNTY DEEDS - BOOK "C"

... by ... sale from Richard Gibbons ... [11 December 1678] ...; [Signed - John Crafford; witnesses - Robt. Hamilton, James Morlin.]

[29 March 1693 - The above deed was acknowledged before Andrew Bowne, Lewis Morris, John Hance.]

[p 38] JOHN SLOCUM to WILLIAM SCOTT

9 December 1688 - ...I, John Slocum of Shrosbury ... Monmouth Yeoman ... [for a compitent sum of money sell to] ... William Scott of Shrowsbury ... all that tract of upland & meadows ... in the County of Monmouth ... upon Narumpsous Neck ... [adjacent land owners or names - Peter Tilton, Peter Parker, Navesink river] ... [66 acres] ... also ... [4 acres] ... of meadow ... in the patten at Long Branch upon Quenhownenarak creek, excepted John Slocum and not sold unto William Scott ... Together with the pattent ... granted to me by the Proprietors ...; [Signed - John Slocum, Meribah Slocum; witnesses - Mary Thropp, Remembrance Lippincott.]

[p 40] POWER OF ATTORNEY

14 April 1679 - I, Christopher Almy of Rhoad Island ... constitute my son-in-law, Lewis Morris of Shrewsbury ... Monmouth ... East New Jersey to be my true ... Attorney for me ...; [Signed - Christopher Almy; witnesses - John Slocum, Robert West made his mark when signing.]

[p 41] SARAH REAPE ET AL to ANTHONY PINTARD

23 November 1693 - ...Sarah Reape widdow and her son William Reape ... [sold to] ... Anthony Pintard Merchant ... all of Shrowsbury ... Monmouth ... East New Jersey ... [for 8 pounds] ... All that tract of land containing ten acres ... at Norawaticonck in ... Shrowsbury ... [adjoining land owners or names - Joseph Parker, north of a highway & south of Shrowsbury river] ... [which was grant to] ... Sarah Reape by Pattent ... [dated - 24 May 1693] ... amongst other tracts from ye propriators of ye said P'vince ...; [Signed - William Reape, Sarah Reape; witnesses - Lewis Maddock made his mark when signing, Caleib Shrive; acknowledged in Court on 27 December 1693; Tho. Webley, Clk.]

[p 42] JOHN REID to JOHN RUCKMAN, JUNIOR

9 June 1692 - ...John Reid ... County of Monmouth ... East New Jersey ... [for 3 pounds, 10 shillings sold to] ... John Ruckman Junior of the same county, Weaver ... all that tract of land ... [adjoining land owners or names - South of the 9 acres of John Wilson Junir, East by John Ruckman Senir & North by Robert Hamilton & West by Morhorn's brook] ... granted ... to ... John Reid ... from Thomas Gordon on 3 June 1692 ...; [Signed - John Reid; witnesses - Robert Hamilton, Elisha Lawrence; acknowledged before Andrew Bown, John Hance on 27 September 1693.]

MONMOUTH COUNTY DEEDS - BOOK "C"

[p 43] MORDECAI GIBBONS to JOHN RUCKMAN, JUNIOR

8 September 1690 - ... I Mordecai Gibbons of Middletown ... East Jersey Gent. ... sell ... unto John Ruckman Junir of the same town ... meadow ... [6 acres] ... in ... Middletown ... [adjoining land owners or names - West by Shoale Harbour creek, east by upland of John Ruckman Senir & Garret Wall, North by 1 acre formerly of Thomas Cox, south by meadow of John Ruckman senir] ... [for 5 pounds] ... formerly paid to my father Mr. Richard Gibbons of ye said town ...; [Signed - Mordecay Gibbons; witnesses - Samuell Leonard, Obidiah Bown, Garett Wall; acknowledged - 27 September 1693 before Andrew Bown, John Hance.]

[p 44] THOMAS WHITELOCK SENIOR to JOHN RUCKMAN, JUNIOR

9 November 1688 - ... I, Thomas Whitelock Sen of Middletown, Yeoman, for ... [3 pounds, 12 shillings] ... already received of John Ruckman Junir ... [of the same place] ... sell unto him ... All that lot ... [8 acres] ... upon Mohorn's brook West, upon land of Ruckman Sen'r East and between the land of James Grover south & land late of Edward Tart's ...; [Signed - Thomas Whitelock made his mark when signing; witnesses - Daniell Seabrook, Ia. Fullertone.]

[p 45] JOHN PEARCE to THOMAS WHITELOCK

4 September 1693 - ...I, John Pearce of Middletown ... Monmouth ... [sold for 5 pounds to] ... Thomas Whitelock ... Six acres of meadow ... [adjoining land owners or names - West side of Shoale Harbour Neck, betwixt John Bown's & James Robinson, bounded on the upland by William Whitelock formerly of Benjamin Devill] ...; [Signed - John Pearce made his mark when signing; witnesses - Henery Marsh, Garrett Wall; acknowledged before Andrew Bown, John Hance on 26 September 1693.]

[p 47] JOHN BOWNE to THOMAS WHITELOCK

26 March 1689 - ...I, John Bowne of Middletown ... Monmouth ... East New Jersey planter for ... a competent sum of money ... [sold to] ... Thomas Whitelock of Middletown ... lott of meadow or salt marsh ... at Shoale Harbour within ... Middletown ... [6 acres] ... [adjoining land owners or names - north by William Lawrence, South by Creek, East & West by upland] ...; [Signed - John Bowne; witnesses - James Bowne, Tho. Webley; acknowledged before Andrew Bowne, John Hance on 26 September 1693.]

[p 48] JOHN GIBBONSON to DANIEL HENDRICKSON

23 September 1693 - John Gibbonson & Daniel Hendrickson of Flatt bush of Kings County on Long Island ... [sold to] ... William Whitlock of ... Middletown ... Monmouth ... East New Jersey ... in

MONMOUTH COUNTY DEEDS - BOOK "C"

strabery field ... [104 acres] ... [plus] ... fifthty acres of land at the bogg meadow ... which ... John, John & Daniell ... leased ... to ... William Whitlock by deed ... [dated 22 September 1692 and to be paid at 20 pounds a year to be completed on 10 March 1697] ...; [Signed - John Gibbonson, Daniell Hendrickson; witnesses - James Dorsett, Clemment Masters, John Bown; acknowledged in Court per Tho. Webley, Clk.]

[p 49] JOHN CRAFFORD to JOHN WHITLOCK

22 August 1693 - ...I, John Crafford of Middletown ... Monmouth ... New East Jersey ... [for valuable consideration sold to] ... John Whitlock ... [of the same place] ... Carpenter ... all that tract ... at Shaole Harbour ... [13 acres] ... [adjoining land owners or names - West by William Whitlock, East by Thomas Cox, North by ye creek, South by Sarah Reape] ... assured unto me by patent ... [dated 10 June 1677] ...; [Signed - John Crafford; witnesses - Thomas Whitlock made his mark when signing, Robert Hamilton; recorded - 27 September 1693 by Tho. Webly, Clk.]

[p 50] MARY MASTERS to CLEMMENT MASTERS

12 July 1691 - ... Mary Masters widdow ... of Shrowsbury ... Monmouth ... East New Jersey sole executrix of Francis Masters deceased late of said town ... [sold for a sum of money from] my loving son Clemment Masters ... [of the same place] ... severall tracts of uplands ... one tract ... at horss neck ... [173.5 acres] ... [adjoining land owners or names - land of the orphans of Jacob Coale deceased, Clemment Masters, salt water creeks] ... Also ... [3 acres] ... [Goose Neck, Elizabeth Hutton, John Williams] ... likewise ... [1.5 acres] ... [adjoining land owners or names - Rackoon Island, Edward Williams] ... in all ... [178 acres] ...; [Signed - Mary Masters made her mark when signing; witnesses - Abiah Edwards, John Whitelock; acknowledged before Andrew Brown, L. Morris on 29 June 1693.]

[p 52] EDWARD WOOLLEY to JOHN LEONARD

5 April 1692 - Edward Woolley of Rhode Island, Hatter ... [sold to] ... John Leonard of Shrowsbury, Yeoman ... [for 50 pounds] ... land ... in ... Monmouth ... [adjoining land owners or names - Mannusquan river, John Hance, Edmond Laffetra] ... [60 acres] ...; [Signed - Edward Woolley; witnesses - Nicholas Brown made his mark when signing, William West, Sam^{ll} Leonard; acknowledged before Andrew Bowne, L. Morris on 29 June 1693.]

[p 53] PAYMENT OF DEBT

21 September 1693 - Middletown - William Lawrence, I desire thee to pay to the weaver John Shoan ... [30 shillings] ... which thee and I, agreed for when thee paid me ... [5 pounds, 1 shilling] ... his receipt shall be your full discharge of all that money by the Court ordered ... to me ....; [Signed - John Tilton.]

MONMOUTH COUNTY DEEDS - BOOK "C"

Then received of William Lawrence ... [30 shillings] ... by order and upon the accott of John Tilton, I say received by me...; [Signed - John Shoan made his mark when signing.]

[p 54] **TAVERN LICENSE**

These are to Lycense & authorize Pouncett Stelle of Shrewsbury to keep a publick house or house of entertainment in the house where he now lives ... for ... one whole yeare ... and to sell ... wine, brandy, rum, strong beare & Cyder or other strong drinks or lickquors he being bound with sufficient surities in a recognizance of ... [20 pounds] ... according to Law...; [Dated - 8 January 1693; signed - And. Hamilton.]

[p 54] **MARRIAGE LICENSE**

22 February 1694 - George Allen of Shrewsbury and Elizabeth Hulett of the same town after lawfull publication came before me and did take each other in marriage before severall witnesses until Death parted them; [Signed - Peter Tilton.]

[p 55] **THOMAS WEBLEY to NICHOLAS BROWN**

13 January 1693 - Thomas Webley ... Shrewsbury ... Monmouth ... East New Jersey, Yeoman ... [sold to] ... Nicholas Brown ... [of the same place] ... yeoman ... [for 40 pounds] ... All the tract of Land ... lying & being neare the Leonard's Saw Mill ... [adjoining land owners or names - Swiming River, John Leonard, Lewis Morris of Tinton Mnaor] ... land & premises ... [250 acres] ...; [Signed - Tho. Webley; witnesses - John Satton - Sutton written over name in pencil, John West.]

[27 June 1694 - The above deed was acknowledged before John Hance and Peter Tilton.]

[p 57] **JOHN HAVENS to GEORGE ALLEN**

18 September 1693 - ... I, John Havens ... Town of Shrewsbury ... Monmouth ... East New Jersey planter for ... [50 acres] ... of land & meadow ... being on both sides of Manusquan river ... Monmouth ... [30 acres] ... thereof to be taken on the Southeast side joyning to Joseph West, alias Robert West, his lands of a tract ... lying on the North side of Manusquan river ... bounded ... [adjoining land owners or names - southeast by the river, northwest with a highway, southwest with lands of Joseph West alias Robert West, and on the northeast with lands of Richard Hartshorne] ... And ... [20 acres] ... more, the remainder thereof to be taken from the north side Joyning to Tobias Hanson ... [sells unto] George Allen, of ye said Town of Shrewsbury ... weaver All that one quarter part of upland ... on ye east side of a certain tract ... in ... Shrewsbury town ... bounded in ... my mother-in-law's name, Anna Havens, bearing date ... [25 March 1688] ... [adjoining land owners or names - along the highway, west by Edmond Lafetra, east by Judah Allen, north by a highway, south by unsurveyed land] ... Also one quarter part of Meadow ... bequeathed to me by my loving father

MONMOUTH COUNTY DEEDS - BOOK "C"

John Havens, late of the said Shrewsbury ... by his last will ... [dated 14 March 1686 or 87] ... and since by deed ... [Dated 15 April 1693] ... under the hands ... of ... Anna Havens my mother-in-law, Relict of the said John Havens my father deceased ...; [Signed - John Havens; witnesses - Jedeiah Allen, John West, Sam^{ll} Dennis; 27 June 1694 - The above deed was acknowledged before Tho. Webley.]

[The term "alias" may not have had the meaning that it has today. It probably refers to "at another time" meaning the previous owner of the land.]

[p 59] JUDAH ALLEN to DANIELL ALLEN

12 December 1685 - ... I Judah Allen ... township of Shrewsbury ... Monmouth ... East New Jersey ... for a valuable consideration to me in hand paid by my brother Daniell Allen of the town of Sandwich ... of New Plimouth in New England ... for certain parcells of upland & meadow ... [sell to] ... Daniell Allen All that my said parcells of upland & meadow and one parcel of upland ... [of 7 acres] ... [adjoining land owners or names - east by Catherine Brown & John Chamness alias Jedediah Allen, west by John Havens, south by unsurveyed land, north by a highway] ... [60 acres] ... Item ... [4 acres of upland and meadow] ... [adjoining land owners or names - lying upon a branch of Shresbury river, notheast by Ephraim Allen alias John Woolley, southeast by a highway, and nothwest by said branch] ... to remain ... [3 acres forever] ... also a third part ... of my salt meadow ... in Shrewsbury ... with all privileidges ... in my patten to ... Daniell Allen ... Also another parcell of upland & meadow ... [.5 acres] ... at a place caled Manusquan ... [for 50 acres] ...; [Signed - Judah Allen, Mary Allen his wife; witnesses - Remembrance Lippincott, Jedediah Allen.]

15 December 1685 - Both Judah and Mary Allen acknowledged the above deed before John Hance - Justice.]

[p 60] MARRIAGE

... All to whom it may concern that on the tirteenth day of December old stile 1694, Richard Compton and Providence Usselton were by me Lewis Morris one of his Majesties Justices of the peace, joyned in the hand of holy wedlock, And this to be their sufficient Certificate as witness my hand this day & year above wrighten; [Signed - Lewis Morris.]

[p 61] RECORDING BY DANIELL ALLEN

3 May 1687 - ... Daniell Allen of Sandwich ... County of Barnstable ... Collony of New Plimmouth in New England ... husbandman sendeth Greeting: I ... Daniell Allen ... for a valuable parcell of lands to me by Deed secured by my father George Allen of Sandwich ... in the behalf of my youngest brother George Allen now under covert ... sold ... unto him my said borther George Allen ... All that

MONMOUTH COUNTY DEEDS - BOOK "C"

severall p'cells of upland and swamp ... and marsh and meadow ... within the Township of Shrewsbury ... Monmouth ... East New Jersey and is all that which I, ye said Daniell Allen bought of my brother Judah Allen of Shrewsbury ... one of the p'cells of upland ... [70 acres] ... [adjoining land owners or names - east by Catharine Brown & John Champnes alias Jedediah Allen, west by John Havens, south by unsurveyed land, north by a highway].

[Signed - Daniell Allen ... to the said George Allen for ye use of sd. George Allen his brother; witnesses - William Bassitt, Shuball Smith. Daniell Allen appeared before a Stephen Stieffe, Justice of Peace.]

[This deed is for the same property in Item #35 above.]

[p 63] GEORGE ALLEN to NICHOLAS BROWN

1 March 1693 - ...I, George Allen ... town of Shrewsbury ... Monmouth ... East New Jersey weaver ... [for] ... all that tract of meadow land ... [2 acres] ... in the said Shrewsbury at Goose Neck ... [adjoining land owners or names- west by Ephraim Allen, south by a small creek, north by Shrewsbury river, east by Francis Masters] ... & though in the patten thereunto belonging by mistake John Worthley's ... sell ... unto Nicholas Brown of ye Shrewsbury ... all that tract ... [of 2 acres] ... in Shrowsbury, upon Long branch alias Racoon neck or Island ... [adjoining ing land owners or names - south southwest by John Havens, west southwest by the River, northeast by Thomas Vickers, east southeast by Gideon Freeborn] ... same was granted to me by a deed ... [dated 3 May 1687 from] ... Daniell Allen of Sandwich ... Barnstable ... New Plimmouth ... my loving brother ...; [Signed - George Allen; witnesses - John Slocum, Saml Dennis.]

[27 June 1694 - The above deed was acknowledged before John Hance and Peter Tilton, Justices.]

[p 65] ELIAKIM WARDELL to JOSEPH WEST

17 December 1691 - ... Eliakim Wardell of ye town of Shrewsbury ... Monmouth ... East New Jersey, gent. And Lydia his wife ... [sold to] ... Joseph West ... [of the same place] ... Carpenter ... [for 15 pounds] ... all those tracts of land ... at Manusquan .. On Southside of Manusquan river ... [39 acres] ... [adjoining land owners of names - north by Remembrance Lippincott, south by Richard Hartshorne, east by the sea, west by a highway] ... also ... [19.5 acres] ... on the South side of ye river ... [adjoining land owners or names - north by Richard Hartshorne, south by John Hance] ... Also on the North side of the said river ... [30 acres] ... [adjoining land owners of names - south by river, north by a highway, east by John Hance, west by William Lawrence] ... also another tract on the North side of said River ... toward the beach ... [60 acres] ... [adjoining land owners or names - south by the River, north by a highway, west by John Williams, and William Woolley on the east by Judah

MONMOUTH COUNTY DEEDS - BOOK "C"

Allen ...; [Signed - Eliakim Wardell; witnesses - Nicholas Brown made his mark when signing, Elizabeth Wainwright made her mark when signing, Tho. Webley.]

[27 June 1694 - The above deed was acknowledged before John Hance and Peter Tilton.]

[p 68] INVENTORY OF ANN CHAMBERLIN

A Record of ye Inventory of the Chattells & Cattells of Ann Chamberlin, deceased, Relicque of Henery Chamberlin of Shrewsbury deceased; the inventory listed numerous animals and other personal items including a Bible; not dated.

[p 69] GEORGE ALLEN to JOHN HAVENS

18 September 1693 - ... I George Allen of the Town of Shrewsbury ... Monmouth ... East New Jersey, weaver for ... all that one quarter tract of upland to be taken of from ye East side of a certain tract ... in ... Shrewsbury, thus bounded in the patten ... [dated 25 March 1688] ... [adjoining land owners or names - west by Edmond Laffetra, east by Judah Allen, north by a highway, south by unsurveyed] ... sells to] ... John Havens of ... Shresbury ... planter ... [50 acres] ... purchased by the said George Allen of my brother Daniell Allen of Sandwich ... County of Barnstable ... New England husbandman ... by deed ... [dated 3 May 1687] ... [30 acres and again refers to Item #34 above] ...; [Signed - George Allen; witnesses - John West, Saml Dennis.]

[p 71] ANNA HAVENS to JOHN HAVENS

15 April 1693 - ... I, Anna Havens ... town of Shrewsbury ... Monmouth ... East New Jersey relict of John Havens deceased ... Whereas my late husband ... John Havens was in actuall possession many years of certain tracts of land and meadow ... [by patent] ... And by his last Will ... [dated 14 March 1686 or 87] ... and since Pattenned, in my name ... Now know yee that I, for and in consideration ... of the Will ... have given ... unto John Havens of the said Shrewsbury second son to the said John Havens deceased ... All that one Quarter part of upland ... to John Havens ...; [Signed - Anna Havens made her mark when signing; witnesses - Nathaniel Leonard, Edward Williams made his mark when signing, Saml Dennis.]

[27 June 1694 - The above deed was acknowledged before John Hance and Peter Tilton.]

[p 73] THOMAS WEBLEY to THOMAS HEARCE

27 December 1691 - Thomas Webley ... Town of Shrewsbury ... Monmouth ... East New Jersey Yeoman ... [to] ... Thomas Hearce ... [of the same place] ... [for 40 pounds] ... all those tracts ... of land ... in ye town ... aforesaid ... [adjoining land owners or names - Ramsouts neck. Highway to

MONMOUTH COUNTY DEEDS - BOOK "C"

Long Branch, west by Samuell Wollcott, north by branch of Neversink river, road that goes to the Iron Mill, east by a highway] ... Also ... [3.5 acres] ... [adjoining land owners or names - west by Robert West, east by Mr^s Kathrine Brown, south by a small creek, north by upland] ... also ... [2 acres] ... of upland ... on goose neck ... [adjoining land owners or names - south by Sarah Reape, east by Mr^s Catherine Brown, west by John Chambers, north by Shrewsbury river] ... [66 acres] ... [rented for seven years] ...; [Signed - Tho. Webley; witnesses - George Hulett, Saml Leonard, William West.]

[p 74] RECORD OF RECEIPT

Receaved by me Restore Lippincott ... [125 pounds] ... from ... William Bickley in full payment for ... land & meadow ground ...; [Dated - 2 March 1691; signed - Restore Lippincott made his mark when signing; witnesses - Abraham Brown, John Tilton, William Shattock, Nicholas Brown made his mark when signing.]

[p 75] RESTORE LIPPINCOTT to WILLIAM BICKLEY

1 March 1691 - ...I, Restore Lippincott ... Shrewsbury ... Monmouth ... East New Jersey planter, and Hannah his wife ... [for 125 pounds] ... paid by William Bickley of New York, merchant ... [sells to] ... ye said William ... All ... that tract of upland & meadow ... in ... Shrewsbury ... [adjoining land owners or names - east by John Clayton, north by Neversink River, west by a highway, south by his own & Abraham Brown's meadow] ... also ... [7 acres] ... [adjoining land owners or names - west by Abraham Brown, south and east by two small creeks, north by his own land] ... 200 acres ... [land being in Lippincott's patent dated 21 January 1687] ...; [Signed - Restore Lippincott made his mark when signing, Hanah Lippincott.]

7 May 1692 - Both Restore and Hannah acknowledged the above deed before John Hance and Lewis Morris - Justices.]

[p 77] THOMAS POTTER to JOHN WOOLLEY

11 October 1680 - ... I Thomas Potter of Shrewsbury ... Monmouth ... East New Jersey yeoman ... [for 39 pounds] ... by John Woolley of the same place, smith ... All that tract ... of land ... [adjoining land owners or names - brook that is the bounds of land formerly sold Adam Channelhouse] ... [100 acres] ...; [Signed - Thomas Potter made his mark when signing; witnesses - Jedediah Allen, Thomas Eaton, Sam. Dennis.]

[1 December 1694 - The above deed was acknowledged before John Hance and Peter Tilton.]

MONMOUTH COUNTY DEEDS - BOOK "C"

[p 78] RECEIPT

[1 December 1694 - Receipt from Thomas Potter to John Woolley; received 39 pounds from John Woolley.]

[p 78] RECORD OF WRITING

5 January 1692 - This wrighting doth declare & testafie that I, Remberance Lippincott of Shrewsbury ... Monmouth ... East New Jersey, do freely acknowledge that I have no right or title to any ... parcell of that land lying on ye westerly side of Long neck, alias point creek ... but doth wholly renounce the same ... unto William Worth ... although it is expressed in ye pattent that doth belong to my land at Long point ... my bounds reacheth no further then William Worth's meadow ...; [Signed - Rembrance Lippincott.]

[29 September 1694 - The above writing was acknowledged before John Hance and Lewis Morris - Justices.]

[p 79] THOMAS POTTER to JOHN TUCKER

28 December 1692 - I, Thomas Potter of Shrewsbury ... Monmouth ... East New Jersey ... planter ... [for 120 pounds] ... paid by John Tucker ... planter ... [sell] ... all that tract of land ... in Monmouth ... at a place called Deale, belonging to Shrewsbury ... [460 acres] ... [adjoining land owners or names - Thomas White, Francis Jeffres, by the sea] ... also another tract ... [92 acres] ... [adjoining land owners or names - whole pond brook, east by Francis Jeffreys, Benjamin Roggers & John Iresones, south by a highway, west by ye barren land] ... also another tract ... [40 acres] ... [adjoining land owners or names - formerly John Iresones land lying at Deale, southwest by aforesaid lands, northeast by Francis Jeffreys land] ... [592 acres] ... conveyed to ... [Potter] ... by pattent ... [20 January 1687] ...; [Signed - Thomas Potter made his mark when signing; witnesses - William Shattock, Peter White, William Worth, Remberance Lippincott.]

[p 81] POWER OF ATTORNEY

1 December 1694 - ...I, Thomas Potter ... Town of Shrewsbury ... Monmouth ... East New Jersey, Yeoman ... have assigned ... in my stead & place ... constitute my loving son-in-law & loving friend John Woolley of ... [Shrewsbury] ... yeoman, to be my true, sufficient & lawful Attorney for me ..; [Signed - Thomas Potter made his mark when signing; witnesses - Lewis Morris, Justice and Tho. Webley, Clerk of Peace.]

MONMOUTH COUNTY DEEDS - BOOK "C"

[p 82] POWER OF ATTORNEY

9 September 1693 - ... I, Benjamin Devile ... Gloucester in West Jersey ... constitute my friend Samuell Leonard of Shrewsbury ... to be my true & lawfull Attorney for me ...; [Signed - Benjamin Devell; witnesses - Thomas Leonard, Henery Leonard made his mark when signing.]

[26 September 1694 - Thomas Leonard and Henerey Leonard acknowledged that they saw "Benjamin Devill" sign the above letter; before Tho. Webley, Clerk.]

[p 83] JOSEPH PARKER, JR to THOMAS HEARSE

17 September 1694 - ... I, Joseph Parker of ye Town of Shrewsbury ... Monmouth ... East New Jersey cordwainer, Whereas my loving father Joseph Parker late of ... Shrewsbury, Esqr deceased did sometime in his lifetime ... sell unto Thomas Hearse of ye same Town ... planter ... [for 10 pounds] ... which ye said Joseph Parker my father deceased reserved ... a certain tract ... of Land hereafter menconed & through negligence of ye said Hearse got no assurance for ye same, therefore Now know yee for ... ye same ... [10 pounds] ... doth hereby ... sell ... unto him the said Thomas Hearse ... All that tract ... of land ... on ye Northeast side of a brook commonly cal'd ... by the name, alewife brook ... in ... Shrewsbury ... [adjoining land owners or names - Gideon Freeborn] ... since it became myne being heir to my loving father the said Joseph Parker, Esqr., deceased ...; [Signed - Joseph Parker; witnesses - Saml Dennis, Tho. Webley.]

[26 December 1694 - The above deed was acknowledged before Lewis Morris and John Hance.]

[p 85] WILLIAM LAWRENCE, SR to WILLIAM LAWRENCE, JR

26 December 1694 - ...I, William Lawrence of the Town of Middletown ... Monmouth ... East New Jersey, yeoman ... Greeting: for and in consideration of ye naturall Love and affection which I beare to my loving son William Lawrence ...[of the same place] ... Junior ... [for 17 pounds sell] ... All those severall tracts of land & meadow ... [100 acres] ... heretofore purchased by him the said William Lawrence, Sen'r of Robert Barclay of Ury in the Kingdom of Scotland, Esq'r by John Reid of Hortencie ... County of Monmouth his attorney ... lying ... in ye said Middletown ...on the south side of Hopp river by Burlington path ... Also another Tract ... in ... Middletown ... on the north side of hop-river ... [100 acres] ... also one moiety or half part of a certain tract of lands ... in Monmouth on ye South side of Manusquan River ... [adjoining land owners or names - north and south of land of Richard Hartshorne, east by the sea, west by a highway] ... same conveyed to me by ... Robert Barclay by his Attorney ... 10 August 1688 and by Patten ... [dated 5 January 1685] ... and another instrument ... [dated 19 January 1692] ...; [Signed - William Lawrence; witnesses - Thomas Roberts, Mordecia Gibbons, James Lawrence, John Lawrence, John Cox made his mark when signing.]

MONMOUTH COUNTY DEEDS - BOOK "C"

[27 March 1695 - William Lawrence acknowledged the above deed before Andrew Bowne and John Hance.]

[p 88] WILLIAM LAWRENCE, SR to JOSEPH LAWRENCE

6 March 1695 - ...I, William Lawrence, of Middletown ... Monmouth ... East New Jersey, Yeoman, Sen'r ... for and in consideration of ye naturall love & affection, that I beare to my son Joseph Lawrence of ye town of Shrewsbury ... and a competent sum of money ... sell ... unto him ye said Joseph Lawrence ... All those severall tracts ... of land & meadow ... on both sides Manusquan river ... in ... Shrewsbury ... heretofore purchased by him ... William Lawrence ... [by patent dated 19 January 1692] ... the one moiety or half part .. [adjoining land owners or names - southside of Manasquan River, Richard Hartshorne] ... and ... half part of another tract ... [adjoining land owners or names - sea, Richard Hartshorne] ... also ... half part ... [adjoining land owners or names - north side of Manasquan River, Richard Hartshorne, Joseph West] ... [180 acres] ... Also another tract on the north side of ye said River ... [adjoining land owners or names - Richard Hartshorne, John Hance] ... [60 acres] ...; [Signed - William Lawrence; witnesses - Thomas Roberts, Mordecia Gibbons, James Lawrence, John Lawrence, John Cox made his mark when signing.]

[27 March 1695 - William Lawrence acknowledged the above deed before Andrew Bowne and John Hance.]

[p 90] WILLIAM LAWRENCE, SR to JOHN LAWRENCE

26 December 1694 - ...I, William Lawrence, of Middletown ... Monmouth ... East New Jersey, Yeoman, Sen'r ... for and in consideration of ye naturall love & affection, that I beare to my son John Lawrence of ye town of Shrewsbury ... and a competent sum of money ... sell ... unto him ye said John Lawrence ... All those severall tracts ... of land ... in ... Shrewsbury ... [heretofore purchased by William Lawrence by patent dated 19 January 1692] ... [adjoining land owners or names - John Hance, Ephraim Allen] ... [78 acres] ... [also other land of 269 acres] ... [adjoining land owners or names - Richard Hartshorne, Judah Allen, Manasquan River, Remembrance Lippincott, the sea] ...; [Signed] - William Lawrence; witnesses - Thomas Roberts, Mordecia Gibbons, James Lawrence, John Lawrence, John Cox made his mark when signing.]

[27 March 1695 - William Lawrence acknowledged the above deed before Andrew Bowne and John Hance.]

[p 102]   RENTAL AGREEMENT

7 February 1689 - ... Peter Tilton of Middletown ... Monmouth ... East Jersey ... [for 20 shillings paid by Thurley Swiny of ye same County ... for ye use of his son John Swiney ... one piece of Reedy

MONMOUTH COUNTY DEEDS - BOOK "C"

Mash ... [1.5 acres] ... in Tilton's farm called Marvill hill ...; [Signed - Peter Tilton; witnesses - John Hance, Elisha Lawrence.]

[27 March 1695 - Peter Tilton acknowledged the above deed before Andrew Bown and John Hance.]

[p 103]   **RECORD OF RECEIPT**

[7 February 1689 - Record of Peter Tilton receiving 20 shillings from Thurley Swiney made before John Hance.]

[p 103]   **MARRIAGE**

In Middletown ... East Jersey the 9 Day of January ... 1694/5 Nathaniell Leonard of Middletown & Hannah Grover of the same Town after lawfull publication did before me & severall witnesses take each other in Marriage till death part them. [Signed - Peter Tilton.]

[p 104]   **COURT OF SESSIONS FOR YE COUNTY OF MONMOUTH**

March ye 26 Anno 1695 - It is the order of the Court that upon application made by James Grover Senir, Cap[n] Safety Grover, William Lawrence Sen'r and William Lawrence Jun'r the nearest relations to Joseph Grover & Hanah Leonard late wife of the said Joseph Grover, deceased, that William Lawrence Sen'r, grandfather of ye children of the aforesaid Joseph Grover & Hannah his late wife shall have the oversight of the said children.

Joseph Grover son of the aforesaid Joseph Grover late deceased came into Court and did make choice of his grandfather William Lawrence Senir, and his Uncle William Lawrence, Junir to be his Guardians.

Mary Grover Daughter of the aforesaid Joseph Grover & Hanah his late Wife lately deceased, did make choice of William Lawrence Senir, her grandfather to be her Guardian. John Swiney Son of Thurlough Swiney late of Middletown, deceased did make choice of William Lawrence Junir & Capt. Grover to be his Guardians.

All of which was allowed by the Court and ordered to be recorded. By Order of the Court - [Signed - Tho. Webley, Clerk.

[p 105]   **ROBERT BARCLAY to THOMAS WARNE**

20 March 1689 - Robert Barclay of Ury in ye Kingdom of Scotland ... [sold to] ... Thomas Warne ... Monmouth ... East New Jersey ... Witnesseth that ... Barclay by John Reid of Hortencie ... County of Monmouth aforesaid his Attorney ... [for a] ... competent sum of money to ... John Reid ... [sells

MONMOUTH COUNTY DEEDS - BOOK "C"

to Warne] ... all that tract of land ... in ... Monmouth ... neare the Rockie Hill on the Burlington Road ... [adjoining land owners or names - Samuel Foreman's land, Daniell Harker's land, to ye mine brook, to the Topp of Rockie Hill, Aron Foreman, James Miller] ... [claimed by Barclay through a patent dated 29 September 1686] ...; [Signed - John Redir made his mark; witnesses - John Barclay, Ja. Fullertone.]

[26 March 1695 - John Reid acknowledged the above in Court before Andrew Bowne and John Hance.]

[p 106]   **JAMES MILLER to THOMAS WARNE**

12 March 1689 - James Miller of Carshore in ye Kingdom of Scotland by John Reid of Hortencie ... Monmouth ... East New Jersey ... [sold to] ...Thomas Warne ... County of Monmouth ... [for a] ... competent sum of money ... all that tract of Land neare Rockie Hill on Burlington Road ... Monmouth ... [adjoining land owners or names - Samuell Foreman, G. Lawrie's land, Daniell Harker, R. Barclay] ... [which Miller claims by a deed] ... from John Mollison ... in ... [August 1689] ...; [Signed - John Reid made his mark; witnesses - John Barclay, Ja. Fullertone.]

[26 March 1695 - the above was acknowledged in Court by Reid before Andrew Bowne and John Hance.

[p 108]   **ROBERT BARCLAY to ARON FOREMAN**

15 January 1688 - Robert Barclay of Ury ... Kingdom of Scotland esquire by John Reid of Hortencie ... Monmouth ... East New Jersey ... [sold to] ... Aron Foreman of the sais County, planter ... [for 10 pounds] ... All that tract of Land ... in ... Monmouth ... neare to a place called ye Rockie Hill on Burlington Road ... [adjoining land owners or names - Samuell Foreman, Dry Spring, Robert Barclay] ... [Barclay claimed rights by part of his patent of 29 September 1686] ...; [Signed - John Reid made his mark; witnesses - James Scott, Andrew Bowne.]

[26 March 1695 - John Reid acknowledged the above deed before John Hance, Tho. Webley.]

[p 110]   **THOMAS COX to JAMES COX**

20 March 1695 - ... I, Thomas Cox of Middletown ... Monmouth ... East New Jersey Planter ... for & in consideration of the naturall love & affection which I have to my brother James Cox ... [plus 40 shillings sold] ... All that Tract of Land Beginning at ye Southeast corner of my ... [240 acres] ... where I live ... containing ... [80 acres] ... Also ... [1 acre] ... of meadow ... [adjoining land owners or names - Richard Gibbons, Northeast by another acre which I bought of George Job] ... the siad tracts of land & meado; Together with othe tracts were granted to my father Thomas Cox by pattent ... [dated 1 December 1676] ... and also ye forementioned acre of meadow which I bought of george

MONMOUTH COUNTY DEEDS - BOOK "C"

Job by Deed ... [dated 15 December] ...; [Signed - Thomas Cox made his mark when signing; there were no witnesses shown.]

[Proved before Andrew Bowne, John Hance.]

[p 111]   **JANE SADLER to JOHN JOBS**

8 May 1691 - ... Jane Sadler of Middletown ... Monmouth ... East New Jersey in America, Administrix of Richard Sadler of ye foresaid Town, County & province, sends greeting: Now Know yee that I ... Jane Sadler for ... [5 pounds] ... paid to me by John Jobs of ye ... [same place] ... Yeoman ... grant unto him the said George Jobs ... [Notice - This first name is circled in pencil and the name John Job is listed throughout the rest of the deed] ... [sells 5 acres of meadow] ... within Middletown granted by pattent ... [dated 2 June 1677] ... [adjoining land owners or names - John Stout] ...; [Signed - Jane Sadler made her mark when signing; witnesses - John Crafford, Rob. Hamilton, George Crafford; 26 March 1695 - The above deed was proved before Justices Andrew Bowne and John Hance.

[p 113]   **JOSEPH WEST to THOMAS HEARCE**

14 September 1694 - ... I, Joseph West of ... Shrewsbury ... Monmouth ... East New Jersey Yeoman ... [for 11 pounds] ... [sold to] ... Thomas Hearce of ye same ... [place] ... yeoman ... all that tract ... in Shrewsbury ... lying on a certain neck, commonly cal^d ... Long neck ... [adjoining land owners or names - West by Edmond Laffetra, East by Stephen West, alies Thomas Hearse, South by a creek that comes from Shrewsbury] ... howsoever since ye ame was conveyed to me by ... Deed ... from ... my loving brother Robert West of ye said Shrewsbury ... [on 2 April 1688] ...; [Signed - Joseph West; witnesses - Nicholas Brown made his mark when signing; Saml Dennis.]

[27 March 1695 - The above deed was proved in Court - Tho. Webley.]

[p 114]   **JOSEPH WEST to THOMAS HEARSE**

1 January 1693 - ... Joseph West of ... Shrewsbury ... Monmouth ... East New Jersey, carpenter ... [sold to] ... Thomas Hearse ... [of the same place for 40 shillings] ... all them severall tracts of meadow ... [5.5 acres] ... in ... Shrewsbury formerly ... surveyed to Stephen West late of the said Shrewsbury ... surveyed to Stephen West lying at Norwodiconk ... [adjoining land owners or names - Robert West, Mr^s Katherine Brown] ... also ... [2 acres] ... in the Long Neck but is called Goose Neck ... [Sarah Reape, Mistress Katherine Brown, John Chambers, Shrewsbury river] ... purchased by ... Joseph West of Willm of Middletown ... Senir, and Coopper ... [by deed dated 1 March 1693 or

MONMOUTH COUNTY DEEDS - BOOK "C"

1692] ...; [Signed on 1 October 1693 by Joseph West; witnesses - L. Morris, Nathaniell Leonard, Saml Dennis.]

[27 March 1695 - The above deed was proved in Court - Tho. Webley.]

[p 116]   **WILLIAM WEST to JOHN WEST**

30 September 1694 - William West of ... Shrewsbury ... Monmouth ... East New Jersey, Carpenter and Margarett his wife ... [sold to] ... John West brother of ... William West ... [of the same place] ... [for 20 pounds] ... the moiety or half part of a certain tract ... in ... [the same place] ... [adjoining land owners or names - George Allen, Jedediah Allen, William West] ... [60.5 acres] ... [Also] ... Ye moiety or half part of ... [14 acres] ... At Norwaticonck ... [adjoining land owners or names - Stephen West, Francis Burden, John Havens] ... [Also 3 acres] ... lying at Goose Neck ... being a triangle ... by a branch of Shrewsbury River ...; [Signed - William West, Margarett West; witnesses - Samuell White, Francis Jackson, Tho. Webley.]

[26 March 1695 - Both William and Margaret West appeared and acknowledged the above deed in Court before Lewis Morris and John Hance.]

[p 118]   **HANANIAH GIFFORD to FRANCIS JACKSON**

4 March 1694 - Hananiah Gifford of ... Shrewsbury ... Monmouth ... East New Jersey Yeoman & Elizabeth his wife ... [sold to] ... Francis Jackson ... Yeoman ... [for 14 pounds] ... a certain tract ... at Shark river ... [adjoining land owners or names - John Chambers, Shark river] ...; [Signed - Both Hananiah and Elizabeth Gifford made their marks when signing; witnesses - Job Lawrence, Joseph Lawrence, Robert West made his mark when signing.]

6 March 1694/5 - Robert West and Tho. Webley acknowledged in Court before Lewis Morris and John Hance that they saw the grantors sign the above deed.]

[p 120]   **THOMAS WHITELOCK to JOHN WHITELOCK**

26 March 1695 - Thomas Whitlock ... Town of Middletown ... Monmouth ... East New Jersey Yeoman ... [sold to] ... John Whitelock ... [of the same place] ... Yeoman ... [for 10 pounds] ... all that tract ... at Shoal Harbour ... [in Middletown] ... [9 acres] ... [adjoining land owners or names - Richard Sadler alias John Whitelock, Edward Tart, alias John Stoutt, Shoal Harbour creek] ..., [Signed - Thomas Whitelock made his mark when signing; witnesses - Obidiah Bowne, James Bowne, Jr.]

[27 March 1695 - Whitelock acknowledged the above deed in Court before Tho. Webley.]

MONMOUTH COUNTY DEEDS - BOOK "C"

[p 121]   GARWIN DRUMMOND to NICHOLAS BROWN

25 July 1693 - ... Garwin Drummond of Lor [Long?] Harbour ... Monmouth ... East New Jersey ... planter ... [sold for 8 pounds to] ... Nicholas Brown of Shrewsbury ... planter ... All that ... [50 acres] ... of land lying in ye barrens including the half of ye bogg where William West & William Woolley moved their hay ... [land claimed by Drummond by pattent dated 2 November 1692] ...; [Signed - Garvin Drummond; witnesses - Clemment Masters, William Woolley, Tho. Webley.]

[1 May 1695 - The above deed was acknowledged in Court before Lewis Morris and John Hance.]

[p 123]   NICHOLAS BROWN to JOHN TILTON

24 April 1695 - Nicholas Brown of ... Shrewsbury ... Monmouth ... East New Jersey yeoman & Katherine his wife ... [sold to] ... John Tilton of Middletown ... [for 42 pounds] ... All that tract of land ... neare ye Leonard's saw mill ... [adjoining land owners or names - some of the tract in Middletown and some in Shrewsbury, branch of the Swiming river, saw mill brook, land formerly John Leonard's, Lewis Morris Esq'] ... which said tract of land by ... Lewis Morris was granted unto Thomas Webley ... on 26 December 1692 and Webley sold it on 3 January 1693 to ye Nicholas Brown] ...; [Signed - Both Nicholas Brown and Katherine made their marks when signing; witnesses - Sarah West, Robert Parker, Tho. Webley; Nicholas Brown acknowledged the above deed before L. Morris.]

[p 124a]   EBONEZER COOKE to THOMAS HUETT

26 April 1695 - ... Ebonezer Cooke of ... Shrewsbury ... Monmouth ... East New Jersey, Yeoman & Mary his wife ... [sold to] ... Thomas Huett ... [of the same place] ... Whereas Edward Pattison father of the abovesaid Mary Cook did purchase a Right ... in Narrumson Neck ... in the Town bounds of ... Shrewsbury ... [amounting to one equal share] ... of land within ye said town ... Now ... Ebenezer Cooke & Mary his wife Daughter & one of the Coheireses of the ... Edward Pattison deceased ... [sold for 10 pounds the] ... interest in a ... share of land ... of ye town ...; [Signed - Ebenezer E. Cooke, Mary made her mark when signing; witnesses - Gawin Drummond, Thomas Parker, Tho. Webley.]

[9 May 1685 - Garwin Drummond and Thomas Webley upon their oath, before Lewis Morris and John Hance, stated that they saw both of the Cookes sign the above deed.]

[p 126]   GARWIN DRUMMOND to JOHN TUCKER

13 May 1693 - ...I, Garwin Drummond of Long Harbour ... Monmouth ... East New Jersey ... planter ... [sold for 16 pounds to] ... John Tucker of Deale ... planter ... All that hundred acres of land ... [adjoining land owners or names - poplar swamp brooke, by Tucker's land] ... [Drummond claimed

MONMOUTH COUNTY DEEDS - BOOK "C"

the land by his patent dated 2 November 1692] ...; [Signed - Garwin Drummond; witnesses - Thomas White, John Woolley.]

[1 May 1695 - The above deed was acknowledged in Court before L. Morris and John Hance.]

[p 127] **RICHARD SADLER to JAMES GROVER**

27 July 1688 - ... I Richard Sadler ... Monmouth ... East New Jersey send Greeting; ... whereas Phillip Carteret late Governor of East Jersey ... did ... grant unto me Richard Sadler a house lott containing ... [10 acres] ... [sold land to James Grover] ... [adjoining land owners or names - James Grover, Thomas Whitelock] ... [Also 12 acres] ... of upland at Cocouders ... [adjoining land owners or names - James Grover, William Whitelock, Richard Hartshorne] ... [land granted to Sadler by Patent on 20 June 1677] ...; [Signed - Richard Sadler and Jane Sadler made their marks when signing; witnesses - James Dorsett, John Stoutt.]

[26 March 1695 - The above was proved before Andrew Bowne and John Hance.]

[p 128] **THOMAS WARNE to HENERY BELL**

21 March 1694 - ... Thomas Warne ... Monmouth ... East New Jersey, Carpenter ... [for 10 pounds sold to] ... Henery Bell ... [of the same place] ... planter ... all that tract of land ... [and premises] ... in ye said County ... [adjoining land owners or names - Aaron Foreman, Samuel Foreman, Burlington Road] ... [the land claimed by Thomas Warne by a sale from John Reid attorney of Robert Barclay on 12 March 1689] ...; [Signed - Tho. Warne; witnesses - Samuell Foreman, Samuell Thropp.]

[26 March 1695 - The above deed was acknowledged in Court before Andrew Bown and John Hance.]

[p 129] **MARRIAGE**

27 May 1695 - Then joyned Thomas Foreman & Mary Allen in marriage, which is to satisfie all whom it may concern that this is to be their Certificate - given under my hand this day & yeare above wrighten. [Signed - L. Morris, quorm.]

[p 129] **MARRIAGE**

These are to certifie any whom it may concern that Thomas Potter & Sarah Lawrence both of Shrewsbury in East New Jersey did come before me in ye presence of ye under mentioned witnesses I did joyne them lawfully in marriage as witness my hand ye 29 day of ye first month 1695. [Signed - John Hance; witnesses - Thomas Cooke, William West, Elisha Allen, Richard Chambers, Abraham Bickley, Susanah Bickley, Margarett West, Elizabeth Cooke .]

MONMOUTH COUNTY DEEDS - BOOK "C"

[p 130]   EPHRAIM ALLEN to ABRAHAM BROWN

17 November 1691 - Ephraim Allen ... Shrewsbury ... Monmouth ... East New Jersey yeoman ... [sold to] ... Abraham Brown Sen'r ... [of the same place] ... [for 21 pounds] ... All that tract of land ... in ... Monmouth ... [adjoining land owners or names - Manalapan brook which runs along the rear of Job. Jenckin's & Elizabeth Hutton's lot that lye upon Burlington Path neare the pynes, Gideon Freeborn ...; [Signed - Ephraim Allen; witnesses - George Hulett, William West, Tho. Webley.]

[3 July 1695 - The above deed was acknowledged in Court before John Hance and Tho. Webley.]

[p 132]   JAMES REID to THOMAS FORMAN

3 February 1691 - ... I, James Reid ... Monmouth ... East New Jersey ... [sold for 26 pounds to] ... Thomas Forman of the same County ... All that tract of land in ... Monmouth ... adjoining to the lands of Gawin Lawrie deceased containing ... [200 acres] ... [adjoining land owners or names - Gawin Lawrie land on Spotswood brook] ... also ... [4 acres] ... [adjoining land owners or names - Spotswood brook below James Miller's corner] ... [Reid claimed the land by patent dated 20 January 1687 & recorded on 8 & 9 February 1687 in Liber B-Folio 281 of public records] ...; [Signed - Ja. Reid, Jein Reid; witnesses - Alex'r Meikle, George Reid; acknowledged before L. Morris.]

[p 133]   SARAH PARKER to PETER WHITE

10 May 1688 - Sarah Parker ... County of Burlington ... West New Jersey, widdow, George Parker & William Parker sons of ye said Sarah Parker both ... [of the same place] ... [sold to] ... Peter White of Shrewsbury ... East New Jersey Taylor ... [sells for 30 pounds] ... All their right ... of that parcell of land, meadow & premises late apertaining to George Parker deceased whereupon ye said Peter White doth now dwell ... [in Shrewsbury] ... [adjoining land owners or names - Neversincks River, John Hance, John Chambers] ... [also 3.5 acres] ... of meadow ... [adjoining land owners or names - branch of the Shrewsbury River, John Clayton, Calieb Shreive] ...; [Signed - Sarah Parker, George Parker, William Parker made his mark when signing; witnesses - Henry Borr, Joseph Parker made his mark when signing, Symon Charles.]

[4 September 1695 - The Parkers appeared in Court and acknowledged the above deed before John Tatham and John Hollinghead, Justices.]

[p 135]   SOLDIER'S POWER OF ATTORNEY

13 December 1695 - ...I, Nicholas Havens, Soldier, in his Majestie's fort of New York, have ... in my stead & place put & deputed my trusty & loving friend Calieb Allen of ... Shrewsbury ... East New Jersey, Smithi, my true & lawfull Attorney ... and to take possession of my estate of land in ... Shrewsbury formerly belonging to John Havens my father ... Excepting always from this Letter of

MONMOUTH COUNTY DEEDS - BOOK "C"

Attorney my proportion & Share of Carpenters tools ...; Havens made his mark when signing; witnesses - David Vilants, Thomas Bills, George Reid.]

[8 November 1695 - Bills acknowledged the above deed in Court before John Hance.]

[p 136]   **NICHOLAS HAVENS to CALEB ALLEN**

8 February 1695 - Nicholas Havens, soldier in his Majestie's fort of New York, ... [sold to] ... Caleb Allen ... Shrewsbury ... Monmouth East New Jersey, blacksmith ... [for 12 pounds] ... All the Quarter part or tract of ... land ... in sd. Shrewsbury ... [claimed by patent dated 20 March 1688] ... [adjoining land owners or names - Edmond Laffetra, Judah Allen alias George Allen, unsurveyed land given to me by my father John Havens late of ye sd Shrewsbury deceased, one quarter part bounded on East by my loving brother John Havens] ... [the Will of John Havens deceased was dated 14 March 1686/7 and recorded in East New Jersey records] ...; [Signed - Havens made his mark when signing; witnesses - Miles Foster, William Bradford, Obadiah Haig, Nichaoll West; acknowledged before L. Morris, Clerk.]

[p 138]   **GEORGE ALLEN to CALEB ALLEN**

4 March 1695 - George Allen of ... Shrewsbury .. Monmouth ... East New Jersey, weaver & Elizabeth his wife ... [sold to] ... Caleb Allen ... [of the same place] ... [for 10 pounds] ... a certain tract ... of land ... in Ye Town aforesaid ... [adjoining land owners or names - John West, John Havens alias George Allen & Nicholas Havens, up to the highway, Calieb Allen] ...; Signed - Both George Allen and Elizabeth made their marks when signing; witnesses - Tho. Webley, Ann Hulett made her mark when signing.]

[4 March 1695/6 - The above deed was acknowledged before L. Morris.]

[p 139]   **WILLIAM LEEDS, SR to WILLIAM LEEDS, JR**

19 September 1694 - William Leeds Senior & resident in ... County of Burlington ... West New Jersey, Cooper ... [sold to] ... William Leeds Junior his second son ... [for 30 pounds] ... All that ... land ... in ... Middletown ... Monmouth ... East New Jersey ... along Swiming River ... [184 acres] ... [Leeds claimed the land by his patent of 30 June 1676 which was granted to Richard Stout] ... [Adjoining land owners or names - Swiming River, falls neck, where the said river meets Hop River, neare a house of late sett up by the widow Grover's negro Tom] ...; [Signed - William Leeds Senir; witnesses - Francis Davenport, Peter Stillwell, Daniell Leeds.]

[p 142]   **THOMAS HEARSE to CALEB ALLEN**

16 March 1695 - Thomas Hearse ... Shrewsbury ... Monmouth ... East New Jersey, yeoman ... [sold

MONMOUTH COUNTY DEEDS - BOOK "C"

to] ... Caleb Allen ... [of the same place] ... blacksmith ... [for 3pounds, 6 shillings] ... All that one quarter part of Meodow ... in ... Shrewsbury ... on ... [land commonly called Norawaticonck alias Long Neck] ... heretofore purchased of William Havens of ... Freehold ... [on 11 February 1695] ...; [Signed - Thomas Hearse made his mark when signing; witnesses - Thomas White, Nicholas Brown mark, Sam¹ Dennis.]

[3 June 1696 - Thomas Hearse appeared in Court and acknowledged the above deed before John Hance and Tho. Webley.]

[p 142] **RECEIPT**

[26 March 1696 - Receipt from John Reid to William Lawrence where Reid acknowledged he received a competent sum for use of Robert Barclay in full satisfaction from William Lawrence; signed - John Reid; acknowledged before John Hance, Justice.]

[p 144] **WILLIAM WOOLLEY to STEPHEN COOK**

23 May 1691 - ...I, William Woolley of Shrewsbury ... Monmouth Planter ... [sold to] ... Stephen Cook Planter of the same place ... All that tract of upland & meadow ... in ... Shrewsbury containing ... [93.5 acres] ... [joyning and bounding by lands of Henery Boman now is the possession of William Case, the bounds of lands of Daniell Leeds & Henery Boman] ... [90 acres] ... [claimed by Woolley by patent dated 10 December 1681] ... [adjoining land owners or names - Sarah Reape's land, Henery Boman's land, Daniel Leeds] ... [also 3.5 acres] ... of meadow at Potaapeck ... [adjoining land owners or names - Restore Lippincott, Tobias Hanson] ... [which was conveyed to Woolley by Rembrance Lippincott on 17 February 1684] ...; [Signed - William Woolley, Ann Woolley; witnesses - Nicholas Brown made his mark when signing, Rembrance Lippincott.]

3 June 1696 - William Woolley appeared and acknowledged the above deed before John Hance and Tho. Webley.]

[p 145] **MARRIAGE**

This may Certifie That I, joyned Gershom Mott & Sarah Clayton in the holy setate of marriage, this fourth day of March 1696. [Signed - Andrew Bown.]

[p 146] **JOHN BOWNE to PETER WILSON**

17 February 1695 - ... I, John Bowne of Middletown ... Monmouth ... East New Jersey merchant ... [sold for 9 pounds to] Peter Tilton ... [Notice - Throughout the rest of the deed and in the heading, the name was Peter Wilson] ... of ye same place planter ... All that lott of meadow ... at Shoal

MONMOUTH COUNTY DEEDS - BOOK "C"

Harbour ... within ... Middletown ... containing ... [6 acres] ... [adjoining land owners or names - meadow formerly of Edward Tart but now of Richard Stout, land formerly of John Throckmorton & now Garrett Wall] ... [which Bowne bought of John Stout on 25 March 1689] ...; [Signed - Jno. Bowne; witnesses - James Dorsett, Francis Harbert, John Brown.]

25 March 1696 - The above deed was acknowledged before Andrew Bowne and John Hance.

[p 147]   **ABRAHAM BROWN SENIOR to SAMUELL THROPP**

2 October 1695 - ... I, Abraham Brown Sen'r ... of Shrewsbury ... Monmouth ... East New Jersey yeoman ... [sold for 5 pounds] ... to Samuell Thropp of ... Shrewsbury ... All that tract of land and meadows ... in ye Town of Freehold ... [adjoining land owners or names - Gideon Freeborn's corner on the north side of Manalapan brook, to an Indian path, Abraham Brown] ... [Brown claimed the land as being sold to him by James Johnston on 10 July 1690] ...; [Signed - Abraham Brown of Shrewsbury; witnesses - Thomas Potter made his mark when signing; Nathaniel Cammock made his mark when signing, Saml Dennis.]

[1 July 1696 - Abraham Brown appeared in Court and acknowledged the above deed before John Hance and L. Morris.]

[p 149]   **THOMAS HILBOURN to RICHARD JAMES**

4 June 1696 - Thomas Hilbourn of ... Shrewsbury ... Monmouth ... East New Jersey yeoman & Elizabeth his wife ... [sold to] ... Richard James ... of Middletown ... yeoman ... [for 25 pounds] ... All that ... land & meadow ... in the Town of Freehold ... Monmouth ... [adjoining land owners or names - on the northside of Burlington Path in the Indian purchase called Pesaqunoqua, Job Jenkins] ... [100 acres] ... [Claimed by Hilbourn by patent dated 22 March 1687] ...; [Signed - Thomas Hilborn, Elizabeth Hilborn; witnesses - Jno. Bowne, Peter White, Sam Dennis.]

[23 September 1696 - Capt. John Bowne and Peter White appeared before Andrew Bowne and John Hance and acknowledged they saw the Hilborn's sign the above deed.]

[p 151]   **COURT OF SESSIONS - MONMOUTH**

23 September 1676 - Upon application of John Hance, Esqr on ye behalf of John Worthley ... Town of Shreswbury ... yeoman concerning one Jonathan Maryson Case son of Mary Sutton the said Jonathan being now nine years of age which said Jonathan Maryson, the said John Worthley hath maintained & bred up from his infancie and doth humbly desire this Court that ye said Jonathan Maryson may be bound an apprentice unto him the said John Worthley ...

Judgement of ye Court is ... Jonathan Maryson ... shall serve the said John Worthley ... after the

MONMOUTH COUNTY DEEDS - BOOK "C"

manner of apprentice from the day of the date hereof until he shall be of the age of Twenty one yeares; he ye said Worthley shall find and allow his said apprentice sufficient meat, drink, aparrell, washing & lodging during his said time, and at ye expiration of the said time to give and allow his said apprentice as is usuall in ye said province.

[p 152]   **JAMES JOHNSTONE to WALTER KERR**

30 January 1690 - ...I, James Johnstone ... Monmouth ... East New Jersey, for favor & other consideration moving me, have ... sold ... to Walter Kerr of ye said County ... for the use ... of James Kerr his second son one tract of land containing ... [100 acres] ... lying in ... Monmouth ... upon the North siad of a brook ... [adjoining land owners or names - below wemcooke point, tract of land sold by me to William Davisson ajoyning William Oliphant's land] ... [owned by him through survey of ye said Tract under the hand of John Barcklay for laying of ye survey in Right of Robert Turner's propriatie purchase by me] ... and which Tract is bounded West & North by barren land ..., east by William Davisson ...; [Signed - James Johnstone; witnesses - William Naughty, Thomas Powell.]

[3 December 1696 - William Naughty acknowledged the above deed in court before L. Morris.]

[p 153]   **SAMUELL CHIELD to WILLIAM AUSTIN**

3 April 1693 - ...I, Samuell Chield of ye Town of Shrewsbury ... Monmouth ... East New Jersey Cordwainer ... [sold for 62 pounds] ... paid by William Austin of ye same ... weaver ... All that tract of upland & meadow ... in ... Shrewsbury ... [adjacent land owners or names - on ye Northeast by Abraham Brown, Southwest by Robert Leacock, Northwest by Neversinke River, Southeast by a small creek that comes from Chrewsbury River] ... [116 acres] ... Also four acres of meadow ... [adjacent land owners or names - on the South by John Hance, North by Francis Burdon, East by a highway, West by a small creek] ... [purchased by Child from Thomas Potter on 1 February 1689] ...; [Signed - Samuell C/Shield; witnesses - Thomas White, Sam¹ Dennis.

[9 January 1696 - The above deed was acknowledged before John Hance and Tho. Webley.]

[p 154]   **MORTGAGE FROM JOHN STRAKE to THOMAS POTTER**

20 March 1692 - ... John Starkee ... Monmouth ... East New Jersey and Mary his Wife in name & behalf of Mary Channelhouse, daughter of ye deceased Adam Channelhouse late of ye place aforesaid on ye one part and Thomas Potter of ye said place on ye other part ... [for 70 pounds] ... All that ... land ... on the North siad of ye saw mill brooke ... also a slipp of boggie meadow ... on ye southeast side of ye said tract of land esteemed two acres, As also another peece of land in ye County of Philadelphia ... Pensilvania containing ... [500 acres] ... [adjoining land ownes or names - Beginning at Sarah Fuller' sland, by Richard Jugelos land] ... Thomas Potter and Anna, his wife ...; [Signed -

MONMOUTH COUNTY DEEDS - BOOK "C"

John Starkee and Mary Starkee made their marks; witnesses - Daniell Harcutt, Thomas Partridge, Ja. Fullertone.]

[4 January 1696 - Mary Starkey did sign the above within wrighten Instrument before us - John Hance, Tho. Webley.]

[p 157]   **JEDEDIAH ALLEN to ROBERT DENNIS**

25TH of the third month called May 1691 - ... I, Jedediah Allen of Shrewsbury ... Monmouth ... East New Jersey ... in consideration of a compitent sum of money to me ... by Robert Dennis of Portsmouth on Rhode Island in New England ... All those tracts of upland & meadow ... in ... Monmouth ... contained in ye late purchase called by ye Indian name pese quenocque, lying on the south side of Burlington path ... [adjoining land owners or names - John Burden's corner tree, near Burlington Road, Jedediah Allen, Peter Simmans, Job Jenckius, William North] ... [150 acres] ... [Signed - Jedediah Allen, Elizabeth Allen made her mark; witnesses - Margarett Lippincott, Richard Lippincott, Rememberance Lippincott; acknowledged before John Hance, Justice.]

[p 158]   **JOHN NEWMAN to WILLIAM SCOTT**

28 March 1691 - ... John Newman ... of Shrewsbury ... Monmouth Carpenter and Mary his wife ... [sold to] ... William Scott ... Whereas ... John Newman on ... [8 February 1687] ... by deed of Sale ... by George Curliss of ye Town & place aforesaid ... Now ... [Newman and wife sell for 1 pound] ... land ... [adjoining land owners or names - North river, William Scott line, John Newman] ...; [Signed - John and Mary Newman made their marks; witnesses - Peter Tilton, Andria Webley, the mark of Excercise Cole, Alex Green, Tho. Webley; acknowledged before Peter Tilton and Tho. Webley.]

[p 161a]   **DANIELL ESTELL to ROBERT HOLMAN**

4 February 1689 - Daniell Estell of Middletown ... Monmouth ... East Jersey planter ... [for 5 pounds] ... paid by Robert Holman of ye same place ... [50 acres] ... of land as it is surveyed which warrent beares Date ye ... [11th, month left blank, 1688] ...; [Signed - Daniell Estill made his mark when signing; witnesses - Richard Hartshorne, John Stoutt, William Whitlock.]

[26 March 1695 - Hartshorne and Stout acknowledged the above deed before Andrew Bown and John Hance.]

[p 162]   **ROBERT HOLDMAN to GERSHOM MOTT**

28 February 1694 - ... I Robert Holdman of Middletown planter ... [sold for 13 pounds] ... paid by Gershom Mott of Middletown ... [50 acres] ... in ... Middletown ... [by Robert Hartshorne] ...;

MONMOUTH COUNTY DEEDS - BOOK "C"

[Signed - Robert Holdman made his mark when signing; witnesses - James Dorsett, Zebulon Clayton.]

[26 March 1695 - Holdman acknowledged the above deed before Andrew Bown and John Hance; this was the same piece of property in the previous deed.]

[p 163]   **ILOSECHCOTE, SACHEM ET AL to LYDIA BOWN**

10 August 1690 - Ilosechcote, Tascalaway and Talinquanecan Indian Sachems of Mecaponects ... [sold to] ... Lydia Bown of ... Monmouth ... East New Jersey widdow ... [for 7 pounds] ... a tract of land commonly Known by the name of Mowhingsunge neck ... [500 acres] ... [adjoining land owners or names - Mohingsunge neck, Thoˢ Warn's land, Gershom Bown's corner tree, Middletown path from Amboy, Mowhingsung brook, Matewan Creek, Thoˢ Warns's Creek]...; [Signed by the marks of the Indian Schems; witnesses - Richard Salter, Richard James, John Bown.]

[28 March 1696/7 - Capt John Bown and Richard Salter acknowledged that they saw the above named Indians sign and seal the above instrument before Andrew Bown and Peter Tilton.]

[p 164]   **RICHARD HARTSHORNE to WILLIAM LAYTON, JUNIR**

22 August 1690 - Whereas ye Propriators of East Jersey by Pattent unto Restore Lippincott of Shrewsbury ... [100 acres] ... as by Pattent ... [dated 2 January 1687] ... and ... Restore Lippincott did by deed convey the abovesaid ... [100 acres] ... to Remberance Lippincott of ye same place and ...[Remberance Lippincott sold it to Richard Hartshorne of Portland ... Monmouth] ... Now know ye that I, ... Richard Hartshorne ... [for 20 pounds] paid by William Layton of Middletown ... sold unto William Layton, Junir ... All that tract ... of land ... in the late purchase lying by Pasaquequa ... [adjoining land owners or names - William Scott, George Keith, Peter White, John Havens as] ... granted unto ye Richard Hartshorne by deed from Edward Woolley ...[dated 4 August 1690] ...; [Signed - Richard Hartshorne; witnesses - John Stout, Hener[-] Marsh.]

[24 March 1696/7 - Hartshorne acknowledged the above deed befroe Andrew Bown and John Havens.]

[p 165]   **REMEMBRANCE LIPPINCOTT to EDWARD WOOLLEY**

29 November 1688 - ...I, Remembrance [Lippincott] ... of ye Town of Shrewsbury ... Monmouth planter, in consideration of ... [10 pounds] ... paid by Edward Woolley of Shrewsbury ... All that tract ... in Monmouth ... in ye late purchase lying by Pesaquanoqua brook ... [adjoining land owners or names - Richard Stout Junir, William Scott, George Keith] ... [100 acres] ... [this land is the same land in the above deed] ...; [Signed - Remembrance Lippincott; witnesses - Judah Allen, John Tucker, Ruth Tucker.]

MONMOUTH COUNTY DEEDS - BOOK "C"

[24 March 1696/7 - Rembrance Lippincott acknowledged the above deed before Andrew Bowne, Peter Tilton.]

[p 166]   **RICHARD HARTSHORNE to PETER TILTON**

10 November 1696 - ... Richard Hartshorne of Portland in Middletown ... Monmouth ... East Jersey ... [for 25 pounds] ... by Peter Tilton ... [of the same place] ... [sells land in Monmouth] ... [adjoining land owners or names - John Grover's line, rear of Benjamin Burden's lott of Plain Dealing] ... which was granted to me by George Willocks Deed ... [dated 6 October 1696] ...; [Signed Richard Hartshorne; witnesses - Robt. Hamilton, John Salton [Salter?], John Stout.]

[24 March 1696/7 - Hartshorne acknowledged the above deed before Tho. Webley.]

[p 167]   **WILLIAM LAWRENCE to ELISHA LAWRENCE**

2 March 1690 - ... William Lawrence of Town of Middletown ... Monmouth ... New East Jersey ... [for good causes, etc plus 40 pounds paid by] ... Elisha Lawrence of ye same place ... [130 acres] ... [as by patent from Phillip Carterett Governor unto Thomas Herbert, who sold it to Robert Hamilton, and by Hamilton] ... to me ...; [Signed - William Lawrence, Ruth Lawrence made her mark; witnesses - John Stout, John Vachon.]

[25 March 1697 - William Lawrence Junior acknowledged the above deed to be his act before Andrew Bown and John Hance.]

[p 168]   **JOHN REID to ELISHA LAWRENCE**

9 June 1692 - ... I John Reed ... Monmouth ... East New Jersey ... [for 9 pounds] ... [sold to] ... Elisha Lawrence of the same County planter ... All that peece of land ... on hogg pound neck ... granted to me ... by ... Thomas Gordon ... [on 3 June 1692] ...; [Signed - John Reid; witnesses - Robert Hamilton, John Rackman.]

[25 March 1697 - Reid acknowledged the above deed before Andrew Bown and John Hance.]

[p 169]   **JAMES GROVER SENIR to SAFETY GROVER**

18 November 1685 - ... this deed of gift ... I, James Grover Senir of Middletown ... Monmouth ... New Jersey ... for the naturall love & affection I have & beare to my son Safety Grover of Middletown ... a cetain tract ... in bounds of Middletown ... [185 acres of upland and 6 acres of meadow] ... [adjoining land owners or names - mill creek and called by the name of Grover's New Invention, Charles Haines, John Stout] ... which was granted to me ... by Phillip Carterett Governor

MONMOUTH COUNTY DEEDS - BOOK "C"

... [on 20 June 1677] ...; [Signed - James Grover Senir; witnesses - James Grover Junir, Benjamin Burdin.]

[28 September 1686 - James Grover Junir and Benjamin Burden acknowledged that above deed before Andrew Bown and Richard Hartshorne.]

[p 171]   **JOHN HAMTON to BENJAMIN BURDEN**

7 October 1696 - John Hamton of ye Town of Freehold ... Monmouth ... East New Jersey planter ... [sold to] ... Benjamin Burden ... Middletown ... planter Whereas Peter Soumans ... [was seized of land & meadow ... in the Town of Freehold which he claimed by patent dated 10 May 1688] ... [adjoining land owners or names - Burlington path, Jedediah Allen, Robert Barclay's corner, Manalapan Brook, Manusquan Brook] ... which ... [Soumans by his Attorney Miles F. Forster did convey & assure to George Keith and Keith sold it to John Hamton on 5 August 1690, 25 October 1693 and whereas John Reid of Freehold was seized of a tract adjoining this tract by patent of 23 June 1696] ... [adjoining land owners or names - Clemment Plumsteeds, Manasquan Brook] ... and ... John Reid ... [sold it to John Hamton] ... Now this Indenture John Hamton ... [for 100 pounds sells to Benjamin Burden] ...; [Signed - John Hamton; witnesses - John Reid, Elisha Lawrence, William Lawrence Junir.]

[24 March 1696/7 - John Reid and William Lawrence acknowledged, that they saw Hamton sign the above deed, before Andrew Bown, Lewis Morris, Richard Hartshorne.]

[p 173]   **THOMAS WARN to SAMUELL FORMAN**

5 March 1696 - Thomas Warn of Middletown ... East New Jersey, gent, ... [sold to] Samuell Forman ... Township of Freehold ... Monmouth .. [for 25 pounds, 3 shillings] ... Already paid to and for the use of ... Thomas Warne ... All that ... land ... in ... Monmouth ... [adjoining land owners or names - Shrewsbury Road to Burlington, Samuell Forman, Shrewsbury men's land, Gawin Lawrie's land, mine brook] ... [148 acres] ...; [Signed - Thomas Warn; witnesses - Edward Woolley, Thomas Forman.]

[p 175]   **ARON FORMAN to ALEXANDER FORMAN**

3 November 1696 - Aron Forman & Dorathie his wife of Freehold ... Monmouth ... East New Jersey planter ... [sold to] ... Alexander Forman lawfull son of ye siad Aron & Dorathie Forman ... for ... ye affection to their son Alexander Forman and also for ... [20 bushels of good merchantable wheat & 25 busels of ... Indian corn to be payed yearly ... during all ye term of ye naturall life of ye said Aron Forman and Dorathie Forman & the naturall life of the longer of them at or within ye dwelling house of ye said Aron at or before ye 25th day of the third month ... viz ninety & eight and likewise fodder for four head of cattell to be sett in a convenient placed and firewood for their fire yearly ... [in return

for] ... All that tract ... in ... Monmouth ... [adjoining land owners or names - Samuell Forman's land, Burlington Road, Henery Bell] ... [50 acres] ...; [Signed - Aron Forman made his mark; witness - William Laing.]

[p 177]   **MARRIAGE**

... Now Know ye That ... on the ... [4 September 1696] ... John Chambers of ... Shrewsbury ... Monmouth ... and Bridgett Huett was joyned in the holy estate of Matrimony by me - Peter Tilton, Justice.

[p 177]   **MARRIAGE**

The seventh & twenty day of the seventh month Cal^d September ... [1696] ... Thomas Higham and Jane Sadler of Middletown came before me and did take each other in Marriage before severall witnesses till death part them, they being lawfully published - Peter Tilton, Justice.

[p 178]   **CHERAWAS ET AL to WILLIAM LEEDS**

29 March 1680 - ... I Cherawas & Metshatt & Cheslis & Puropa and Hendrick & Iraseak & Nestoa & Pouraas, & Potroas & Secpha & Secoes, owners of a Tract of land called Pessesick amesslofe & which land ... [adjoins the land owners or names - Ben. Burden, Jacob Truwaxe, road from Shrewsbury to Middletown, down by Tho. Aplegats land, Peter Tilton's land, Joseph Grover's land, Richard Stout Junior] ... [and the above Indians sold to] ... William Leeds Coopper of Shrewsbury ...; [Signed - with the marks of the above Sachems; no witnesses or date of the recording shown.]

[p 180]   **POWER OF ATTORNEY**

8 October 1695 - ... I, Gideon Freeborn of Portchmouth on Rhode Island ... New England yeoman ... have ... constituted my loving friend Abraham Brown Senir, of Shrewsbury in East Jersey yeoman, to be my true & lawfull Attourney ...; [Signed - Gidion Freebourne; witnesses - Daniell Houland, John Smith.]

[8 October 1695 - Gidion Freebourne acknowledged that above item before Sam^{ll} Cranston, Asist.]

[p 182]   **SHOUGHAM, SACHEM to EDWARD WEBLEY**

14 January 1686 - ... Between Shougham Sachem of Crosswicks Indian Town being between Delaware River and Raritan River ... [sold to] ... Edward Webley late of Shrewsbury ... Monmouth ... [for 10 pounds] ... land ... neare Crosswicks ... [adjoining land owners or names - a small river

MONMOUTH COUNTY DEEDS - BOOK "C"

called Croswicksum] ... [1,000 acres] ...; [Signed - Shougham made his mark; witnesses - John Slocum, the mark of Edward Williams.]

[24 September 1696 - Acknowledged before Andrew Bown and Lewis Morris.]

[p 184]   **EDWARD WEBLEY to THOMAS WEBLEY**

15 January 1686 - Edward Webley late of Shrewsbury ... [sold to] ... Thomas Webley ... Monmouth ... [the same land in the above deed] ... [for 50 pounds for the above] ... tract of land & ye p^{r}mises ...; [Signed - Edward Webley; witnesses - John Slocum, Edward Williams made his mark.]

[24 September 1696 - John Slocum and Edward Williams acknowledged the above deed before Andrew Bown and L. Morris.]

[p 186]   **GEORGE MOUNT to RICHARD MOUNT**

13 April 1698 - George Mount of ... Middletown ... Monmouth ... East New Jersey & Catherine his wife ... [sold to] ... Richard Mount ... [of the same place] ... [land in Middletown of 76 acres] ... [adjoining land owners or names - Mill brook, Thomas Cox, Safety Grover, William Layton] ... [100 acres] ... granted to ye ... George Mount ... by ye said pattent ... Another Tract of land ... lyeing at ye Poplar field ... [9 acres] ... [adjoining land owners or names - John Smith, mill run, William Layton] ... granted ... to ... George Mount by Richard Hartshorne ... [on 10 December 1680] ... Now Know Yee that ... George Mount & Catherine ... [sell for 50 pounds] ...; [Signed - Both George Mount and Catherine Mount made their marks when signing; witnesses - A. Pintard, Thomas Bills, Tho. Webley.]

[p 190]   **FRANCIS BURDEN to THOMAS VICKARS**

... 7th day of the 7th month called October 1684 - ... I, Francis Burden ... Shrewsbury ... Monmouth ... [for 23 pounds] ... [sells to] ... Thomas Vickars of ... Shrewsbury ... [adjoining land owners or names - 50 rod road by John Lippincott's land, neck belonging to Norawaticonck, Catherine Brown's meadow, John Havens, Gidion Freeborn's meadow, Rackoone Island, Judah Allen, Nicholas Brown] ...; [Signed - Francis Burden; witnesses - Peter Tilton, Judah Allen, Rememberance Lippincott.]

[p 191]   **WILLIAM SHATTOCK to GEORGE CURLISS**

6 July 1695 - ...I, William Shattock ... Shrewsbury ... Monmouth ... East New Jersey yeoman ... as well for and in consideration of the naturall affection and fatherly Love which I have and beare unto my Loving Son-in-Law George Curliss & Exercise Curliss his wife my own child and to my grand children on [of] their bodyes ... also for ... [6 pounds, 15 shillings] ... and also ... [17 pounds] ... land ... in ... Shrewsbury ... And it is hereby to be noted that it shall ... be lawfull ... in for ... George

MONMOUTH COUNTY DEEDS - BOOK "C"

Curliss, after my decease to give & bequeath ye said land to either of the said children or amongst all ye said children ... [of George and Exercise] ...; [Signed - William Shattock; witnesses - William West, Francis Jackson, Tho. Webley.]

[12 May 1698 - William Shattock acknowledged the above deed before John Hance and Tho. Webley.]

[p 195]   **JOHN JOHNSTON to THOMAS WINWRIGHT**

9 May 1692 - ...I, John Johnston ... Monmouth ... East New Jersey Esqr ... [for a competent sum of money paid by] ... Thomas Winwright Carpenter & Planter ... sell to him ... All that Tract of Land ... [adjoining land owners or names - Pine Brooke, Tinton Iron Works] ... [300 acres] ... Also about ... [4 acres] ... of boggie meadow at ye head of ye said Pine Brook ... [Johnston claimed right to the land by a Patent dated 24 May 1690] ...; [Signed - John Johnston; witnesses - John West, Geo, Willoks, John West.]

[p 197]   **EDWARD WILLIAMS to THOMAS COOKE**

29 September 1694 - I, Edward Williams ... Shrewsbury ... Monmouth ... East New Jersey yeoman ... [for 24 shillings sold to] ... Thomas Cooke ... [of the same place] ... Coopper ... a certain neck of ground ... callled long neck ... situate in ... Shrewsbury ...; [Signed - Edward Williams made his mark when signing; witnesses - Samuell White, George Curliss, Lewis Morris.]

END OF BOOK "C"

I, Joseph Mc Dermott, Clerk of the County of Monmouth, certify the foregoing copy of "BOOK C" to be a true copy of the original Book in my office ... [Ordered to be done because of the bad condition of the original on 9 February 1900] ...; Signed - Joseph McDermott, 10 August 1903.]

MONMOUTH COUNTY DEEDS - BOOK "D"

[p 1]   ROBERT SKELTON to REBECCA STILLWELL

20 March 1696/7 - Robert Skelton ... Citty of New York ... Taylor ... [sold to] John Stillwell of Staten Island ... Richmond ... New York ... Esqr. High Sheriff of ... County of Richmond and Rebecka his wife, Daughter of John Throckmorton of Garrots hil, Middletown ... Monmouth ... East New Jersey deceased ... Whereas ye said John Throckton ... ye seventh Day of July ... [1690] ... by his last will ... did ... bequeath unto his loving wife Alie ... [Alce written in pencil] ... Throckmorton : All that ... tenement at Garrots Hill ... with ye orchard ... [100 acres & 20 acres of meadow] ... for ... her naturall life ... And whereas ... Robert Skelton is since Jaster ... [inter written in pencil] ... -married unto ye said Alie ... [Alce written in pencil] ... Throckmorton: Now This Indenture, Witnesseth, That ye said Robert Skelton & Alie his wife for ... the naturall Love and affection, That they have and beare unto ye said Rebecca wife of ye said John Stillwell ... also ... [10 pounds, sold] ... the said messuage together with the Dwelling house and orchard ...; [Signed - Robert Skelton, Alce made her mark when signing; witnesses - Daniell Butts, Gustavus Horn, John Stephens.]

[23 April 1697 - New York - Robert Skelton and Alce acknowledged the above deed before Stephanis Vn. Courtland.]

[p 3]   CALEB ALLEN to WILLIAM SCOTT

7 April 1697 - ... I, Caleb Allen ... of Shrewsbury ... Monmouth ... East New Jersey blacksmith for ... a certain tract ... of land and meadow ... in Shrewsbury ... Delivered to me by William Scott ... [of the same place] ... planter ... [adjoining land owners or names - ye Partition line between Caleb Allen's and Scott's land] ... in Shrewsbury ...; [Signed - Caleb Allen; witnesses - Clement Masters, Saml Dennis, Tho. Webley.]

[p 4]   JOHN REID to JOHN WEST

20 June 1697 - ... John Reid of Hortencie ... town of Freehold ... Monmouth ... East New Jersey ... [for 8 pounds sold to] ... John West of Shrewsbury ... All y't Tract of land ... at Shark River ... [adjoiing land owners or names - John West, William West] ... [which Reid claims right to by a grant dated 7 April 1695] ...; [Signed - John reid; witnesses - Sam^{ll} Dennis, Gawin Drummond; the above deed was acknowledged before L. Morris.]

[p 6]   THOMAS POTTER to JOHN STARKEY

9 July 1697 - ... I, Thomas Potter of ... Shrewsbury ... Monmouth ... East New Jersey planter ... Whereas John Starkey of Middletown ... by a certain Deed ... [dated 20 March 1692, sold] ... unto ye said Thomas Potter All that ... land on ye North side of ... sawmill brook now in ye occupation of ye said Starkey ... [2 acres] ... upon ye condition ye said Starkey shall procure ... a

MONMOUTH COUNTY DEEDS - BOOK "D"

Deed or Release of Mary Channelhouse Daughter of ye deceased Adam Channelhouse at her full age one and twenty years ... land at Poplar awamp formerly: To have been conveyed unto ye ... Mary Channelhouse by ye said Thomas Potter ... Now ... for ... [15 pounds and a penall bond of 15 pounds] ... of ye said Starkey ... quitt claimed ... unto ye said John Starkey ...; [Signed - Thomas Potter who made his mark when signing; witnesses - Sam^{ll} Leonard, John Reid.]

[12 July 1697 - Thomas Potter acknowledged the above deed before Lewis Morris.]

[p 7] GEORGE WILLOKS to RICHARD HARTSHORNE

6 October 1696 - To all X'Pian people ... George Willocks of Perth Amboy ... Middlesex ... [for 20 pounds sold to] ... Richard Hartshorne of Middletown ... Monmouth ... All that tract of land ... in Monmouth ... [adjoining land owners or names - Joseph Grover, Benjamin Burden's lott of Plain Dealing] ... [which Willocks claimed by patent dated 1 May 1690] ...; [Signed - George Willocks; witnesses - Rob. Hamilton, John Stout, Samuell Forman.]

[26 March 1697 - Hamilton and Stout acknowledged the above deed before Andrew Bowne and John Hance.]

[p 8] THOMAS WAINWRIGHT to NICHOLAS WAINWRIGHT

10 August 1697 - ... Thomas Wainwright of ... Shrewsbury ... Monmouth ... East New Jersey yeoman & Alce his wife ... [sold to] ... Nicholas Wainwright ... [of the same place] ... yeoman ... [for 14 pounds] ... All y't tract of land in ... Shrewsbury ... [adjoining land owners or names - Iron Works, Prudence Limings corner, Lewis Morris of Tinton, Thomas Wainwright] ... [100 acres] ...; [Signed - Thomas Wainwright, Alce Wainwright made her mark when signing; witnesses - Benjamin Burden, Sarah Kilmaster made her mark when signing.]

[10 August 1697 - Both Thomas and Alce Wainwright acknowledged the above deed before T. Webley.]

[p 10] THOMAS WAINWRIGHT to PRUDENCE LIMMING

14 July 1697 - ... Thomas Wainwright ... Shrewsbury ... Monmouth ... East New Jersey yeoman ... [sold to] ... Prudence Limming of ... Middletown ... widdow ... [for 14 pounds] ... All that Tract of land ... in Shrewsbury ... [adjoining land owners or names - Iron Works, Thomas Wainwright, Pine Brook] ...; [Signed - Thomas Wainwright, Alce A. Wainwright made her mark when signing; witnesses - Catherine Brown made her mark when signing; Andria Webley, Tho. Webley.]

MONMOUTH COUNTY DEEDS - BOOK "D"

[15 July 1697 - Both Thomas Wainwright and wife acknowledged the above deed before Tho. Webley.]

[p 12] THOMAS COOKE to THOMAS WEBLEY

6 June 1696 - Thomas Cooke ... Shrewsbury ... Monmouth ... East New Jersey yeoman & Elizabeth his wife ... [sold to] ... Thomas Webley ... [of the same place] ... yeoman ... land in Shrewsbury ... [for 37 pounds] ... certain tracts ... of land ... commonly cal^d ... Little Silver ... [24 acres] ... [adjoining land owners or names - Samuell Woollcott alias Edward Williams & Joseph Parker] ... which said share of upland doth lye upon a Neck commonly cal^d by ye name of long neck, excepting and it is hereby excepted three rods square of land for a buring place where John John (sic) Havens is intered lying at ye southwest corner of the said of ye said tract of land called little silver, with free egress & regress to and from ye said burying place ...; [Signed - Thomas Cooke, Elizabeth Cooke; witnesses - Francis Jackson, John West, Thomas Hearss made his mark when signing.]

[Excepted out of the present grant a piece of fresh meadow betwixt ... Thomas Cooke's and Edward William meadow ...]

[6 June 1696 - Both Thomas Cooke and wife acknowledged the above deed before John Hance.]

[p 15] JOHN STARKEY to THOMAS BILLS

10 July 1697 - ... I, John Starkey of Middletown ... Monmouth ... East New Jersey planter ... [for 35 pounds, sold to] ... Thomas Bills of Burlington ... West New Jersey weaver ... All that ... land now in the occupation of myself on ye North side of the saw mill brook ... [2 acres] ... [land which Starkey purchased from Thomas Potter on 18 March 1692] ...; [Signed - John Starkey, Mary M. Starkey made her mark when signing; witnesses - Sam^{ll} Leonard, John Reid.]

[12 July 1697 - Both John Starkey and wife acknowledged the above deed before Peter Tilton, Justice.]

[p 16] SAMUELL DENNIS to JOHN WILLIAMS

3 March 1696 - Samuell Dennis of ... Shrewsbury ... Monmouth ... East New Jersey planter ... [sold to] ... John Williams ... of Shrewsbury ... Yeoman ... [for 5 pounds] ... All that ... meadow ... in ... Shrewsbury ... [adjoining land owners or names - Shrewsbury River, Nicholas Brown, Judah Allen alias ye said John Williams] ... [2 acres] ... [which was conveyed to him by Thomas Potter on 5 November 1688] ...; [Signed - Samuell Dennis; witnesses - L. Morris, Tho. Webley.]

MONMOUTH COUNTY DEEDS - BOOK "D"

[p 18] CALEB SHREVE to JOHN LIPPINCOTT, JUNIOR

4 January 1692 - ... Caleb Shreve ... Shrewsbury ... Monmouth ... East New Jersey yeoman & Sarah his wife ... for ... severall tracts ... of land and meadow ... [250 acres] ... in the late purchase called by the Indian name Pessaquenocqua ... [dated 24 December 1692] ... [sold to] ... John Lippincott Junior ... [of the same place] ... land ... [on Rumson's neck] ... [adjoining land owners or names - John Chambers, Neversink River, Shrewsbury River, George Parker, John Clayton] ... Shreve claims by patent granted on 22 January 1687] ...; [Signed - Caleb Shreve, Sarah Shreve made her mark when signing; witnesses - Saml Dennis, Abiah Edwards, John Lippincott Senior.]

[1 October 1697 - The above deed was acknowledged before Andrew Bown and John Hance , Justices.]

[p 20] JOHN WESTGATE'S AFFIDAVIT

12 December 1697 - ... John Westgate late Master of the Sloope Endeavor, burthened Thirty Tuns ... belonging to Rhode Island ..., the owners which is Mr. William Earle of ye said Island and Capt. Timothy Brooks late of Swanzy in New England: That Whereas ... John Westgate some time in November last post did sett saile in ye said Sloope from Rhode Island ... being by his orders and bill of Loadening bound for Salem, or Cohowzy in West New Jersey, but with all to take ye advice of the said Timothy Brooks for ye management of ye said voyage: I ye abovesaid John Westgate do hereby declare that I being intended to saile directly from my Port of Rhode Island to Salem ... and to goe on ye South side of Long Island to one of ye abovesaid Ports; he ye abovesaid Timothy Brooks by his orders and avice caused me to saile on ye inside of Long Island and so by New York to East New Jersey, there to land a company of whalemen in pursuance of ye said Brooks, his orders; that on ... [December 11 last past] ... I landed ye said company of whalemen with their goods on Sandy Hook, after which did arise a storme at most so that all our anchors & cables would not hold us to ride by and being neare the shore, by ye orders & advice of ye said Brooks did lett slipp our cables and run on shore on ye said hook, ... and being so ashore at was pleased God, to send such a time of hard freezing winter so that I could no ways proceed on my voyage as intended, all which hath been to my great Damage: for which I do make this my protest against ye abovesaid Timothy Brooks & the weather, for not proceeding on my voyage as by God's grace was intended to be faithfully P^r formed by me...; [Signed - John Westgate, Master; Richard Cally, Mate; the above was acknowledged before John Hance Esqr, Justice.]

[p 22] WILLIAM SCOTT to CALEB ALLEN

7 April 1697 - ...I, William Scott ... Shrewsbury ... Monmouth ... East New Jersey planter ... [for 12 shillings, sold to] ... Caleb Allen ... [of the same place] ... Blacksmith ... a small peece of meadow in ... Shrewsbury ... [adjoining land owners or names - William Scott, Caleb Allen,

MONMOUTH COUNTY DEEDS - BOOK "D"

Neversink River] ...; [Signed - William Scott made his mark when signing; witnesses - Tho. Webley, Clement Masters, Sam^ll Dennis.]

[p 24] ANNA HAVENS to NICHOLAS HAVENS

26 November 1697 - ...I, Anna Havens alias Stannard of ... Shrewsbury ... Monmouth ... East New Jersey Relict of John Havens of ... Shrewsbury deceased ... Whereas my late husband ... was in actuall possession many years of certain tracts of land and meadow ... by his last Will ... [dated 14 March 1686/7] ... and since patented in my name ... Now Know yea that I ... [sell for a competent sum] ... by ... Nicholas Havens of ... Shrewsbury ... said Third son of ye said John Havens deceased ... [adjoining land owners or names - Edward Laffetra, Judah Allen, George Allen, Nicholas Havens] ... the said Quarter part of land is bounded on ye east by my son in law John Havens alias ye said George Allen ...; [Signed - Anna Havens alias Stannard made her mark when signing; witnesses - William Laing, Sam^ll Dennis, Edmond Laffetra.]

[p 26] NICHOLAS HAVENS to CALEB ALLEN

11 December 1697 - Nicholas Havens late of ... Shrewsbury ... Monmouth ... East New Jersey, planter ... [sold to] Caleb Allen ... Shrewsbury ... blacksmith ... [for 12 pounds] ... land and meadow ... [owned by patent dated 25 March 1688] ... [adjoining land owners or names - Edmond Laffetra, Judah Allen alias George Allen, bequeathed to me by my loving father John Havens late of ... Shrewsbury ...] ...; [Signed - Nicholas Havens made his mark when signing; witnesses - William Woolley, Nicholas Wainwright, Tho. Webley.]

[p 28] THOMAS POTTER to JOHN WOOLLEY

9 February 1697 - Thomas Potter ... Shrewsbury ... Monmouth ... East New Jersey yeoman ... [sold to] ... John Woolley ... [of the same place] ... yeoman ... [Potter owned the land by patent dated 20 January 1688] ... at Poplar swamp ... [for 60 pounds] ... [500 acres] ...; [Signed - Thomas Potter made his mark when signing; witnesses - Abiah Edwards, Tho. Webley.]

10 February 1697 - Thomas Potter acknowledged the above deed before John Hance and Tho. Webley.]

[p 31] RECORD OF DEBT OWED

9 February 1697 - ...I, Thomas [Potter] of ye Town of Shrewsbury ... Monmouth ... East New Jersey Yeoman Do ow and stand Duly indebted unto John Woolley of ... [the same place, for 120 pounds] ... The Condicon of ye above obligation is such that whereas ye above bounden Thomas Potter ... by Deed of Sale ... conveyed unto ... John Woolley ... land at Poplar swamp ... as also a mortgage for ... [500 acres] ... being in the County of Philadelphia ... Pensilvania as also an

MONMOUTH COUNTY DEEDS - BOOK "D"

assignment of a bill ... due from John Starkey to ye abovesaid Thomas Potter ...; [Signed - Thomas Potter made his mark when signing; witnesses - Abiah Edwards, the mark of Thomas Concarskee, Tho. Webley.]

[10 February 1697 - The above deed was acknowledged by Thomas Potter before John Hance and Tho. Webley.]

[p 33] RECORD OF DEBT OWED

9 February 1697 - I, John Woolley ... Town of Shrewsbury ... Monmouth ... East New Jersey yeoman ... indebted unto Thomas Potter ... Three score or sixty pounds ... [referenceing the above deed] ...; [Signed - John Woolley; witnesses - Abiah Edwards, the mark of Thomas Concarskee, Tho. Webley.]

[10 February 1697 - The above deed was acknowledged by Thomas Potter before John Hance and Tho. Webley.]

[p 34] WILLIAM SHATTOCK to RESTORE LIPPINCOTT

20 August 1687 - ...I, William Shattock, of Shrewsbury ... Monmouth ... East New Jersey ... for a valuable sum ... sold ... unto Restore Lippincott ... one half share of upland & meadow ... on Rumsons Neck bounded ... on East by John Clayton, North by Neversinck River, West by his own land bought of Eliakim Wardell, South by his own meadow] ... [claimed his rights to the land by surveyor's certificate dated 6 November 1679]...; [Signed - William Shattock; witnesses - Peter White, George Curlis, Saml Dennis.]

[p 36] THOMAS HIGHAM to JOHN STOUT

6 November 1696 - Whereas Richard Sadler of Middletown ... East New Jersey was seized of an estate of inheritance of lands lying in Middletown as by Pattent ... 10 June 1677 ... And ye said Sadler by his ... Will ... did give ... all his lands ... unto Jane Sadler his wife ... and ye said Jane Sadler being so seized did marry one Thomas Highham now dwelling in Middletown ... Now Know ... that I, Thomas Higham and Jane my wife ... [for 40 pounds] ... paid by John Stout of Middletown ... do ... sell ... All that tract ... belonging ... [to] ... Richard Sadler ...; [Thomas Higham, Jane Higham; witnesses - William Wright, Sarah Wright.]

[10 November 1696 - Both Thomas and Jane Higham acknowledged the above deed before Richard Hartshorne, Justice.]

MONMOUTH COUNTY DEEDS - BOOK "D"

[p 38] RICHARD ASHFIELD to WILLIAM CLARK

3 December 1695 - Richard Ashfield of New York ... merchant and Mary his wife ... [sold to] ... William Clark of Monmouth ... of East New Jersey ... [these same lands were patented to Thomas Hart on 25 June 1687] ... in ye Town of Wickatuck ... Monmouth ... [480 acres] ... also another Tract ... [in the same place consisting of 32 acres] ... and ... Thomas Hart ... [sold the land to Richard Ashfield on 25 April 1692] ... Now This Indenture ... [sells for 70 pounds] ... unto ... William Clark ... [adjoining land owners or names - Peter Sunnans, Walter Beuthall, north by the highway, Elizabeth Gibson] ... 480 acres and also 32 acres ...; [Signed - Richard Ashfield and Mary Ashfield both made their marks when signing; witnesses - Thomas Boell, Jno. Bowne.

[p 41] JOHN WORTHLEY to SAMUELL DENNIS

14 January 1688 - ... I, John Worthley ... Town of Shrewsbury ... Monmouth ... East New Jersey Planter ... in consideration of a certain Tract ... lying upon a branch of ye said Shrewsbury River ... [of 30 acres] ... [adjoining land owners or names - Ephraim Allen, John Worthley, Samuell Dennis] ... [sold to] ... Samuell Dennis ... All that ... house lott lying neare or at Norawaticonck ... [7 acres] ...; [Signed - John Worthley made his mark when signing; witnesses - Peter White, Thomas Vickars.]

[p 43] SAMUEL LEONARD to JONATHAN MARSH

2 January 1696 - ... I, Samuell Leonard ... Town of Shrewsbury ... Monmouth ... East New Jersey Capt ... [for 5 pounds] ... paid by Jonathan Marsh of Newport ... Collony of Rhode Island ... mariner ... All that ... land and meadow ... in ... Monmouth ... purchased of ye Indian owners ... [adjoining land owners or names - Job Throckmorton's land on Manasquan River commonly called Squanacoung] ...; [Signed - Samuell Leonard; witnesses - Mary Chambers made her mark when signing, Sam^{ll} Dennis.]

[p 45] SAMUELL DENNIS to JOHN WORTHLEY

14 January 1688 - ...I, Samuell Dennis ... Town of Shrewsbury ... Monmouth ... East New Jersey ... for ... a certain house lott neare ... Norawaticonck in ... Shrewsbury ... [7 acres] ... [adjoining land owners or names - by a highway, branch of Shrewsbury River, Ephraim Allen] ... [sold to] ... John Worthley Planter ... 30 acres] ... [which he claims from Thomas Potter on 5 November 1688; [Signed - Samuell Dennis; witnesses - Peter White, Thomas Vickars.]

[6 April 1698 - Samuell Dennis acknowledged the above deed before John Hance and Tho. Webley.]

MONMOUTH COUNTY DEEDS - BOOK "D"

[p 47] LETTER OF ATTORNEY

20 August 1696 - ...I, Samuell Webb of ye Island of Barbadoes, Joyner for divers ... considerations ... apointed ... my trusty & well beloved friend John Hance of Shrewsbury ... Yeoman & Mathew Ling Merchant ... City of New York my true & lawfull attoneys ...; [Signed in New York on 1 July 1697 - Sam^{ll} Webb; witnesses - John Vinsentt, Robt Livinstone.]

[1 July 1697 - Acknowledged before And. Hamilton.]

[p 49] WILLIAM BICKLEY to THOMAS POTTER

20 August 1696 - ... William Bickley of New York, shopp-Keeper & Susannah his wife for divers ... consideration ... especially ... [125 pounds] ... paid by Thomas Potter of Shrewsbury ... Monmouth ... East New Jersey husbandman ... [sold to] ... Abraham Bickley of Burlington All that ... upland & meadow ... in Shrewsbury ... [adjoining land owners or names - John Clayton, Newasenck River, Abraham Brown] ... [200 acres] ... [claimed by by patent granted to restore Lippincott and transferred to William Bickley by deed 1 March 1691] ...; [Signed - William Bickley and Susannah Bickley both made their marks when signing; witnesses - S. Van Cortland, Brand Schuyler.]

[p 51] ABRAHAM BICKLEY to THOMAS POTTER

2 December 1696 - Abraham Bickley of Burlington ... West New Jersey and Elizabeth his wife ... [sold to] ... Thomas Potter of Shrewsbury ... East New Jersey husbandman & Sarah his wife ... All that Tract of upland & meadow ... in Shrewsbury ... [this is the same property described in the above deed] ... Now this Indenture ... Abraham Bickley ... [sells for 125 pounds, 200 acres] ... in Shrewsbury ...; [Signed - Abra. Bickley, Elizabeth Bickley; witnesses - Thomas Raper, Samuell Kemble, Tho. Midgley; acknowledged before Peter Freettwell, Justice.]

[p 54] ABRAHAM BROWN SENIOR to NICHOLAS BROWN

2 October 1694 - ...I, Abraham Brown senior of Shrewsbury ... Monmouth ... East New Jersey yeoman ... for consideration of the naturall affection & fatherly Love which I have & Bear unto my Loving son Nicholas Brown if ye Town of Freehold ... and for ... [25 pounds, sell] ... All that tract of land & meadow ... in the Town of Freehold ... [adjoining land owners or names - Elizabeth Hutton's corner, Burlington Path, south side of Manasquan brook] ... [380 acres] ... [which Abraham claimed by deed from James Johnstone on 14 June 1690] ...; [Signed - Abraham Brown Senior; witnesses - Thomas Jacobs, Sam^{ll} Dennis.]

[On the side and under the other signatures is the name "Mary Williams".]

MONMOUTH COUNTY DEEDS - BOOK "D"

[p 56] **BOND**

9 February 1697 - ...I, John Woolley ... Town of Shrewsbury ... Monmouth ... East New Jersey yeoman do ... stand ... indebted unto Thomas Potter ... [this has the same language as the previous Bond between these two subjects except it reads] ... And whereas their is or may be some ambiguity in making good the said ... assignments by reason of a confirmation of ye said Deed to be confirmed by Mary Channelhouse at ye age of her ye said Channelhouse ...[of 21 years] ... then if ... Woolley shall then acept of the aforesaid ... land ... lawfully conveighed unto him by ye said Channelhouse without fraud ... then this obligation to be void & of none effect or else to remain in full force ...; [Signed - John Woolley; witnesses - Abiah Edwards, the mark of Thomas Concarskee, Tho. Webley.]

[10 February 1697 - The above deed was acknowledged by Thomas Potter before John Hance and Tho. Webley.]

[p 57] **REMEMBRANCE LIPPINCOTT to FRANCIS BURDEN**

9th day of the eight month 1697 - ...I, Remembrance Lippincott of ye Town of Shrewsbury ... Monmouth yeoman ... [for 40 pounds] ... by Francis Burden of Shrewsbury yeoman ... Monmouth ... East New Jersey ... [sells] ... All that ... land ... in ye late purchase called by the Indian name Pesaquanockqua and by the English Freehold ... [200 acres] ... [adjoining land owners of names - John Worthley, Pesaquanocaqua brook, Geroge Keith, John Clayton] ... [193 acres plus 7 acres of meadow] ... [bounded on the west with meadow belonging to his mother Abigail Lippincott] ... Together with ye Pattent thereof granted to my brother Jacob Lippincott by ye Propriators ... [dated 25 March 1687] ...; [Signed - Remembrance Lippincott; witnesses - Thomas Bills, A. Pintard.]

[4 May 1698 - the above deed was acknowledged before John Hance and Tho. Webley.]

[p 59] **EDWARD WILLIAMS to FRANCIS BURDEN**

4 May 1696 - Edward Williams ... Town of Shrewsbury ... Monmouth East New Jersey yeoman, ... [sold to] ... Francis Burden ... [of the same place] ... [for 14 pounds] ... All ... land ... in ... Town of Freehold in ye purchase ... Indian name of Pesquanocqua ... [100 acres] ... [adjoining land owners or names - Burlington Path, Francis Burden] ... [the land claimed by Williams by patent dated 25 March 1687 ...; [Signed - Edward Williams made his mark when signing; witnesses - John Hance, Joseph Wardell, Saml Dennis.]

MONMOUTH COUNTY DEEDS - BOOK "D"

[p 62] THOMAS HEARSE to THOMAS VICARS

28 December 1695 - ... I, Thomas Hearse ... Town of Shrewsbury ... East New Jersey Planter ... [for 400 pounds, 10 shillings] ... paid by Thomas Vickars of ... Town of Shrewsbury ... Blacksmith ... All that ... land & meadows ... in Shrewsbury ... [2 acres of meadow] ... in the long neck butt is cald goose neck ... [adjoining land owners and names - Sarah Reape, Mrs. Katherine Brown, John Chambers, Shrewsbury River] ... heretofore purchased by him ye said Thomas Hearnse of Joseph West of ye ... Town of Shrewsbury ... [by deed of 1 March 1692/3] ...; [Signed - Thomas Hearse made his mark when signing; witnesses - John Worthley made his mark when signing, Nicholas Brown made his mark when signing, Sam^{ll} Dennis.]

[4 May 1698 - Thomas Hearse acknowledged the above deed before John Hance, Tho. Webley.]

[p 64] ABRAHAM BROWN to ANTHONY PINTARD

10 February 1695 - Abraham Brown ... Town of Shrewsbury ... East New Jersey yeoman & Mary his wife ... [sold to] ... Anthony Pintard ... Merch^t ... [for 35 pounds] ... All that ... land & meadow ... [200 acres] ... in Shrewsbury ... [adjoining land owners or names - North River, land of Samuell Dennis alias William Auston, Neversincke River, Abraham Brown] ... [Brown claims the land by a patent dated 10 May 1688] ...; [Signed - Abraham Brown ; witnesses - Thomas Cooke, Abraham Brown, Jun'r, Sam^{ll} Dennis.]

[1 June 1698 - The above deed was acknowledged before John Hance and Tho. Webley.]

[p 66] ABRAHAM BROWN to ANTHONY PINTARD

1 June 1698 - Abraham Brown ... Town of Shrewsbury ... Monmouth ... East New Jersey yeoman ... [sold to] ... Anthony Pintard ... [of the same place] ... Merch. ... [for 5 pounds, 10 shillings] ... All that ... land and meadow ... in the Town of Shrewsbury ... at Norawaticonck being a house lott ... of 6 or 7 acres ... [adjoining land owners or names - John Lippincott, land of John Chambers alias Mary Chambers widdow, Shrewsbury River] ...; [Signed - Abraham Brown; witnesses - Thomas Cooke, Sam^{ll} Dennis, Tho. Webley.]

[1 June 1798 - The above deed was acknowledged before John Hance.]

[p 67] RECORD O F THOMAS WEBLEY'S EAR MARK

Which is a slitt on ye off eare, and a half penny on ye fore part of ye same eare, and a cropp & kind of a swallow ford on the neare eare.

MONMOUTH COUNTY DEEDS - BOOK "D"

[p 68] SUSANNAH BARNES ET AL to JOHN STUART

20 October 1697 - ... wee Susannah Barnes & Mary Barnes both of the City of New York, spinsters, heirs by law of ye estate of Thomas Barns our Loving father, late of the Town of Shrewsbury ... Monmouth ... East New Jersey deceased, ... [for 40 pounds] ... to be paid by John Stuart ... cooper ... All that ... land & meadow ... in ... Shrewsbury ... [adjoining land owners or names - land surveyed by Abiah Edwards in right of Mrs. Sarah Reap, John Williams, Lewis Mattock, Remembrance Lippincott alias John Lippincott] ... [excepting a small spote of land three rods square where our loving father and mother Mary Barnes deceased lyes intered throw inadvertance was not excepted in ye body of this present Deed] ...; [Signed - Susannah Barnes and Mary Barnes both made their marks when signing; witnesses - Peter Tilton, Joseph West, Sam^{ll} Dennis; Peter Tilton Esq and Samuell Dennis acknowledged that they signed the above deed.]

[p 70] ISACK ONG, SENIOR to JOHN STUART

23 March 1698/7 - ... Isaac Ong Senior late of Shrewsbury ... [for 37 pounds] ... do ... discharge to ... ye said John Stuart ... a certain Tract of land ... in ye town of Shrewsbury ... [44 acres] ... [adjoining land owners or names - Nathaniell Cammock, highway going to Mrs. Sarah Reape, land of ye orphans of Thomas Barnes deceased, Shrewsbury River] ... also ... meadow ... also ... [140 or 240 acres] ...; [Signed - Isack Ong made his mark when signing; witnesses - James Lawrence, Benjamin Lawrence, Abiah Edwards; acknowledged before Andrew Bowne and Richard Hartshorne in Court.]

[p 72] DANIEL LEEDS to JOHN LIPPINCOTT

29 January 1689 - Daniel Leeds of Springfield ... Burlington ... West Jersey, Cooper, ... [sold to] ... John Lippincott of Shrewsbury ... East New Jersey, Yeoman ... Whereas Thomas Leeds late of Shrewsbury ... by his last will ... [dated 13 September 1686] ... bequeather unto ye said Daniel Leeds from & after ye decease of Margaret Leeds then wife of the said Thomas Leeds: All that his house and homestead wherein ... Thomas Leeds did dwell ... at Shrewsbury ... Now ... [for 7 pounds and 10 shillings] ... and [7 pounds mechantable pay] ... by ... John Lippincott ... All ye aforesaid houses, lands and premises ...; [Signed - Daniel Leeds made his mark when signing; witnesses - Tho. Ollive, Abraham Brown, Symon Charles, Christo Werrill; acknowledged before Daniel Wells, John Hollingshead - Justices.]

[p 74] FRANCIS BURDEN to JOHN LIPPINCOTT

16 February 1688 - ...I, Francis Burden of ye ... Shrewsbury ... East New Jersey, planter, ... [for 5 pounds] ... [sold to] ... John Lippincott of Shrewsbury ... all y^t ... upland or house lott ... at Norawaticonck ... [adjoining land owners or names - John Chambers, John Slocum, Shreswbury

MONMOUTH COUNTY DEEDS - BOOK "D"

River] ...; [Signed - Francis Burden; witnesses - Thomas Potter made his mark when signing, Sam¹¹ Dennis.]

[p 75] JOSEPH WEST to JOHN LIPPINCOTT, SENIOR

10 May 1697 - Joseph West ... Town of Shrewsbury ... Monmouth ... East New Jersey, Yeoman ... [sold to] ... John Lippincott Senior ... Towne of Shrewsbury ... Yeoman ... [for 3 pounds] ... land and meadow ... in town of Shrewsbury ... at Narawaticonck ... [adjoining land owners or names - Shrewsbury River, Hanah Jay alias Cooke, Joseph Parker] ... 6 acres] ... excepted out of ye p^rsent granted ... tract of land four rods lying on the east side of ye said land runing south from ye north end of ye burying place where my Loving Father Robert West lyes intered and some others, and two rods in breadth, And also free liberty of ingress, egress, regress ... to & for Edmond Laffetra of ... Shrewsbury ... his heirs ... friends & Relations at all tymes forever hereafter to come to ye excepted small ... piece of Land & burying place to bury dead corps there no ways to be disturbed nor molested ...; [Signed - Joseph West; witnesses - Sam¹¹ Dennis, Tho. Webley.]

[p 77] REMEMBRANCE LIPPINCOTT to JOHN LIPPINCOTT

15 December 1688 - ... I, Remembrance Lipincott ... of Shrewsbury ... Monmouth ... East New Jersey & Margarett Lippincott wife ... [for 12 pounds] ... [sold to] ... John Lippincott of ye same Town ... one house lott ... at Norawaticonck ... in Town of Shrewsbury ... [13 acres] ... [adjoining land owners or names - John Lippincott, Hanah Jay alias Cooke, Shrewsbury River] ... [which he claimed by his patent of 10 December 1681] ...; [Signed - Remembrance Lippincott, Margaret Lippincott; witnesses - Sam¹¹ Dennis, A. Pintard, Thomas Hearse made his mark when signing; acknowledged before John Hance and Peter Tilton.]

[p 79] RECEIPT AND BOND

25 September 1697 - ... I Samuell Dennis ... Shrewsbury ... Monmouth ... East New Jersey yeoman ... am firmly bound and obligated unto John Lippincott senior ... of Shrewsbury ... [for 16 pounds.]

The Condicon of this obligation is such that ... Samuell Dennis ... [that no suit be between he and] ... John Lippincott concerning a fether bed and bolster, two pillows one coverlid and two blankets, given to ye said Samuell Dennis, his Youngest Daughter Rachell Denniss by Abigail Lippincott late of ye said Shrewsbury ... widdow deceased own mother to ye above named John Lippincott & mother-in-law to the said Samuell Dennis and delivered unto ye possession of him ye said Samuell Dennis for the use of ye said Rachel Dennis ...; [Signed - Sam¹¹ Dennis; witnesses - Peter White, William Scott.]

MONMOUTH COUNTY DEEDS - BOOK "D"

[p 80] ABRAHAM BROWN to WALTER WALL, JUNIOR

29 December 1697 - Abraham Brown ... Shrewsbury ... Monmouth ... East New Jersey, Yeoman ... [sold to] ... Walter Wall, Junior of Middletown ... yeoman ... [for 35 pounds] ... All that ... land ... in ... Freehold ... [adjoining land owners or names - Manillapan brooke, Job Jenkins, Elizabeth Hutton, Burlington Path, Gideon Freeborn] ... [anc conveyed to him by deed dated 17 November 1691] ...; [Signed - Abraham Brown; witnesses - Joseph Parker, William Brinley, Samll Dennis; acknowledged by Brown in Court on 24 March 1697/8.]

[p 82] JOHN CHAMBERS to JOHN LIPPINCOTT, JUNIOR

1 March 1695 - ... I, John Chambers of ... Shrewsbury ... Monmouth ... East New Jersey planter ... for one moiety or half part of a certain Tract of land & meadow ... in ... Shrewsbury upon Rumsonl neck ... [adjoining land owners or names - John Chambers, Shrewsbury River, Caleb Shreeve, George Parker alias Peter White, Neversinck River, Alecwife brook] ... [sold to] ... John Lippincott, Junior of ... Shrewsbury ... [claimed by him as it was given] ... unto me by my loving father John Chambers as doth ... apeare by his last will ... [dated 13 August 1687] ...; [Signed - John Chambers; witnesses - Richard Lippincott, Sam^{ll} Dennis, Joseph Parker; acknowledged before John Hance.]

[p 84] RELEASE OR QUIT CLAIM

20 March 1695 - ... I, John Lippincott ... Shrewsbury ... Monmouth ... East New Jersey, Junior, Tanner ... [quit claimed] ... for one moiety or half part ... [discharge the land in the previously recorded deed to] ... ye sd. John Chambers ...; [Signed - John Lippincott; but note signed by him until 30 March 1698; witnesses - Richard Lippincott, Peter White, Sam^{ll} Dennis, Joseph Parker.]

[p 87] RECORD OF YE COURT'S PUTING OUT OF FRANCIS JACKSON'S CHILDREN

29 September 1698 - Whereas the Court is well informed of ye honesty & integrity of George Allen, they have thought fit to put out one child of Francis Jackson called William Jackson ... and ... put him to ye sd. George Allen and Elizabeth his wife, he being seaven years old last March until he arive to ye age of twenty one years and with him as a servant to live ye full time & term as afforesaid, In consideration whereof ye sd. George Allen & Elizabeth his wife do ... promise to teach and instruct ye said William Jackson in ye art and mystery of a weaver ... and to find him goo suficent meate, drink, washing lodging and apparel dureing ye whole time & at ye end of ye said time to give ye sd. William two good sutes of apparrel & to teach him to Read, write & sifer...; [Signed - George Allen; witnesses - Andrew Bowne, President of the Court and James Bollen, Clerk.]

MONMOUTH COUNTY DEEDS - BOOK "D"

Whereas the Court is well informed of ye honesty & integrity of John Worthley they have thought fitt to putt out one child of Francis Jackson called Mary & do ... put her out to John Worthley & Elizabeth his wife untill she ... [is 18 years old] ... or till she marry, and with him as a servant ... [in return they promised to teach her] to reade, Knit & sew ... [in addition to providing her keep and giving her two good suites of clothes at the end of her time] ...; [Signed - Name was written John "Worley" and he made his mark when signing; witnesses - before Jahn Hance and Jas. Bollen.]

29 September 1698 - Whereas Application has been made by Samuel Leonard, Administrators to ye Estate of Francis Jackson Desceased, Francis Borden & Jane his wife to ye Court concerning Francis Jackson's children Elizabeth Jackson & Francis Jackson ... ye order of ye Court with ye consent of ye aforesd, Leonard, & Francis & Jane Bordin is yt. Elizabeth Jackson aged twelve years is bound to ye said Francis Bordin & Jane his wife, untill ... [18 years of age] ... but in case they dye or shee marry before ye expiration of ye sd. Time then shee is to be free ... [and the Bordins agreed to teach her to read, knit and sew including] ... all other things nesescary to be thought her; and att ye end of her time ... to give her two sutes of aparel. And Francis Jackson ye son of Jackson about ... [13 months old] ... to be, abide & continue with the said Francis Borden & Jane his wife ... untill he be twenty one years of age ... [and they to teach him to Reade, write & sifer, his lodging, and to have two good suits of clothes at the end of his term] ... and to teach him husbandre or other trade to get an honest liven ... And ... Samuel Leonard ... to pay ... Francis Bordin and Jane ... [20 pounds; 5 pounds in money and 8 pounds in apparel, puter & other household goods, and 40 shillings] ... making in all ... [15 pounds] ... which is to be pay'd to ... [the Bordins at or before the next Court at Midletown] ... and ... [5 pounds them from Leonard before 24 September 1700] ... and ... [the Bordins promise to pay to] ... Elizabeth Jackson ... [8 pounds] ... at the end of her time & ... [40 shillings] ... to Samuel Leonard ... at ye said Term ... five pounds of ye abovesaid Twenty pounds ye Leonard paid to ye aforesaid Bordin & his wife in ye presence of ye Court ...; [Signed - Samuel Leonard, Francis Bordin; witnesses in Court - Andrew Bowne-President and Jas. Bellen, Clerk.]

[p 90] OBADIAH BOWNE to GERSHOM MOTT

10 November 1697 - Obadiah Bowne of Middletown ... Monmouth ... East New Jersey yeoman ... [sold to] ... Gershom Mott, yeoman, of ye same place ... [for 80 pounds] ... All that track of land ... at Shepakarneck in Middletown ... [for 250 acres] ... [adjoining land owners or names - James Dorsett, Obidiah Bowne] ...; [Signed - Obadiah Bowne; witnesses - John Bowne, Jon Geysbertson, Alexander Wilson; acknowledged before Andrew Bowne and John Hance.]

[p 92] WALTER WALL to CAPT. JOHN BOWNE

10 November 1698 - Walter Wall of Freehold Junior ... East New Jersey ... yeoman ... [sold to] ... Capt. John Bowne of Middletown marchant ... Monmouth ... [for 52 pounds] ... All that ... land ...

MONMOUTH COUNTY DEEDS - BOOK "D"

in ... Freehold ... [being the same property Wall purchased in previous described deed] ...; [Signed - Walter Wall made his mark when signing; witnesses - Jerat Wall, James Bollen, George Rorie; acknowledged by James Bollen & George Roruy before Richard Hartshorne.]

[93] MARRIAGE

24 February 1698/9 - These may Certifie All persons ... upon ye ... [date] ... James Bollen of Midletowne ... East New Jersey & Elizabeth Godfree of Nasan ... [Nassua?] ... Island ... of New York, came before me John Tredwell one of his Majesties Justices and were lawfully joyned together in Matrimony ...; [Signed - John Tredwell- Justice; witnesses - William Peace, John Okisson.]

[p 93] PETER TILTON, SENIOR to PETER TILTON, JUNIOR

28 March 1699 - Peter Tilton Senior of Midletown ... [sold to] ... Peter Tilton Junior his son ... [for 100 pounds] ... All this Intier tract .. of land ... in Midletowne ... [adjoining land owners or names - Jumping brook, Peter Tilton] ... [100 acres] ...; [Signed - Peter Tilton senior; witnesses - Jno. Bowne, Jas. Bollen, Obadiah Holmes; acknowledged by Peter Tilton Senior before Richard Hartshorne on 14 July 1699.]

[95] JOHN LIPPINCOTT to JEDEDIAH ALLEN ET AL

5 March 1695/6 - John Lippincott ... of Shrewsbury ... Monmouth ... East Jersey ... [sold to] ... Jedediah Allen, Peter Tilton, Remembrance Lippincott ... all yeomen ... for 5 pounds ... land ... [of 1 acre] ... [adjoining land owners or names - John Lippincott, Thomas Vickars] ... [granted for the uses] ... to ye use benifit behoof of ye poor people to ye Religious Society of ye people of God called quakers forever and for a place to erect a Meeting house and make a burying place for ye use ... of ye said ... Quakers ... [who usually met] ... at Francis Borden's house in Shrewsbury ...; [Signed - Jedediah Allen, Peter Tilton, John Lippincott made his mark when signing, Remembrance Lippincott made his mark when signing; witnesses - Peter White, Caleb Allen, George Corleis, Richard Lippincott; acknowledged by John Lippincott Senior before Andrew Bowne, John Hance, Tho. Warne on 28 September 1699.]

[p 97] NICHOLAS BROWNE to STEPHEN COOK

26 December 1696 - Nicholas Browne of ... Shrewsbury ... Monmouth ... East New Jersey yeoman ... [sold to] ... Stephen Cook ... [of the same place] ... [for 6 pounds, 10 shillings] ... All that ... meadow ... [2.5 acres] ... in ... Shrewsbury upon Racone neck alias Racone Island ... [adjoining land owners or names - Francis Borden, Peter Tilton, Racone Island, Shrewsbury River] ... [and he claimed same by patent dated 15 December 1693] ...; [Signed - Nicholas Browne made his mark when signing; witnesses - Joseph Parker, Sam^{ll} Denniss; Brown

MONMOUTH COUNTY DEEDS - BOOK "D"

acknowledged the deed before L. Morris, Tho. Webley on 1 January 1696/7; recorded - 25 September 1700.]

[p 99] POWER OF ATTORNEY

30 October 1700 - ...I, Mary Brown widdow and sole Executrix to the estate of John Brown late of Middletown ... Monmouth ... East New Jersey ... have assigned ... my trusty friend John Stuart my true and lawful Attorney ...; [Signed - Mary Brown made her mark when signing at Shrewsbury; witnesses - Abiah Edwards, Elizabeth Stuart made her mark when signing; Gav^e Drummond; recorded - 8 January 1701.]

[p 101] STATEMENT OF FACT

11 September 1700 - [Appeared before] ... Lewis Morris Esqr ... provincial Judge ... Thomas Potter aged about seaventie years and being engadged according to act of Assembly saies ... That the tract of land called ... Popular swamp in Shrewsbury is bounded by a line of mark't trees ... [adjoining land owners or names - East by Ephraim Potter's cellar, John Woolley's field] ... which said tract of land as is contained in the ... patent I sold all the right I had in it to Adam Channelhouse and ... [100 acres] ... to John Woolley ... and other land ... contained in that tract as is specified by the patent ... I sold not ...; [Signed - Not signed.]

[p 102] JOSEPH WARDELL to ELIAKIM WARDELL

13 November 1691 - ...I, the sd. Joseph Wardell for ... [67 pounds] ... from Eliakim Wardell of Shrosberry aforesd my father whereof I ... Quitt claime and release ... the sd. Eliakim Wardell ... to a certin tract of land ... at port apeck with ... Shrosberry ... [270 acres] ... [adjoining land owners or names - Manahacons creek, toward the sea, John Slocum] ... also a peece of meadow ... [145 acres] ... [adjoining land owners or names - Ananias & Christopher Gifford] ... granted to me by patent ... [10 December 1681] ...; [Signed - Joseph Wardell; witnesses - Ephraim Allen, William Biddle Junior, James Bellover made his mark when signing; 28 September 1699 - Joseph Wardell acknowledged the above deed in Court before Andrew Bowne, Thos. Warne, John Hance.]

[p 104] THOMAS COOKE to NICHOLAS SARRA

2 June 1690 - ... I Thomas Cook of Shrowsbery ... Monmouth Cooper ... [sold to, for 15 pounds] ... Nicholas Sarra of ... Shrowsbery ... planter ... All that tract of upland and meadow ... in the ... Shrowsberry new purchase ... [adjoining land owners or names - Abigail Lippincott, Thomas Cooper, Manasquan brook] ... [100 acres] ...; [Signed - Thomas Cooke; witnesses - Remembrance Lippincott, John West, samll Dennis; 26 August 1702 - Samuel Dennis and John West acknowledged the above deed before Jedediah Allen.]

MONMOUTH COUNTY DEEDS - BOOK "D"

[p 105]   JOHN STEWART to WILLIAM GOODBODY

8 March 1700 - John Steward ... Town of Shrowsbury ... Monmouth ... East New Jersey Chururgerm[?] ... and Elizabeth his wife ... [sold to] ... William Goodbody of ye same towne ... planter ... [for 10 pounds] ... All that tract of land ... [100 acres] ... in ... Shrowsbury ... neare Manasquan ... [adjoining land owners or names - John Hance, William Goodbody, Richard Hartshorne, Thomas Green] ... ye same tract ... was granted to me ... by patten ... [dated 20 December 1700] ...; [Signed - John Stewart, Elizabeth Stewart made her mark when signing; witnesses - Joseph Wing, Samuell Dennis, Thomas Webley; 10 March 1700 - John Stewart acknowledged the above deed before L. Morris.]

[p 108]   JOSEPH LAWRENCE to WILLIAM GOODBODY

2 January 1698 - Joseph Lawrence of ye ... Shrewsbury ... Monmouth ... East New Jersey yeoman and Sarah his wife ... [sold to] ... William Goodbody ... [of the same place] ... [for 17 pounds]... All yt tract of land and meadow ... in ... Shrowsbury ... [adjoining land owners or names - Manasaquan River, Richard Hasrtshorne] ... the same was conveyed to me by ... one deed ... [from] ... my loving father William Lawrence Senior ... [on 26 March 1695] ...; [Signed - Joseph Lawrence, Sarah Lawrence; witnesses - John Williams, Nicholas Browne, Sam^{ll} Dennis, John West, Philip Truax made his mark when signing; 23 August 1704 - Joseph Lawrence acknowledged the above deed in Court.]

[p 110]   JOHN WEST to JOSEPH LAWRENCE

8 January 1701 - John West of Manasquan in ye Town of Shrowsbury ... Monmouth ... East New Jersey, sing man ... [sold to] ... Joseph Lawrence of ye same town ... yeoman ... [for 8 pounds] ... All that ... land ... in ... Shrowsbury ... [adjoining land owners or names - Manasquan river, ye Sea Shore, Remembrance Lippincott, Joseph Lawrence] ... [20 acres] ... Also one halfe of one acre ... by ye said River ... [adjoining land owners or names - Joseph Lawrence, John Hance] ... conveyed to me by ... patten ... [dated 7 October 1695] ...; [Signed - John West; witnesses - John Havens made his mark when signing, John Elis made his mark when signing; 23 August 1704 - John West acknowledged the above deed in Court.]

[p 113]   ROAD COMMISSIONERS

3 December ???? - Wee ... have agreed to ye mending of ye highway by John Throckmorton (to ye Road from Shrewsbury to Burlington) ... between sd. Throckmorton & Thomas Leonard ...; [Signed - Elisah Lawrence, John Woolley, John Hebron - Commissioners.

MONMOUTH COUNTY DEEDS - BOOK "D"

[p 113] ROAD COMMISSIONERS

Laid out a ... Road of two rods wide from ye Road yt goes from Coles bridge by Moses Robens ... opposite to ye house of Miner Reid ... to the corner of Thomas Parker ... land by Richard Borden ... Peleg Smith & over Doctor's brook ... by ye old Path ... wch comes from Pine bridge to Crosswicks creek ... [Laid out 21 April 1713] ...; [Signed - John Reid, Elisha Lawrence - Commissioners.]

[p 114] TO THE OWNERS OF FREEHOLD

Wee do order you to order the continuing and maintaining of Swinging gates in the Road that is laid out by the Commissioners of the County of Monmouth through Benjamin Borden's field of Crosswicks at the going in and out of the sd. Borden's field as ye road is now laid out by the Commissioners. [Signed - John Leonard, John Hebron.]

[p 114] ROAD ALTERING AGREEMENT

Wee ... have agreed to the altering of the highway by Henry Leonard and Thomas Leonard (tis the road from Shrewsbury to Burlington) ...; [Signed - John Reed, John Woolley, Obadiah Bown - Commissioners.]

[p 115] GIDIAN FREEBORNE to JOSEPH ALLEN

17 June 1703 - ... Gidian Freeborne of Portsmouth ... Rhode Island ... [of the] ... plantation in New England ... I ye sd. Gidian Freeborne for ... [for 100 pounds, sell to] ... Joseph Allen of Freehold ... East New Jersey ... Monmouth ... land ... in ye township of Freehold ... which ... formerly belonged unto William Reape deceased ... [being one share of land in ye Township of Shrewsbury] ... ; [Signed - Gidian Freeborne made his mark when signing; witnesses - Thomas Wever made his mark when signing, Thomas Cornell; Freeborne acknowledged the above deed before Walter Clark, dpt. Govr - Newport - 17 June 1703.]

[p 117] NICHOLAS WAINWRIGHT to EPHRAIM POTTER

1 March 1704 - Nicholas Wainwright ... Towne of Shrewsbury ... Monmouth ... New Jersey Planter and Mary his wife ... [sold to] ... Ephraim Potter of ye same ... [place] ... Planter ... [for 60 pounds] ... All that ... Land and meadow ... [104 acres] ... in ye sd Shrewsbury ... being part ... of a sartain tract of Land ... purchased ... [by] ... Nicholas Wain wright of Edward Woolley of ... Shrowsbury ... [by deed dated 1 February 1700] ... [adjoining land owners or names - John James Stell, Jude Allen] ...; [Signed - Both Nicholas and Mary Wainwright made their marks when

MONMOUTH COUNTY DEEDS - BOOK "D"

signing; witnesses - Thomas H. Hearse made his mark when signing, Joseph Clerke, Thomas Woodmansy, Samuell Dennis.]

[p 120]   **WILLIAM CHEASEMAN to THOMAS APLEGATE**

31 October 1696 - ... William Cheaseman of Midletowne ... Monmouth ... East New Jersey ... [for 14 pounds, sold to] ... Thomas Aplegate of ye same place, Juner, ... All that ... upland & meadow ... within the bounds of Middletown, Known ... commonly ... by ye name of Cheasman's fly ... [claimed by Cheaseman by patent dated 15 January 1679] ...; [Signed - Both William and Charity Cheaseman made their marks when signing; witnesses - Ben Lawrence, Thomas Roberts; 15 August 1704 - William Cheaseman Senior acknowledged the above deed before Jeremiah Stillwell - Justice.]

[p 122]   **RICHARD HARTSHORNE to THOMAS BILLS**

19 May 1703 - Richard Hartshorne of ... Towne of Middletown ... Monmouth ... East New Jersey Gent^l and ... Margaret his wife ... [sold to] ... Thomas Bills of ... Shrowsbury ... yeoman ... [for 144 pounds] ... All yt tract of land and meadow ... in ye sd Shrowsbury ... [adjoining land owners or names - Manasquan River, Juda Allen, William Lawrence] ... [144 acres] ... ye same was conveyed to me by Patten ... [dated 18 January 1685 ...; [Signed - Richard Hartshorne, Margret Hartshorne; witnesses - Caleb Allen, Joseph Parker, George Allen Junior, Edward Woolley, James Lawrence, Samuell Dennis; 9 May 1704 - Both Richard and Margret Hartshorne acknowledged the above deed before Jeremiah Stillwell.]

[p 125]   **THOMAS HUETT to STOEFELL LONG STREETT**

17 November 1698 - Thomas Huett ... Towne of Shrewsbury ... Monmouth ... East New Jersey Gent ... [sold to] ... Stofell Longstreet ... [of the same place] ... Planter ... Whereas .... Thomas Huett by a deed ... [dated 1 May 1690 from] ... Samuel Spicer of Burlington ... West New Jersey became seized ... of a tract of land ... at Deale in ye sd. Shrewsbury ... [200 acres] ... [now sold for 50 pounds] ... [adjoining land owners or names - Christopher Gifford, Tobias Hanson] ... Also ... [7 acres] ... of meadow at Patapeck ... [adjoining land owners or names - Hannah Jay alias Cook, Sarah Reape] ... and a small Island of upland ...; [Signed - Thomas Huett; witnesses - Joseph Wardell, William West, Thomas Webley; 23 May 1705 - Huett acknowledged the above deed before Andrew Bowne.]

[p 128]   **TOBIA HANSON to GILBERT LANE**

30 May 1699 - Tobia Hanson ... Towne of Dover ... New Hampshire planter ... [sold to] ... Gilbert Lane of New Utrick on Long Island ... Kings County, yeoman ... [for 50 pounds] ... All that tract of Land and meadow ... [200 acres] ... in ye Towne of Shrewsbury ... Monmouth ...

MONMOUTH COUNTY DEEDS - BOOK "D"

East New Jersey ... [adjoining land owners or names - Edward Wharton] ... Also a piece of meadow ... at Portapeck ... [7 acres] ... [Joseph Wardell, Wharton, Remembrance Lippincott] ... Hanson claims the land per patent to him dated 5 May 1686] ...; [Signed - by John Hance as Attoney for Hanson; witnesses - Joseph Parker, Stoffel Lonngstreet, Sam^{ll} Dennis; 23 May 1705 - Stoffill Longstreet, yeoman acknowledged the above deed before Andrew Bowne.]

[p 131]   **JOHN BRAY to OBADIAH BOWNE ET AL**

17 December 1705 - John Bray ... Township of Middletown ... Monmouth ... New Jersey and Susannah his wife ... [sold to] ... Obadiah Bowne and Jaret Wall ... [of the same place] ... for ... a competant sum ... All yt tract ... of land ... in ye bounds of Midletown ... [adjoining land owners or names - John Braye, Jonathan Holmes] ... [Bray claims the land by a deed from John Reid dated 10 August 1688] ...; [Signed - John Bray, Susannah Bray; witnesses - John Watson, Andrew Bowne Junior; recorded - 29 April 1706.]

[p 134]   **OBADIAH BOWNE ET AL to SOCIETY OF PEOPLE CALLED BAPTISTS**

18 December 1705 - ... Wee, Obadiah Bowne and Jarat Wall ... Township of Midletowne ... Monmouth ... New Jersey, Gentlemen ... Now Know ye that ye before recited Indenture ... [the above deed was for] ... ye only use benefit and behoof of ye Society, community or congregation of people called Baptists forever ...; [Signed - Obadiah Bowne, Jarat Wall; witnesses - John Watson, Andrew Bowne Junior; recorded - 30 April 1706 by James Bollen, County Clerk.]

[p 136]   **SAMUEL CHILD to JOHN BUTLER**

1 February 1695 - Samuel Child of ye Towne of Shrewsbury ... Monmouth ... East New Jersey Cord Warner ... [sold to] ... John Butler of ... Towne of Freehold ... Planter ... [for 20 pounds] ... All yt Tract of land & meadow ... in ye late purchase called by ye Indian name Passequenocqua (alias) in ye sd Towne of Freehold ... [adjoining land owners or names - Burlington path, John Lippincott] ... also ... [3.5 acres] ... of meadow in the great meadow ... at ye head of Manasquan brook ... [adjoining land owners or names - Morris Worth, Henry Chamberline] ... [100 acres with 50 acres being in right of Thomas Huett] ... [land being claimed by Child by a deed from George Corlis on 27 January 1691] ...; [Signed - Samuel Child; witnesses - John Lippincott, John Chambers, Samuell Dennis, Joseph Parker; 3 December 1705 - John Lippincott and Joseph Parker acknowledged the above deed before George Allen, Justice; recorded - 8 May 1706 by Jas. Bollen, Clerk.]

[p 138]   **JOHN BUTLER to JOHN HAMTON**

3 January 1696 - John Butler ... Towne of Freehold ... Monmouth ... East New Jersey, Planter ...

MONMOUTH COUNTY DEEDS - BOOK "D"

[sold to] ... John Hamton ... [of the same place] ... Planter ... [for 44 pounds] ... All that Tract of Land & meadow ... in the Towne of Freehold ... [adjoining land owners or names - Burlington Path, Caleb Sherife] ... Also ,,, [3 acres] of meadow ... [adjoining land owners or names - Manasquan brook, Munrico Worth, Hendry Chamberlaine] ... [being the same land inthe above deed] ...; [Signed - John Butler made his mark when signing; Mary Butler made her mark when signing; witnesses - William Laing, John Astoil made his mark when signing; 24 July 1705 - William Laing of Freehold acknowledged the above deed before John Bowne, Justice.]

[p 140]   **GEORGE CORLIS to SAMUEL CHILD**

27 January 1691 - George Corlis ... Towne of Shrewsbury ... Monmouth ... East New Jersey Cordwainer ... [for 20 pounds sold the land in the above deed to] ... Samuel Child ... Cordwainer ...; [Signed - George Corlis; witnesses - Francis Jackson, Samuell Dennis; 3 December 1705 - Corlis acknowledged the above deed before George Allen.]

[p 142]   **WILLIAM DAVIS to JOHN BOWNE**

18 February 1702 - William Davis ... Citty of New York Marchant & Isabella his wife ye Datter and only child of James Lawry dec'd the sonn of Garvin Lawry dec'd some time Governor of ye ... East New Jersey ... Whereas Miles Foster of Perth Amboy ... of East New Jersey Marchant, intermarried with Rebecca in her life time the Datter of ye said Garvin Lawry, and ye said Rebecca dec'd and Mary haig also dec'd late the widdow of William haig dec'd another of the datters of the said Garvin Lawry by their certain deed ... [sold to] ... John Bowne of Middletown ... All that certain part of the lands of the said Garvin Lawry ... being ... [known as Gov. Lowry's 1,000 acres] ... [adjoining land owners or names - head of Toponemus brook, head of Spotswood brook, Burlington path, Isaac Byran] ... Now Know ye that Wee, the said William Davis and Isabella my wife ... [sold for a competant sum] ... to John Bowne; [Signed - William Davis, Isabella Davis; witnesses - Tho. Cadrington, Wm. Carter, Elihu Antill, Rob. Milwgrd, David Jamison; New York - 19 February 1702 - William and Isabella Davis acknowledged the above deed before John Bridges, Esq; recorded - June 1706.]

[p 145]   **JOHN HAMTON to DAVID HAMTON ET AL**

28 April 1705 - John Hamton of Freehold ... Monmouth ... New Jersey for ... ye last Will ... of his father John Hamton deceased dated ... [23 January 1702] ... and for the natural love which he bares to his brothers (viz, David Hamton, Joseph Hamton, Andrew Hamton, Jonathan Hamton and Noah Hamton ... forever quit claimed ... unto his sd. Brothers ... the lands ... which ware devised in his sd. Father's will to ye sd. Brothers ... all that part of ye Tract wch was granted to his sd. Father deceased by deed of James Miller ...[on 7 October 1696] ... [adjoining land owners or names - head of Spotswood's middle brook on Burlington Path, Rob't Ray, Miller's gulley] ... All that tract ... granted to his said father deceased by deed of John Butler dated ... [3 June 1697] ...

MONMOUTH COUNTY DEEDS - BOOK "D"

And all that tract ... [from Robert Barclay on 10 August 1688 and ½ the land from Thomas Hewit on 29 December 1687, and the land from Abraham Brown on 30 November 1689] ...; [Signed - John Hamton; witnesses - Tho. Bels, Robert Ray, John Reid; 26 March 1705 - John Hamton acknowledged the above deed before Richard Salter; recorded - July 1706.]

[p 147]   **NICHOLAS BROWN to WILLIAM HULET**

8 September 1704 - Nicholas Brown ... Towne of Shrewsbury ... Monmouth ... New Jersey, Gent, ... [sold to] ... William Hulet ... [of the same place] ... yeoman ... [for 80 pounds] ... All that tract of Land and meadow ... in ... Shrewsbury ... [adjoining land owners of names - Long Branch path, Jedediah Allen, widdow Eatton's land] ... [land claimed by patent dated 15 December 1693] ...; [Signed - Nicholas Brown made his mark when signing; Witnesses - Sam^{ll} Dennis, George Allen, Caleb Allen, Tho. Hearse made his mark when signing; recorded - 18 July 1706.]

[p 149]   **EDWARD WOOLLEY to WILLIAM HULLETT**

1 July 1701 - Edward Woolley ... Towne of Shrewsbury ... Monmouth East New Jersey felt marker and Lydia his wife ... [sold to] ... William Hullett of ye same ... [place] ... planter ... [for 14 pounds] ... All that ... Land & meadow ... in ... Shrewsbury ... on Norawataconck point ... [7 acres] ... [adjoining land owners or names - Shrewsbury River, Thomas Leeds alias John Lippincott Senr, Peter Parker alias Caleb Allen] ... Woolley claimed the land by deed of Samuel Webb of ye Island of Barbadoes on 4 May 1699] ...; [Signed - Edward Woollye, Lydia Woollye made her mark when signing; witnesses - George Allen, Edmond Lafetra, Saml Dennis; 30 May 1706 - Edward and Lydia Woolley acknowldged the above deed before George Allen; recorded - 20 July 1706.]

[p 151]   **JOSEPH WEST to WILLIAM HULLETT**

13 January 1702 - Joseph West ... Towne of Shrewsbury ... Monmouth ... East New Jersey Carpenter & Mary his Wife ... [sold to] ... William Hullett ... [of the same place] ... [for 17 pounds] ... All that tract of land and meadow ... in ... Shrewsbury ... [for 6 acres] ... [adjoining land owners or names - John Hance, Edmond Lafetra] ... [land claimed by West by a deed from Edward Williams on 27 September 1698] ...; [Signed - Joseph West, Mary's signature was not present; witnesses - Joseph Parker, Robert Lippincott, Saml Dennis Ser; May 1706 - Joseph West was the only person to acknowledge the above deed before George Allen; recorded - 22 July 1706.]

[p 153]   **RICHARD STOUT SENIOR ET AL to JOSEPH HULETT**

20 December 1705 - Richard Stout Senior ... Towne of Shrewsbury ... Monmouth ... New Jersey

MONMOUTH COUNTY DEEDS - BOOK "D"

yeomⁿ and, Robert Stout ye sd. Richard Stout's own son of ye same ... [place] ... singleman ... [sold to] ... Joseph Hulett of ye said Shrewsbury ... singleman also ... [for 30 pounds] ... [adjoining land owners or names - Hannaniah Gifford, Richard Stout] ... [land conveyed to Richard Stout by Hannahiah Gifford on 10 March 1691 and since was conveyed to Robert Stout by deed dated 7 April 1703] ...; [Signed - Richard Stout Senior made his mark when signing, Robert Stout made his mark when signing; witnesses - Joseph Wardell, Jacob Dennis, Saml Dennis; recorded - 22 July 1706, James Bollen, Clerk.]

[p 155]   **JOSEPH ALLEN to TRUSTROM ALLEN**

24 May 1703 - I Joseph Allin ... Towne of Freehold ... Monmouth ... East New Jersey ... Whereas John Reid of the same Towne ... [sold to Allin] ... all that tract of Land ... at Manalapan ... [adjoining land owners or names - Manalapan Brook, William Davison, Thomas Edwards] ... by a deed ... [dated 2 September 1697] ... Now know yee that I ... Joseph Allen ... for ... ye Love ... I beare to my son Trustrom Allen ...; [Signed - Joseph Allin; witnesses - John Williams, Elizabeth Williams, John Williams Ju^r; 11 December 1704 - Both John and Elizabeth Williams acknowledged the above deed before George Allen; recorded - 27 July 1706 , Ja. Bollen, Clk.

[p 156]   **THOMAS POTTER to WILLIAM REAPE, DECEASED**

2 October 1679 - Thomas Potter of Deale near Shrewsbury ... New East Jersey (sic) ... [for 40 pounds] ... paid before the sealing ... by William Reap deceased the husband of Sarah Reeap of New Port on Rhoad Island late widdow ... [sold] ... one share of land lying & being in ... [the area] ... by the name of Naromsom ... Township of Shrewsbury ... [and Potter claimed it by a deed from Thomas Winterton] ... was lay'd out in five parsels ... which Christopher Allmey sold unto Simon Cooper ... three of them on the mill lott ... wch five lots Thomas Winterton exchange Eliakim Wardell for his great lot ... adjoying to John Clayton & to a hey way by Fransies Borden ...; [Signed - Thomas Potter made his mark when signing; witnesses - Joseph Parker, Remembrance Lippincott; 8 August 1706 - Remembrance Lippincott acknowledged the above deed before George Allen; recorded - 20 August 1706.]

[p 158]   **HENRY LEONARD to CAP'T JOHN BOWNE**

10 June 1704 - Henry Leonard of Shrowsbury ... Monmouth ... New Jersey Esquire ... [sold to] ... Cap't John Bowne of Midletowne ... [for a sum of money] ... All yt tract of Land ... Freehold ... Monmouth ... [adjoining land owners or names - Richard Combes, Daniel Harkers] ... his now dwelling place at Colts Neck ...; [Signed - Henry Leonard; witnesses - Jeremiah Stillwell, Richard Comes, Hugh Hartshorne; 29 May 1706 - Henry Leonard acknowledged the above deed before Richard Salter, Justice; recorded - 24 August 1706.]

MONMOUTH COUNTY DEEDS - BOOK "D"

[p 159]   **JOHN REID to JOHN BOWNE**

12 June 1701 - ... I, John Reid of Hortencie ... Monmouth ... East New Jersey ... [for a sum of money sold to] ... John Bowne ... [200 acres] ... [adjoining land owners or names - Burlington path, land formerely of Sonman, James Reid, R. Barclay] ... conveyed to me ... by deed of Robert Barclay by his Attorneys Thomas Gordon, George Willocks and John Barclay ... [dated 4 November 1699] ...; [Signed - John Reid; witnesses - Richard Clark, Nicholas Brittan; 25 May 1706 - Richard Clark acknowledged the above deed before Andrew Bowne; recorded - 18 September 1706.]

[p 160]   **JACOB COLE to THOMAS COOKE**

20 November 1688 - I Jacob Cole of Shrewsbury ... Monmouth ... Planter ... [for 9 pounds, sold to] ... Thomas Cooke of ye sd Shrewsbury Cooper ... All that tract of upland and meadow ... [100 acres] ... [adjoining land owners or names - George Keith, Morris Worth] ... [claimed by Cole by his patent] ...; [Signed - Jacob Cole made his mark when signing; witnesses - John Laing, Peter Parker made his mark when signing, Sam Dennis; 8 August 1706 - Sam Dennis acknowledged the above deed before George Allen.]

[p 162]   **THOMAS COOK to JOHN BOWNE**

12 December 1698 - Thomas Cooke ... Town of Shrewsbury ... Monmouth ... East New Jersey yeoman and Elizabeth his Wife ... [sold to] ... John Bowne of Middletown ... March't ... [for 4 pounds] ... All that ... land & meadow in ... Town of Freehold ... [adjoining land owners or names - George Keith, Morris Worth alias Caleb Shreeve, John Worthley] also a lott of meadow ... at ye head of Manasquan River ... [adjoining land owners or names - land from Jacob Cole, land late of ye sd. Towne of Shrewsbury deceased dated 24 November 1688]...; [Signed - Thomas Cooke, Elizabeth Cooke; witnesses - Abra. Bickley, Thomas Potter made his mark when signing, Saml Dennis; 21 June 1706 - Samuel Dennis acknowledged the above deed before George Allen; recorded - 23 September 1706.]

[p 164]   **JOHN WORTHLEY to CAPT. JOHN BOWNE**

30 January 1698 - John Worthley ... Towne of Shrewsbury ... Monmouth ... East New Jersey Yeoman & Elizabeth his wife ... [sold to] ... Capt. John Bowne of Middletown ... March't ... [for 25 pounds] ... All that tract of Land & meadow ... in Monmouth ... Freehold ... [100 acres] ... [adjoining land owners or names - George Keith, Jacob Lipppincott] ... [96.5 acres] ... Also ... [3 acres] ... at head of Manasquan River ... [adjoining land owners or names - Edward Williams] ...; [Signed - Both John and Elizabeth Worthley made their marks when signing; witnesses - John Steward, Willm West, Saml Dennis, George Corlis; 21 June 1706 - Both John and Elizabeth Worthley acknowledged the above deed before George Allen.]

MONMOUTH COUNTY DEEDS - BOOK "D"

[p 166]   **THOMAS COOPER to JAMES BOLLEN**

8 December 1705 - Thomas Cooper of London Marchant ... [sold to] ... James Bollen of ye Town of Freehold ... Monmouth ... New Jersey ... [for 84 pounds] ... All that tract of upland and meadow ... [382 acres] ... [adjoining land owners or names - the line between Cooper's and George Keith's land, Clement Plumsted, Manasquan brook, land lately surveyed to Nathaniel Slocum, land formerly of Thomas Cooke]... also ... [17.5 acres] ... of meadow ... [adjoining land owners or names - Manasquan Brook, Clement Plumsted, George Corlis] ... [land claimed by Cooper by his patent of 4 November 1687] ...; [Signed - Richard Salter Attorney for Cooper; witnesses - William Lawrence Junior, Thomas Smith, George Reid; 28 May 1706 - Cap^n Richard Salter acknowledged the above deed before Jo^n Bowne; recorded - 11 October 1706.]

[p 169]   **RELEASE**

5 October 1705 - I, John Stout ... Towne of Middletown ... Monmouth ... New Jersey Yeoman ... Quit claimed unto Benjamin Stout ... [of the same place] yeoman ... all his rights ... to a certain tract of land at Rumanis or Hop River ... in Middletown ... [adjoining land owners or names - Hop River, John Wilson, land formerly David Stouts, land formerly Peter Stout] ... also ... [6 2/3 acres] ... of meadow ... [adjoining land owners or names - land formerly of Peter Stout, Richard Hartshorne] ... Belonging and in the tenure or occupation of Richard Stout my Late father Deceased ...; [Signed - John Stout; witnesses - James Hubbard, Jonathan Stout; 6 October 1705 - John Stout acknowledged the above deed before Obadiah Bowne; recorded - 25 October 1706.]

[p 172]   **MARRIAGE NOTICE**

On the yeare the 5 day of the 5 month in ye yeare 1687 - This is to sarty fie to any persons or person to Know the truth of these folowing lynes we hoes names are under writing being at a meting at bordentowne at the same time When William Worth took Mary Smith to wife before the meeting of friends held at Burlington and ye said Mary Smith came from Burmudos and brought 3 Negroes with her which was children with thar mother, and the siad Mary Smith being willing to make something shorer to herselfe proposed articles for herslefe and hers for the bringing up these children with mine, that is if I should be taken away from them, the which was granted by ye sd. William Worth to give her a deed of gift wherein all his houses and lands whare now he dweleth should be made shur to her during her life ... and also shee requested that the 2 eldest boys might be att William Worth's dispose untill they ware of the age of 30 ty years to the sade William Worth did condesend if the meeting did see it fit ... and that bit of paper was cared in to the meting to have ther sence of that mater and there sence and Judgement was that paper was not to be a Loude of and there senc was that as my estate was left to her by deade of gift so that the Negro should be at his disposing as he saw good to this sined by us, And to this Mary Smith agreed too. We are witnesses - William Shattock, George Corliss, John Lippincott; 24 June 1706 - George Corlis and John Lippincott acknowledged the above notice before George Allen.

MONMOUTH COUNTY DEEDS - BOOK "D"

[p 173]   **JOSEPH WEST to EDMOND LAFETRA**

17 April 1706 - I, Joseph West ... Towne of Shrewsbury ... Monmouth ... New Jersey yeoman am held and firmly bound ... unto Edmond Lafetra of the same towne ... yeom^n in ye som of ... [100 pounds] ...; [Signed - Joseph West; witnesses - George Allen, Saml Dennis, Nathaniel Parker, John West; 3 December 1706 - Joseph West acknowledged the above document before George Allin.]

[p 174]   **JEDIDIAH ALLEN to GEORGE ALLEN**

13 April 1706 - I, Jedidiah Allen of Shrewsbury ... Monmouth ... New Jersey ... [for a sum of money sold to] ... George Allen of the same place All that tract of land in sd Shrewsbury ... [formerly Juda Allen now George Allen, Edmond Lafetra, land formerly John Havens, Exton's land] ... [Allen claimed by patent dated 7 June 1701] ...; [Signed - Jedidiah Allen; witnesses - Thomas Gordon, Joseph West, Nathaniel Parker, John Lippincott Sen., Edmond Lafetra; Allen acknowledged the above deed before Jeremiah Stillwell.]

[p 175]   **JEDIDIAH ALLEN to JAMES WILSON**

10 September 1706 - Jedidiah Allen & Elizabeth his wife of Shrewsbury ... Monmouth ... New Jersey ... [sold to] ... James Wilson of ye towne of Middletown ... yeoman ... [for 250 pounds] ... All them tracts of Land and meadow ... in ye Towne of Freehold ... [adjoining land owners or names - Peter Wilson, Burlington Road, along the Indian line, William Shattock] ... also ... [14 acres] ... of Bogg Meadow ... [claimed by Allen by patent dated 28 October 1687] ... William Shattock his conveyance ... [dated 25 February 1687] ... James Johnston his deed ... [dated 3 June 1690] ... Robert Burnet his conveyance ... [dated 3 May 1706] ...; [Signed - Jedihiah Allen, Elizabeth Allen made her mark when signing; witnesses - Henry Lindly, Thomas Comes, Meribah Allen; 3 December 1706 - Jedidiah Allen acknowledged the above deed before John Bowne.]

[p 177]   **SAMUEL FORMAN to THOMAS FORMAN**

12 March 1699 - Samuel Forman of ye Towne of Freehold ... Monmouth ... East New Jersey yeoman and Mary his Wife ... [sold to] ... Thomas Forman my Loving Brother of ye same ... [place] ... yeoman ... [for [85 pounds] ... and Also for and in consideration of certain tracts purchased ... of James Reid of ye Towne of Freehold and of John Bowne of Middletown ... [dated 3 February 1691 and 1 May 1699] ... except and always reserved four acres of bogg meadow ... All those tracts of Land & Meadow ... in ye. Sd. Freehold ... [adjoining land owners or names - Burlington Path, Robert Barclay, Land called Shrewsburymen's land, Aron Forman, Saml Forman, Garvin Laurie's land, Mine brook] ... [198 acres] ... [Forman claims the land from John Reid and Thomas Warne of 16 November 1688 and 5 March 1696] ...; [Signed - Samuel Forman; witnesses - Nicholas Brown made his mark when signing, Saml Dennis, William Brinley; 10

MONMOUTH COUNTY DEEDS - BOOK "D"

August 1705 - Nicholas Brown acknowledged the above deed before Jnº Bowne; recorded 16 February 1706.]

[p 180]   **JOHN COX to NICHOLAS WAINRIGHT**

15 November 1706 - John Cox of Freehold ... Monmouth ... New Jersey yeoman ... [sold to] ... Nicholas Waineright of Shrewsbury ... yeoman ... [22 pounds] ... All that tract of land & meadow ... in Middletown ... [adjoining land owners or names - John Clayton alias ye sd. Nicholas Wainright, Mordecay Gibbons, Joseph Throckmorton] ... [Cox claimd the above by deed from Nicholas Waineright dated 18 November 1697] ...; [Signed - John Cox; witnesses - Richard Hartshorne, James Bollen; 5 December 1706 - John Cox acknowledged the above deed before George Allin.]

[p 182]   **JAMES BOLLEN to SAMUEL LAYTON**

9 May 1706 - James Bollen of Freehold ... Monmouth ... New Jersey wheelwright ... [sold to] ... Samuel Layton of ye place aforesaid ... [for 14 pounds] ... All yt tract of meadow ... in ye Great meadow, att ye head of Manasquan brook ... [adjoining land owners or names - Clement Plumsted, George Corliss] ... [17.5 acres] ... [Bollen claims the above by deed from Thomas Cooper dated 8 December 1705] ...; [Signed - James Bollen; witnesses - David Stout, Sarah Parent made her mark when signing; 5 December 1706 - James Bollen acknowledged the above deed before George Allin.]

[p 183]   **JOHN REID to JOHN HANCE**

14 December 1706 - John Reid of Hortencie ... Monmouth ... New Jersey ... [sold to] ... John Hance of Shrewsbury ... Whereas ye sd John Reid ... [is seized] ... of an undivided tenth part of an undivided twenty fourth part of All that ... Portion of land formerly called East New Jersey ... excepting ye land of ye first Dividend, ye land of ye second dividend, and ye addition to ye second Dividend land belonging to the sd. Tenth part of ye Propriety. Now this Indenture ... [sells for 5 shillings to John Hance] ... [All that undivided 1/12th of undivided 1/10th of an undivided 1/24th part] ... of All that Eastern Division of ye Provence of New Jersey ... [with the above exception] ... [Reid claims the land by a deed from Marion Cambell and John Cambell dated 1 May last] ...; [Signed - John Reid; witnesses - H. Lindley, George Allin -[Black]Smith, Edmond Lafetra; 14 December 1706 - Reid acknowledged the above deed before George Allin; recorded - 10 June 1707.]

[p 185]   **CAP^T SAMUELL LEONARD to EDWARD TAYLOR JUN^R**

1 May 1701 - Capt Samuell Leonard of Shrewsbury ... Monmouth ... East New Jersey ... [sold to]... Edward Taylor Junr of Middletowne ... planter ... [for a competent sum of money] ...All yt

MONMOUTH COUNTY DEEDS - BOOK "D"

... intire tract of Land ... [200 acres] ... [adjoining land owners or names - Long Brook, John Hankins, Henry Bell, Barclay's Brook, Sarah Reape] ... [Leonard claimed the land by a patent dated 1701] ...; [Signed - Saml Leonard; witnesses - Either Job Throckmorton or David I. Citty made his mark when signing; recorded - 12 June 1707.]

[p 187]   **RICHARD HARTSHORNE to JAMES BOWNE**

10 December 1678 - ... Richard Hartshorne ... [for 20 pounds and other considerations] ... [sold to] ... James Bowne of ye same place ... [Middletown] ... a pece ... of upland and boggy meadow ... at the head of Many Minds spring in Midletowne ... [adjoining land owners or names - Benjamin Devell, John Jobe, James Bowne] ... [Hartshorne claimed the land by patent dated 5 December 1678] ... [80 acres] ...; [Signed - Richard Hartshorne; witnesses - John Throckmorton, Peter Tilton; 22 September 1685 - Richard Hartshorne acknowledged the above deed before John Hance; recorded - 13 June 1707.]

[p 188]   **WILLIAM DOCKWRA to THOMAS RUCKMAN**

15 December 1702 - William Dockwra of London, March't ... [sold to] ... Thomas Ruckman ... Middletowne ... Monmouth ... East New Jersey ... whereas ... Dockwra ... appointed ... Richard Salter ... to be his Attorney to sell ... his land ... with ye consent of Andrew Bowne ... by a certain Instrument ... [dated 25 March 1701] ... Witnesseth that ... Dockwra by his said Attorney ... [sold for 75 pounds to] ... Thomas Ruckman ... All that Tract of Land ... neare Crosswecks ... [adjoining land owners or names - Doctor Johnstone's Great meadow] ... [150 acres] ... also ... [150 acres] ... also a piece of meadow on Rocky Brook ...; [Signed - Andrew Bowne, Richard Salter; witnesses - Richard Hartshorne, Safety Grover, Wm Bowne; 26 February 1705 - Salter acknowledged the above deed before J^{no} Bowne; recorded - 14 June 1707.]

[p 190]   **WILLIAM DOCKWRA to THOMAS COX**

2 April 1701 - William Dockwra, merchant of London ... [sold to] ... Thomas Cox of ye Towne of Freehold ... Monmouth ... East New Jersey yeoman ... [for 25 pounds] ... All that tract of land ... in ... Freehold ... [100 acres] ... [adjoining land owners or names - Chestnut brook, Assunpink brook, land formerly of Richard Davis] ...; [Signed - Andrew Bowne and Richard Salter; witnesses - Thos. Boell, yong eyselertsen; 28 August 1706 - Salter acknowledged the above deed before George Allin; recorded 16 June 1707.]

[p 192]   **GEORGE ALLIN to NICHOLAS WAINWRIGHT**

31 March 1703 - George Allin of Towne of Shrewsbury ... Monmouth ... East New Jersey, Blacksmith, ... [sold to] ... Nicholas Wainwright ... [of the same place] ... [for land & meadow in Shrewsbury] ... heretofore purchased of his Loving Brother Thomas Wainwright ... [on 20 August

MONMOUTH COUNTY DEEDS - BOOK "D"

1697] ... All yt tract of land and meadow ... in Shrewsbury ... being one moiety or half part of that tract of land whereon my loving father Caleb Allin lives ... [adjoining land owners or names - Newasink River, John Slocum] ... ye said tract ... was conveyed to me by my Loving father ye sd. Caleb Allin ... [on 13 November 1700] ...; [Signed - George Allin; witnesses - Caleb Allin, Nicholas Brown made his mark when signing; 30 October 1705 - "George Allin blacksmith" acknowledged the above deed before George Allin, Justice; recorded - 20 June 1707.]

[p 194]   **NICHOLAS WAINWRIGHT to JOHN SCOTT**

7 April 1703 - Nicholas Wainwright ... Shrewsbury ... Monmouth ... East New Jersey, planter ... [sold to] ... John Scott ... [of the same place] ... [for 40 pounds] ... All that Tract of Land & meadow ... in ... Shrewsbury ... [adjoining land owners or names - Newasunk River, John Slocum, Caleb Allin] ... [this is the property in the above deed] ... ye same was conveyed to me by my loving brother-in-law George Allin ... [on 31 March 1703] ...; [Signed - Nicholas Wainwright and Mary Wainwright made their marks when signing; witnesses - Caleb Allin, Saml Dennis, Nicholas Brown made his mark when signing; 30 October 1705 - Both Nicholas and Mary Wainwright acknowledged the above deed before George Allin; recorded - June 1707.]

[p 196]   **JOHN SCOTT to SAMUEL LAYTON**

21 June 1707 - John Scott ... Shrewsbury ... Monmouth ... New Jersey yeoman ... [sold to] ... Samuel Layton ... Freehold ... [for 15 shillings] ... All that tract ... in ye Indian purchase ... [72.5 acres] ... [adjoining land owners or names - Willm Layton's land formerly Willm Scott's, restore Lippincott, Nathaniel Slocum] ... [Scott claims the land which was by patent given to] ... my father William Scott ... [on 22 March 1687] ... as ye same was confirmed to me by virtue of my sd. Father's last Will ...; [Signed - John Scott; witnesses - James Bollen, John West; 21 June 1707 - John Scott acknowledged the above deed before George Allin; recorded - 21 June 1707.]

[p 197]   **JOHN JOHNSTON to THOMAS APPLEGATE**

6 September 1706 - ... John Johnston of Freehold ... Monmouth ... New Jersey Esqr ... [sold for a sum of money to] ... Thomas Applegate of Middletowne ... yeoman ... All that tract of Land in ye sd. Midletowne ... [50 acres] ... [adjoining land owners or names - Applegate's land, William Cheesman, John Johnston] ... [Johnston claimed the land by patent of 7 June 1701] ...; [Signed - John Johnston; witnesses - Richard Stanley, John Reid; 25 September 1706 - Reid acknowledged the above deed before John Bowne.]

[p 198]   **MEMORANDUM CONCERNING A ROAD**

29 November 1714 - Laid out a part of a Drift way from ye way which crosses ye brooke & Dam

MONMOUTH COUNTY DEEDS - BOOK "D"

of Daniel Tilton ... [adjoining land owners or names - Tilton's Mill house] ...; [Signed - John Reid, Obadiah Bowne - Commissioners.]

[p 199]   **A RECORD OF HIGHWAYS**

27 October 1708 - Also a Road laid out in Freehold ... [adjoining land owners or names - Richard James, the Indian Path, David Stout, the Division line of ye province] ... alowing to David Stout one swinging Gate to Marmaduke Horssman, one swinging Gate, to John King, one swinging Gate, and to Anthony Woodward two swinging Gates, laid out by us; [Signed - Obadiah Bowne, Elisha Lawrence - Commissioners.]

22 September 1708 - Laid out a Road of two road wide ... [adjoining land owners or names - David Johnston's house, along the path to ye old skoolhouse, the petition line of Holmes and Cottrill, Cheesman's Brook, as a road now lyes to Middletown ...; [Signed - Obadiah Bowne, John Leonard, Elisah Lawrence - Commissioners.]

22 September 1708 - Also a Road laid out of two road wide ... [adjoining land owners or names - James Grover's in Middletown, the road to Shoale harber, Jonathan Ruckman's field] ...; [Signed - Elisah Lawrence, Obadiah Bowne - Commissioners.]

22 September 1708 - ... Road two roads wide ... [adjoining land owners or names - Swimming River, to the house foremerly where William Hunt dwelt, the road to the bridge over falls River] ...; [Signed - Elisah Lawrence, Obadiah Bowne, John Leonard - Commissioners.]

22 September 1708 - ... Road at Jumping brook ... to ye road by Skunkes hill ...; [Signed - Elisah Lawrence, Obadiah Bowne, John Leonard - Commissioners.]

7 May 1709 - Laid out a By Way for Cap't Anderson, Thomas Mattage, and Arra Matison ... [adjoining land owners or names - the road that crosses Manalapan River at Joseph allen's old bridge, below the mouth of Cleare brook the casway, to where Ben Allin built a bridge, to the landing road before William Davison's Bridge ...; [Signed - John Reid, John Hebron - Commissioners.]

The highway ... [adjoining land owners or names - from Richard Hartshorne, John Havens, to Rack Pound] ... Also a Drift was to ye sea ... [adjoining land owners or names - Robert Stout, John Lawrence] ... also a highway ... [adjoining land owners or names - Joseph Lawrence, hockocson swamp, the line between Morris and Thomas Leonard, the bridge below the saw mill of William Lawrence] ... also a highway ... [to ye falls from the rear of Joseph Lawrence's] ... also a highway ...; [Signed - John Leonard, Obadiah Bowne, Elisah Lawrence and John Woolley - Commissioners; James Bollen, Clerk.]

MONMOUTH COUNTY DEEDS - BOOK "D"

1 March 1709/10 - Also another highway ... [adjoining land owners or names - the meeting house in Shrewsbury between Judah Allen's & Reserve Lippincott's lines as it was ... layd out to ye North River ...; [Signed - John Leonard, Obadiah Bowne, Elisah Lawrence and John Woolley - Commissioners.]

[p 201]   **RICHARD HARTSHORNE re: WHAN DEARA'S FREEDOM**

6 March 1702/3 - I, Richard Hartshorne Yeoman some tim in ye year ... [1699] ... did sell unto Capt Jno Bowne Marchant in Middletowne in East Jersey a sertaine man servant called Whan Deara, now by occupation a Cooper, for ye space ... of which sd. Whan was to serve sd. Bowne or assignees Dewly & Truly, now I, Richard Hartshorne do declare that at ... [the end of the term] ... Whan is to be free and his own man ...; [Signed - Richard Hartshorne; witnesses - John Stout, Moses Lip'ct, Peter Vanderventer.]

[p 201]   **JOHN BOWNE re: WHAN DEARA'S FREEDOM**

1 March 1702/3 - Whereas I, John Bowne of Middletwon did som time in .. [1699] ... buy or purchase a sertaine man servant called Whan Deara by occupation now a Cooper of Mr Richard Hartshorne of Middletown Yeoman ... Now ... Whan Deara has followed duly & truly until this ... 1 March 1702/3] ... I do promise ye sd. Whan if he does serve me ... the full terme ... of one year and eleven months ... [from now to 1 February 1704/5] ... that ... I do promise he shall be free ...; [Signed - Jno Bowne; witnesses - Johannes Rees, Francis Harbert, John Liming, Leser Cottrell made his mark when signing.]

[p 202]   **RECORD OF A HIGHWAY**

10 June 1710 - Also another Drift way or Road ... [adjoining land owners or names - Swimming River, Henry Leonard's sawmill, the road from William Lawrence's to Shrewsbury, Johanes Pollhemus and Ouka Leffers] ...; [Obadiah Bowne, Elisha Lawrence - Commissioners.]

Wee do order you to order swinging gatyes in the road that is laid out ... through Benjamin Borden Junior's field at Crosswicks ...; [Signed - Benjamin Borden, Obadiah Bowne - Commissioners.]

Laid out in Shrewsbury a highway ... [adjoining land owners or names - John Eaton, William Hulet, by the road between ye meeting house & Long Branch, Henry Alen's corner, the road from Manasquan to ye falls, John Lawrence's house] ...; [Signed - John Reid, John Leonard - Commissioners.]

MONMOUTH COUNTY DEEDS - BOOK "D"

[p 203] **ORDER FOR BUILDING A GOAL AND COURT HOUSE**

[This is a great example of the construction techniques used during this period of time. Although not recorded here, this Order also mentioned the type of iron fasteners for the doors, the types of nails to be used, etc in the construction.]

8 June 1710 - Order for building the County Gaol at Middletown and for raising money for the same ... John Williams and Thomas White of Shrewsbury, William Lawrence and William Hartshorne of Middletown, John Okison and Zebulon Claton of Freehold being chosen by the respective Towns, Together with Obabiah Bowne, Anthony Woodward and George Allin Esquire, Justices ... for the County of Monmouth ... Do appoint the Common Gaol for this County to be built in the former place of Middletown, where the ancient Prison formerly stood, which ... is to be built ... [22 feet square, 2 stories high, each story 7' high, the lower story to be built] ... with lime and stone underground, the upper story above ground to be built with Timber, the posts to be six inches square and to stand within four inches one of the other, to be covered on the outside with inch boards, the under floor to be laid with plank two inches thick upon good sleepers within eighteen inches each of the other ... [the lower story to have one window in each room] ... with substantial Doors, locks and Bars fit for the securing of malefactors.

The second floor to be laid with Beams of ... [six and eight inch square] ... within six inches one of the other and the third floor in like manner ... the said house to be covered with cedar or chestnut shingles, square edged, and that there be a good brick chimney built at one end with a fireplace in each Room ... and do nominate James Bollen, William Lawrence Junior and Amos White to be Assessors and Joseph Cox of Middletown Collector ... And do also appoint Richard Stout, Moses Lip'ct, Hugh Hartshorne, all of Middletown to be ye Managers to build the said prison-house ...; [Signed - John Williams, Thomas White, William Lawrence, William Hartshorne, John Okison, Zebulon Clayton, Obadiah Bowne, Anthony Woodward, Geroge Allin.]

[p 204] **ELISHA LAWRENCE to EDWARD TAYLOR**

24 December 1708 - Elisha Lawrence ... of Middletwon ... Monmouth ... New Jersey yeoman and Lucy his wife ... [sold to] ... Edward Taylor ... [of the same place] ... [35 pounds] ... All those two hammoucks of Land at Shoal harbour ... [20 acres] ... [adjoining land owners or names - Thomas Morford] ... [Lawrence claimed the land stating that it was sold by him to John Throckmorton late of Middletown deceased, and he then sold it on 27 May 1690 to Capt. Safety Grover] ... [3 acres] ... the same was conveyed to me by patent ... [on 12 May 1688] ... and my loving Brother Mr William Lawrence, his conveyance on 2 March 1690] ...; [Signed - Elisha Lawrence, Lucy Lawrence made her mark when signing; witnesses - Thomas Stillwell, Joseph Ashton, Jonathan Hildreth made his mark when signing; 7 December 1709 - Joseph Ashton and Thomas Stillwell acknowledged the above deed before Richard Salter and Anthony Woodward.]

MONMOUTH COUNTY DEEDS - BOOK "D"

[p 205]   **MEMORANDUM re: THE GOAL AND COURT HOUSE**

12 March 1710/11 - ... John Reid, John Anderson & Samuel Dennis, Justices; Also David Johnston & Peter Wilson, shosen for Freehold, William Lawrence & William Hartshorne for Middletown, John West & Joseph Wardell for Shrewsbury did meet at ye house of Thomas Forman & discoursed concerning a Goal & Court House ... Twis agreed yt. Middletown ... for building a Goal is a place very in convenient ... Some would have it in Shrewsbury ... others to have it in Freehold some where near John Lockison's, ... Lawrence & Hartshorne sd they would not consent to another place for twas begun & part of ye money levied ... Twas alleged by ye rest that twas better ... loose it all than always ... to suffer so much by yt inconvenient scituation ... for ye mean time twas concluded ... that a stop be put to ye building of ye Goal at Middletown until the next sitting of ye Assembly ... [they then ordered all work to stop.]

[p 206]   **MEMORANDUM OF A HIGHWAY**

3 December 1712 - Laid out a highway from Henry Leonard's Saw mill to Barnegate ... [adjoining land owners or names - John Hankins' path, road to Hay Path, Sarah Reape's meadow, road to Manasquan, Path to Cedar Path, to Metutukonk, road to Goose Creek call's Tom's River, land late of Thomas Hart] ...; [Signed - Jon^h Reid, Elisha Lawrence, Obadiah Bowne - Commissioners.]

[p 206]   **MEMORANDUM OF DRIFT WAYS**

13 October 1713 - Then laid out several drift ways in Middletown ... from Middletown to Chinqnorers ... [adjoining land owners or names - fences of James Hubards & Cornelius Covenhoven, Hop Brook, the line between Benjamin Stout & Hendrick Henderson, Joseph Golder, Obidiah Bown, Mohoras Run, from Daniel to Hendrick Hendrickson, John Wall, Tho. Smith, Cornelius Dorn, Tilton, Wakeck Landing, line between Hendrickson and Peter Wikoff, Andrew Wilson, Sam^{ll} Ruckman, John Ruckman]...; [Signed - John Reid, Obadiah Bowne, John Hebron - Commissioners.]

3 April 1714 - Laid out a drift way from Burlington Road to Thomas Melog's Mill ... [adjoining land owners or names - [Cornelius Thomson's house] ... Tis two Rods wide ...; [Signed - John Reid, John Hepburn - Commissioners.]

[p 206]   **JOSEPH WING to JOHN STEWART**

10 March 1713 - Joseph Wing ... Towne of Shrewsbury ... Monmouth ... East New Jersey, Yeoman ... [sold to] ... John Stewart ... [of the same place] ... Churgion [Surgeon] ... Whereas Thomas Eaton late of Shrewsbury deceased by a atten ... [dated 25 March 1687] ... became seized of ... land at a place called by ye Indians Pesaquanog and by the English, Shrewsbury New

MONMOUTH COUNTY DEEDS - BOOK "D"

Purchase, containing ... [100 acres] ... [adjoining land owners or names - Burlington Path, Manasquan Brook, Jedediah Allen, Francis Burden] ... land Thomas Eaton gave to Joseph Wing his son in Law, as by the will ... of ye said Thomas Eaton ... [dated 11 November 1688] ... Now Know yee ... [sold to John Stewart for 48 pounds] ... ye said tract of land, meadow & premises ...; [Signed - Joseph Wing; witnesses - Saml Dennis, Thomas Green, Joseph Wardell, Tho. Webley; acknowledged before L. Morris, Justice.]

[p 208]   **SAMUEL STEWART to JOHN PEARCE**

29 May 1711 - Samuel Stewart of Lewiston ... County of Susses ... Pensilvania son & heir of John Stewart Late of Shrewsbury ... Monmouth ... New Jersey ... deceased ... [sold to] ... John Pearce of the Township of Freehold ... Monmouth ... yeoman ... [for 70 pounds] ... All that land & meadow ... within ye New Purchase ... [adjoining land owners or names - Burlington Path, Manasaquan Brook, Jedediah Allen, Francis Borden] ... sames was conveyed ... to .... John Stewart by deed ... from Joseph Wing ... [10 March 1700] ...; [Signed - Samuel Stewart made his mark when signing; witnesses - Elisha Lawrence, John Lawrence, Wm Lawrence Junior; 3 September 1711 - Elisah Lawrence acknowledged the above before Thomas Gordon.]

[p 210]   **JEDEDIAH ALLEN to JOHN PEARCE**

7 April 1708 - Jedediah Allen ... Township of Shrewsbury ... Monmouth ... New Jersey, Gent. And Elizabeth his wife ... [sold to] ... John Pearce of ye Town of Freehold ... Cordwainer ... [for 60 pounds] ... land within ye New purchase ... [100 acres] ... [adjoining land owners or names - Burlington Path, George Keith, Manasquan Brook, Thomas Boell, Thomas Eaton's land] ...; [Signed - Jedediah Allen, Elizabeth Allen amde her mark when signing; witnesses - Ralph Allen, Samuel O'Keson, Saml Dennis; 25 June 1708 - Jedediah Allen acknowledged the above deed before William Pinhorn, Justice.]

[p 211]   **MEMORANDUM**

8 March 1714 - Sessions met and appointed Wm Leeds Junior, Gabrial Stelle and John Campell Assesors & John Wall, Collector.

The Appointment for Managers ... John Eaton, Edmond Lafetra, Henry Allen, seven viz: Anthony Pintard, Joseph Wardel, Richard Chambers, Joseph Parker, Henry Allen, James Grover, Safety Grover.

For Henry Leonard, James Wilson, Peter Wilson, nine, viz: John Reid, Jeremiah Stillwell, David Johnston, Lawrence Van-hook, James Wilson, Henry Leonard, John Wilson, John Anderson, Peter Wilson.

MONMOUTH COUNTY DEEDS - BOOK "D"

****

Therefore, John Eaton, Edmund Lafetra, Henry Allen are Managers for the ensuing year to agree with workmen & see the work done that is the Court house & Goal built as twas agreed ... [on 26th of August last] ...; [Signed - Safety Grover, Joseph Parker, James Grover Junior, Henry Alt - Freeholders; Pintard, Joseph Wardell, Richard Chambers - Justices.

7 March 1714 - We the under subscribing surviving Commissioners ... for laying out of highways ... do appoint Capt. Richard Stout & Stophel Longstreet in place of Benjamin Borden who is removed out of the sd. County above a year & Capt. John Leonard deceased above a year ...; [Signed - John Reid, Obadiah Bowne, Elisha Lawrence, John Hepburn, John Wooley - Commissioners.]

[p 212]   **MEMORANDUM**

16 May 1715 - Laid out a drift way from Burlington Road to Thomas Boells on Manalapan ... [adjoining land owners or names - James Borden, Petrer Wilson, Benjamin Johnstone] ...; [Signed - John Reid, John Hepburn - Commissioners.]

7 April 1714 - At a private Sessions held at Shrewsbury - The Justices present - John Reid, Anthony Pintard, James Ashton, Lawrence Van hook, John Anderson, Henry Leonard, John Willson.

Ordered that Simon Van Norwick, William Preston, James Laurie be Constables for Freehold. For Middletown - William Cheaseman.

Ordered that as soon as the Constables bring in ye rates that Mr. Reid sware the new Constables for Freehold - Mr. Leonard sware ye Constable of Shrewsbury and Mr. Wilson sweare the Constable of Middleton.

END OF BOOK "D"

****

I, Joseph Mc Dermott, Clerk of the County of Monmouth, certify the foregoing copy of "BOOK D" to be a true copy of the original Book in my office ... [Ordered to be done because of the bad condition of the original on 9 February 1900] ...; [Signed - Joseph McDermott, 10 August 1903.]

INDEX

A

ALEN: Henry, 133
ALFREE: Elizabeth, 72; Thomas, 72
ALLEN: Caleb, 92, 93, 103, 106, 107, 117, 121, 124; Calieb, 91, 92; Daniell, 78, 79, 80; Elisha, 90; Elizabeth, 92, 96, 115, 128, 136; Epheraham, 43; Ephraim, 34, 35, 45, 58, 59, 61, 63, 64, 71, 78, 79, 91, 109, 118; George, 4, 9, 72, 77, 78, 79, 80, 88, 92, 107, 115, 122, 123, 124, 125, 126, 127, 128; Henry, 136, 137; Jedediah, 41, 64, 78, 79, 81, 88, 96, 99, 117, 118, 124, 128, 136; Jedeiah, 60, 78; Jedidiah, 128; Jedihiah, 128; Jno., 6; John, 6; Joseph, 120, 125, 132; Juda, 41, 42, 121, 128; Judadiah, 41; Judah, 29, 30, 32, 34, 35, 36, 37, 38, 40, 41, 48, 61, 66, 71, 77, 78, 79, 80, 84, 92, 97, 101, 105, 107, 133; Jude, 120; Mary, 78, 90; Meribah, 128; Ralph, 136; Trustrom, 125
ALLEN, JUNIOR: George, 121
ALLENY: Christopher, 5
ALLIN: Ben, 132; Caleb, 131; George, 128, 129, 130, 131; Joseph, 125
ALLIN, ESQUIRE: George, 134
ALLING: Christopher, 1
ALLMEY: X'pher, Mr., 11; Christopher, 5, 6, 13, 15, 16, 17, 18, 19, 21, 23, 48, 125; Christopr., 16, 23; Job, 6; Job., 6; X'pher, 18, 20
ALLMY: C'pher, 9; Christopher, 6, 9, 11
ALMEY: Charistopher, 30; Christopher, 29, 30, 31, 32; Christopr., 34
ALMY: Christopher, 31, 74; Christopr., 32
ANDERSON: Capt., 132; John, 63, 135, 136, 137
ANDREWS: Mary, 35; Mordecay, 35
ANDROS: Edmund, Governor, 25
ANDROSS: E., 25

ANTILL: Elihu, 123
APELGATE: Bartholomew, 24; Thomas, 24
APLEGAT: Tho., 100
APLEGATE: Daniell, 64
APLEGATE, JUNER: Thomas, 121
APLGATE, SENR.: Thomas, 15; Thos., 14
APPLEGATE: Daniel, 49, 60; Samuell, 63; Tho., 45; Thomas, 131
APPLEGATE'S MILL: Thomas, 49
APPLGATE: Bartholomew, 16; Daniell, 21; Tho., 21, 23; Thomas, 16, 20, 23; Thos., 16
APPLGATE, SENIOR: Thomas, 15, 17, 22
APPLGATE, YE ELDER: Thomas, 17
ARNOLD: Stephen, 47, 50, 53, 57, 69, 73; Steven, 1, 6
ARRAMASOAK: Indian Sachem, 64
ASHFIELD: Mary, 109; Richard, 109
ASHLEY: Robert, 38; Robt., 45
ASHTON: Ja., 2; James, 1, 2, 3, 7, 14, 17, 21, 22, 32, 35, 37, 69, 137; Joseph, 134; William, 24, 32, 41, 64
ASTOIL: John, 123
ASTON: William, 35, 36; Willm., 34
ATTWATER: John, 51
AUSTIN: William, 95
AUSTON: William, 112
AWAYEIS: Indian Sachem, 47
AWRNE: Thomas, 90
AXTON: Georg., 23; George, 35, 38, 50, 66

B

BAILEY: Richard, 13
BAKER, 69: John, 60, 64
BARCHLEY: John, 61
BARCKLAY: John, 95
BARCKLEY: John, 64
BARCLAY: John, 59, 62, 86, 126; R., 86,

INDEX

126; Robert, 83, 85, 86, 90, 93, 99, 124, 126, 128
BARNES: Mary, 20, 113; Susannah, 113; Thomas, 14, 15, 113; William, 65
BARNS: Thomas, 113
BARTON: Roger, 66
BASHAN, 7
BASSITT: William, 79
BAYARD: Nicho., 39
BEAST: Richard, 43; Richd., 44
BEEDELL, JUNIOR: William, 58
BEERE: Patience, 56
BEERES: Judah, 3; Richard, 3
BELL: Henerey, 100; Henery, 90; Henry, 130
BELLEN: Jas., 116
BELLOVER: James, 118
BELS: Tho., 124
BENNET: Isack, 20
BENNETT: Isack, 23, 25; Jeremiah, 39, 48, 49, 61; Jeremy, 65
BENNIT: Isack, 25
BERGEN: Morgan, 60
BEUTHALL: Walter, 109
BEYER: Joseph, 6
BICKLEY: Abra., 110, 126; Abraham, 90, 110; Elizabeth, 110; Susanah, 90; Susannah, 110; William, 66, 81, 110; Wm., 50, 51
BIDDLE, JUNIOR: William, 118
BILLS: Thomas, 92, 101, 105, 111, 121
BIRD: John, 7
BODIN: Francis, 21
BOELL: Thomas, 109, 136; Thos., 130
BOELLS: Thomas, 137
BOLLEN: Ja., 125; James, 115, 117, 122, 127, 129, 131, 132, 134; Jas., 116, 117, 122
BOMAN: Henery, 93
BONNE: John, 53, 56
BORDEN: Benja., 35, 36; Benjamin, 30, 32, 39, 49, 137; Francis, 59, 60, 116, 117, 136; Fransies, 125; James, 137; Jane, 116; Richard, 6, 120

BORDEN, JUNIOR: Benjamin, 133
BORDIN: Ben, 6; Benjamin, 6; Fra., 14, 23; Jane, 116; Richard, 5, 6; Sam., 12; Samuel, 11; Samuell, 12
BORR: Henry, 91
BOURNE: Gerard, 7; Jarrad, 13; Jurratt, 13
BOWLES: Thomas, 41
BOWMAN: Henry, 27
BOWN, 72, 73: Andrew, 74, 75, 85, 90, 93, 96, 97, 98, 99, 101; Andrew, Capt., 59; Gershom, 97; John, 72, 73, 75, 76, 97; John, Capt., 97; Lydia, 97; Obadiah, 120; Obidiah, 75, 135
BOWN, JUNIOR: Andrew, 122
BOWNE: Andrew, 74, 75, 76, 84, 86, 87, 90, 94, 98, 104, 113, 115, 116, 117, 121, 122, 126, 130; Gerard, 6; James, 1, 2, 3, 5, 6, 7, 8, 11, 14, 23, 25, 28, 46, 48, 51, 52, 75, 130; Jno., 5, 94, 109, 117, 129, 130, 133; Jno., Capt., 133; Jo., 2; John, 2, 4, 5, 6, 7, 8, 14, 16, 17, 19, 25, 27, 42, 43, 46, 51, 52, 53, 55, 62, 75, 93, 116, 123, 126, 128, 131; John, Capt., 15, 17, 21, 22, 28, 94, 116, 125, 126; Lidia, 35; Nicholas, 6; Obadiah, 51, 122, 127, 132, 133, 134, 135, 137; Obidiah, 88, 116; Thomas, 118; Widow, 69; William, 51; Wm., 3, 6, 7, 130
BOWNE, JR.: James, 88
BOWNE, JUNIOR: Andrew, 122
BRADFORD: William, 92
BRAY: John, 69; Susannah, 122
BRAYE: John, 122
BRENEWAX: Jacob, 20
BRIDGES, ESQ.: John, 123
BRINDLEY: Francis, 6
BRINLEY: William, 115, 128
BRITTAN: Nicholas, 126

(140)

INDEX

BRNES: Richard, 60
BROCKHOLLS: Antho., 46
BRODEN: Francis, 117
BROOKS: Timothy, Capt., 106
BROWN: Abraham, 43, 56, 59, 63, 64, 72, 81, 94, 95, 110, 112, 113, 115, 124; Andrew, 73, 76; Catherine, 78, 79, 101, 104; Catherine, Mrs., 81; David, 59; Elizabeth, 72; John, 6, 47, 94, 118; Katherine, 89, 112; Katherine, Mistress, 70, 87; Katherine, Mrs., 70, 87; Kathrine, Mrs., 81; Lidia, 35; Mary, 72, 112, 118; Niccollis, 43; Niccollos, 45; Nicho., 5, 20, 21, 29, 31, 33, 34, 35, 37, 38, 39; Nicholas, 6, 8, 22, 23, 30, 31, 32, 37, 41, 60, 61, 66, 70, 71, 76, 77, 79, 80, 81, 87, 89, 93, 101, 105, 110, 112, 124, 128, 129, 131
BROWN, JUNR.: Abraham, 112
BROWN, SENIOR: Abraham, 110
BROWN, SENIR: Abraham, 100
BROWN, SENR.: Abraham, 91, 94
BROWNE: Abrah., 34; Abraham, 13, 14, 22, 25, 31, 32; John, 25, 39; Kathrine, 32, 48; Nicho., 38, 39, 40; Nicholas, 17, 23, 32, 39, 58, 59, 117, 119
BRUISS: George, 17
BRYA: John, 122
BRYAN: Isaac, 31, 123; Morgan, 46, 63
BRYON: Isaac, 30; Morgan, 39
BUCK: John, 41
BULL: Henerey, 6; Henery, 4, 6
BURDEN: Ben., 100; Benjamin, 7, 62, 98, 99, 104; Francis, 88, 101, 111, 113, 114, 136; John, 96
BURDIN: Benjamin, 99
BURDING: Benjamin, 42; Francis, 43
BURDON: Francis, 95; John, 72
BURKMAN: John, 6
BURNET: Robert, 128
BURNYEATT: John, 8

BURYEAT: John, 8
BUTLER: John, 122, 123; Mary, 123
BUTTS: Daniell, 103

C

C/SHIELD: Samuell, 95
CADRINGTON: Tho., 123
CAHECK: Indian Sachem, 55
CALLY: Richard, 106
CAMBELL: John, 129; Marion, 129
CAMMOCK: Nathaniel, 94; Nathaniell, 60, 61, 113
CAMPBLE: John, 42, 43, 44
CAMPELL: John, 136
CARFFORD: John, 54
CARR: Robart, 10; Robartt, 10; Robert, 6
CARRERITT: Phillip, 62
CARTER: Wm., 123
CARTERET: Phillip, 90
CARTERET, ESQR.: Phillip, Governor, 15
CARTERETT: George, 19; Governor, 55; Phillip, Governor, 98
CARTERETT, ESQR.: Phillip, Governor, 14; Phillip, Governr., 47
CARTON: Jessie, 73
CARTRET: Phillip, 55
CARTRETT: Phillip, Governor, 54
CARTRIGHT: Phillip, Governor, 56
CASE: William, 27, 93
CASSE: William, 44
CATERETT, ESQR.: Philip, Governor, 19
CAWSEHOE: Indian Sachem, 47
CHAMBERLIN: Ann, 80; Henery, 58, 80
CHAMBERLINE: Henry, 122
CHAMBERS: John, 70, 81, 87, 88, 91, 100, 106, 112, 113, 115, 122; Mary, 109, 112; Richard, 90, 136, 137; Thomas, 38
CHAMNES: John, 24
CHAMNESS: John, 20, 78

INDEX

CHAMPEST: John, 24
CHAMPINS & COMPA.: John, 23
CHAMPNES: John, 79
CHAMPNIS: John, 20, 24
CHANNELHOUSE: Adam, 81, 95, 104, 118; Mary, 95, 104, 111
CHARLES: Symon, 91, 113
CHEASEMAN: Charity, 121; William, 121, 137
CHEASEMAN, SENIOR: William, 121
CHECAUCAS: Indian Sachem, 47
CHEDLEY: Anthony, 54
CHEEKELY: Anthony, 50
CHEEKLEY: Anthony, 49
CHEESEMAN: William, 47; Wm., 7
CHEESMAN, 69: William, 41, 131
CHERAWAS: Indian Sachem, 100
CHESLIS: Indian Sachem, 100
CHIELD: Samuell, 95
CHILD: Samuel, 122, 123; Samuell, 73
CHOCOCUS: Indian Sachem, 53
CHREIVE: Caleb, 35
CHRISTOPR., 23
CHUTE: Georg., 6; George, 9, 14
CHUTTE: Geo., 6
CITTY: David I., 130
CLARCK: Walter, 5, 9
CLARCKE: John, 10
CLARK: Richard, 126; Walter, 4, 6; Walter, dpt. Govr., 120; William, 109
CLARKE: James, 63; Jno., 6; John, 36, 38, 40, 41; Walter, 3, 6, 63; West, 63
CLATON: Zebulon, 134
CLAYTON: John, 62, 81, 91, 106, 108, 110, 111, 125, 129; Sarah, 93; Zebulon, 97, 134
CLERKE: Joseph, 121
CLIFTON: Thomas, 6, 56
COALE: Jacob, 13, 76; Robert, 63, 64; Robt., 64
CODDINGTON: Nathaniel, 13; William, 6; William, Gov., 56
CODINGTON: Chr., 10; Wm., 6
COGGSHELL: John, 6; Joshua, 4, 6
COGSHELL: Jos., 6
COLE: Edward, 7; Excerise, 96; Jacob, 23, 30, 31, 126
COLEMAN: Joseph, 6
COMBES: Richard, 125
COMES: Richard, 125; Thomas, 128
COMPTON: Richard, 78; William, 28
CONCARSKEE: Thomas, 108
CONG: Isack, 20
CONGE: Isack, 20
CONSARSKEE: Thomas, 111
COOK: Hannah, 121; Stephen, 93, 117; Thomas, 30, 118
COOKE: Ebenezer E., 89; Ebonezer, 89; Elizabeth, 72, 90, 105, 126; Hanah, 114; John, 6; Mary, 89; Stephen, 60; Thomas, 32, 35, 36, 42, 44, 55, 71, 72, 90, 102, 112, 118, 126, 127
COOKE THOMAS, 105
COOPER: Simon, 125; Thomas, 118, 127, 129
CORLEIS: George, 117
CORLESS: George, 42
CORLIS: George, 122, 123, 126, 127
CORLISS: George, 127, 129
CORNELL: Thomas, 120
COTTRELL: Elizar, 69; Leser, 133
COTTRILL, 132
COVENHOVEN: Cornelius, 135
COX: James, 86; John, 83, 84, 129; Thomas, 6, 7, 14, 15, 21, 22, 25, 69, 75, 76, 86, 87, 101, 130
CRAFFORD: George, 87; John, 25, 31, 32, 35, 36, 38, 39, 40, 46, 47, 48, 49, 50, 54, 62, 65, 73, 74, 76, 87
CRAFFORS: John, 62
CRAFOORD: John, 54, 55, 56
CRAFORD: John, 29, 42, 44, 59

INDEX

CRANSTON: Samll., 100
CRAWFORD: John, 21, 22, 23, 59, 61
CULLIVER: Samuell, 22
CULLVER: Samuell, 22
CULVER: Samuell, 64, 65
CUMING: John, 20
CUMPTON: William, 69
CUNKIN: John, 5
CURLIS: George, 34, 48, 63, 108
CURLISS: Exercise, 101; Georg, 60; George, 71, 96, 101, 102

D

DAVENPORT: Francis, 92
DAVIA: Nicholas, 11
DAVIS: Aaron, 52; Isabella, 123; Nicho., 6, 15, 18, 20, 22; Nicholas, 6, 15, 18; Richard, 61, 69, 130; Robart, 9; William, 123
DAVISON: William, 125, 132
DAVISSON: William, 95
DEARA: Whan, 133
DENALL: Benjamin, 17
DENIS: Samll., 44
DENNIS: Charles, 33; Jacob, 125; Robert, 96; Sam, 94, 126; Sam., 81; Sam.ll, 114; Saml., 79, 80, 83, 87, 88, 93, 94, 95, 103, 106, 108, 111, 124, 125, 126, 128, 131, 136; Samll., 34, 45, 73, 78, 103, 107, 109, 110, 112, 114, 115, 118, 119, 122, 124; Samuel, 36, 118, 126, 135; Samuell, 29, 30, 32, 39, 41, 56, 64, 71, 72, 105, 109, 112, 114, 119, 121, 122, 123
DENNIS, SENR.: Saml., 124
DENNISS: Rachell, 114; Samll., 117
DEVALL: Banja., 40; Ben, 23; Benja., 37, 38, 43, 45; Benjamin, 20, 27, 37, 41, 60, 61, 69; Benjm., 29
DEVEL: Benjamin, 24
DEVELL: Benj., 42; Benja., 44; Benjamin, 28, 64, 130
DEVILE: Benjamin, 83
DEVILL: Benjamin, 63, 75, 83
DICKMAN: Hugh, 31, 32, 34, 73
DOCKWRA: William, 130
DORN: Cornelius, 135
DORSATT: James, 45
DORSET: James, 25, 55
DORSETE: John, 55
DORSETT: James, 14, 15, 17, 21, 22, 35, 36, 37, 38, 48, 52, 76, 90, 94, 97, 116
DOSSET: James, 45
DRUMMOND: Garvin, 89; Garwin, 89, 90; Gave., 118; Gawin, 89, 103
DUNGUN: Thomas, 7

E

EARLE: William, 106
EASON: Peter, 72
EASSEN: Peter, 6
EASTALL: Daniell, 43, 44
EASTELL: Daniell, 42, 43
EASTON: John, 3; John, 56; Peter, 63
EASTON, JUNIOR: Nicholas, 4
EATON: John, 133, 136, 137; Thomas, 41, 81, 135, 136
EATTON: Widow, 124
ECCLES: Charles, 21, 25
EDON: The Indian, 61
EDWARDS: Abia, 45; Abiah, 30, 31, 32, 53, 60, 76, 106, 107, 108, 111, 113, 118; Obiah, 61; Thomas, 125
ELIS: John, 119
ELLIS: Roger, 6
EMORAS: Indian Sachem, 48
EMOROAS: Indian Sachem, 48
EMOTT: James, 41, 61
ESSIN: Petter, 5
ESTALL: Daniell, 41, 42

INDEX

ESTELL: Daniell, 7, 96
ESTILL: Daniell, 96
EYSELERTSEN: Yong, 130

F

FENWICKE: John, 17; Major, 22
FENWICKE, ESQ.: John, 16
FENWICKE, ESQR.: John, 17, 18
FLIPSON: Frederick, 52; Fredryck, 53
FONICKER: John, Major, 15
FOREMAN: Aaron, 90; Aron, 86; Samuel, 86, 90; Samuell, 86, 90; Thomas, 90
FORMAN: Alexander, 99; Aron, 99, 100, 128; Dorathie, 99; Mary, 128; Saml., 128; Samuel, 128; Samuell, 60, 72, 99, 100, 104; Thomas, 91, 99, 128, 135
FOSTER: Miles, 92, 123; Miles F., 99
FRANCKE: [Black woman], 40
FREEBORN: Gideon, 79, 83, 94, 100, 115; Gidion, 101
FREEBORNE: Gideon, 7; Gidian, 120
FREEBOURNE: Gidion, 100
FREEHORN: Gideon, 66
FREETTWELL: Peter, 110
FULLER: Sarah, 95; William, 10
FULLERTONE: Ia., 75; Ja., 71, 86, 96

G

GANT: Armias, 3; Isaroll, 3; Zachary, 3, 6
GARDINER: R., 27, 46, 49, 50, 51, 52, 53; Rich., 46; Richard, 24, 41, 42, 69; Richd., 28, 29, 30, 46, 47, 48
GARDNIER: Richd., 46
GARRETT, 73
GAUNT: Zachary, 6
GEYSBERTSON: Jon, 116
GIBBINS: Rich., 7; Richard, 1, 2, 3, 5, 7, 8, 74
GIBBON: Edmo., 39; Edmund, 16, 18, 22
GIBBONS: Mordecai, 75; Mordecay, 60, 75, 129; Mordecia, 83, 84; Rd., 2; Richard, 4, 6, 21, 22, 47, 75, 86; Richd., 5, 39; Ruth, 48
GIBBONSON: John, 75, 76
GIBINS: Richard, 5
GIBONE: Richard, 54
GIBONS: Richard, 56, 57, 62
GIBSON: Elizabeth, 109
GIFFORD: Ananias, 118; Christopher, 118, 121; Elizabeth, 88; Hanaiah, 64; Hananiah, 88; Hannaniah, 125; Wm., 7
GODFREE: Elizabeth, 117
GOLDER: Joseph, 135
GOODBODY: William, 119
GORDON: Thomas, 74, 98, 126, 128, 136
GOULD: Daniel, 6; Daniell, 4, 6, 9; Samuel, 4
GOULDING: Will, 5, 7; William, 6; Wm., 2, 4, 7
GOULDSMITH: Ralph, 6, 7
GREEN: Alex, 96; H., 20; Henerey, 20; Thomas, 119, 136
GREENER: Richard, 33
GREEVENZAAT: Andreis, 39
GREEVER: Richard, 39
GROVE: Joseph, 30
GROVER: Capt., 85; Hannah, 85; Ja., 8; James, 2, 3, 4, 5, 6, 7, 8, 14, 15, 16, 17, 21, 23, 25, 40, 41, 43, 47, 69, 75, 90, 132, 136; James, Leiut., 21; John, 98; Jose, 42; Joseph, 21, 22, 29, 36, 42, 47, 48, 49, 60, 85, 100, 104; Mary, 85; Richd., 38; Safety, 29, 37, 39, 98, 101, 130, 136, 137; Safety, Capn., 85; Safety, Capt., 134; Widow, 92
GROVER, JR.: James, 30
GROVER, JUNIOR: James, 7, 21, 137
GROVER, JUNIR: James, 99
GROVER, JUNR.: James, 30, 32, 35
GROVER, SENIOR: James, 20, 22

INDEX

GROVER, SENIR: James, 85, 98, 99
GROVER, SENR.: James, 21, 35, 37, 47
GROVER, SR.: James, 21
GROVER, YE ELDER: James, 21
GROVES: Ja., 2

H

HAIG: Mary, 123; Obadiah, 92; William, 123
HAINES: Charles, 98
HALL: Jno., 6; John, 7; Sarah, 60
HAMBLTON: Robert, 21
HAMILTON: And., 44, 77; Andr., 70; Andrew, 58; Andrew, Coll., 61, 63, 64; Andrew, Governor, 62; Rob., 43, 44, 49, 53, 54, 57, 87, 104; Robert, 38, 39, 42, 50, 59, 62, 69, 73, 74, 76, 98; Robt., 25, 40, 42, 54, 55, 56, 59, 74, 98; William, 39; Willm., 40
HAMPTON: John, 41, 69
HAMTON: Andrew, 123; David, 123; John, 99, 123, 124; Jonathan, 123; Joseph, 123; Noah, 123
HANCE: Jahn, 3; Jno., 5, 7; Jo., 2; John, 3, 4, 5, 6, 7, 8, 12, 27, 28, 30, 31, 32, 33, 35, 36, 37, 38, 39, 40, 41, 42, 43, 44, 45, 47, 48, 49, 50, 51, 52, 53, 54, 55, 56, 57, 58, 59, 60, 61, 62, 63, 64, 65, 66, 70, 72, 73, 74; John, 75; John, 75, 76, 79, 80, 81, 82, 84, 85, 86, 87, 88, 89, 91, 93, 94, 95, 96, 97, 98, 102, 104, 107; John, 108, 109, 110, 112, 114, 115, 116, 117, 118, 119, 122, 124, 129, 130; Joseph, 25
HANCE, ESQR.: John, 94, 106
HANDEY: Richard, 4
HANDSON: Tobiah, 6; Tobias, 6
HANKINS: John, 130, 135
HANKINSON: Peter, 65; Thomas, 65
HANS: John, 10
HANSE: John, 62

HANSON: Tobias, 58, 77, 93, 121; Tonia, 121
HARBART: Thomas, 28
HARBERT: Francis, 30, 39, 40, 94, 133; Thomas, 37, 69; Walter, 30, 39, 66
HARCUTT: Daniell, 96
HARKER: Daniell, 86
HARKERS: Daniel, 125
HART: John, 63; Thomas, 7, 109, 135
HARTSHORNE: Hugh, 125, 134; Margaret, 121; Margret, 121; Rich., 44; Richard, 5, 16, 17, 18, 22, 25, 28, 29, 32, 35, 36, 40, 41, 43, 45, 46, 48, 50, 51, 52, 54, 55, 56, 57, 58, 59, 62, 64, 65, 66, 69, 73, 77, 79, 83, 84, 90, 96, 97, 98, 99, 101, 104, 108, 113, 117, 119, 121, 127, 129, 130, 132, 133; Richd., 29, 38, 40, 48; Robert, 96; William, 134, 135
HARWOOD: John, 61; Jon., 61
HAVEN: John, 32, 40, 48
HAVENS: William W., 67; Anna, 77, 78, 80, 107; John, 15, 22, 25, 38, 77, 78, 79, 80, 88, 91, 92, 97, 101, 105, 107, 119, 128, 132; Nicholas, 91, 92, 107; William, 93
HAYNES: Charles, 12
HAZARD: Robert, 7
HEARCE: Thomas, 50, 51, 66, 80, 87
HEARD: James, 3
HEARS: Thomas, 70
HEARSE: Tho., 124; Thomas, 83, 87, 92, 93, 112, 114; Thomas H., 121
HEARSS: Thomas, 105
HEART: Thomas, 60
HEARTS: Thomas, 66
HEBRON: John, 119, 120, 132, 135
HEIRS: Thomas, 53
HENDERSON: Hendrick, 135
HENDRICK: Indian Sachem, 100

(145)

INDEX

HENDRICKSON: Daniel, 75, 135; Daniell, 76
HENRY, 137: John, 24
HEPBURN: John, 137
HERBERT: Thomas, 37, 98
HERS: Thomas, 20
HEUET: Tho., 45
HEULETT: George, 45
HEULIT: George, 44
HEWETT: Thomas, 29
HEWIT: Tho., 42; Thomas, 124
HEWITT: Thomas, 41
HICK: Joseph, 61
HICKEY: Gabriel, 27
HIGHAM: Jane, 108; Thomas, 100, 108
HIGHHAM: Thomas, 108
HIGS: John, 24
HILBORN: Elizabeth, 94; Thomas, 94
HILBOURN: Elizabeth, 94; Thomas, 94
HILBOURNE: Thomas, 72
HILDRETH: Jonathan, 134
HILL: Enoch, 61
HOLDMAN: Robert, 96, 97
HOLLINGHEAD: John, 91
HOLLINGSHEAD: John, 113
HOLLMAN: Samuel, 6
HOLMAN: Robert, 96; Robt., 43, 45; Samuel, 6
HOLMES, 132: Jonathan, 1, 25, 55, 69, 122; Obadiah, 117
HOMES: Jonathan, 6, 22
HOOD: Jeremiah, 30, 31
HOOLMAN: Robt., 44
HORABIN: Jno., 7; John, 6, 8, 12, 20, 21
HORN: Gustavus, 103
HORSSMAN: Marmaduke, 132
HOUGHAM: Indian Sachem, 64
HOULAND: Daniell, 100
HOURDELL: Jno., 7
HOWARD: Hester, 2; Mathew, 2
HOY: John, 61
HUBARD: James, 135; Samuel, 10
HUBBARD: James, 127
HUEITT: Thomas, 25
HUET: Ann, 8; Joseph, 8; Margret, 8; Randall, 3, 5, 8; Thomas, 8
HUET, JUNR.: Randall, 7
HUET, SENR.: Randall, 7
HUET, THE ELDER: Randall, 8; Randull, 8
HUETT: Bridgett, 100; Randall, 11, 12, 14; Thomas, 59, 73, 89, 121, 122
HUIT: Randall, 12; Tho., 25; Thomas, 21
HUITT: Joseph, 15, 17, 21; Randall, 11, 17, 21; Thomas, 16
HULET: George, 30; William, 124, 133
HULETT: Ann, 92; Elizabeth, 77; George, 14, 21, 30, 32, 37, 71, 81, 91; Joseph, 125; William, 61, 63
HULLETT: William, 124
HULLMES: Jonathan, 3, 6, 53; Obidiah, 3, 6
HULMES: Jonathan, 2, 15, 17, 21, 52, 53; Obadiah, 6
HUNT: Anne, 48; William, 38, 48, 132
HUTON: Samuel, 23, 24; Samuell, 22
HUTTON: Elizabeth, 76, 91, 110, 115; Sam, 23; Samuel, 17, 22; Samuell, 23

I

IANSEN: Ian, 50
IAXSONE: Frances, 45
ILOSSECHCOTE: Indian Sachem, 97
ILTONT: Peter, 32
INGRAM: Thomas, 38
IRASEAK: Indian Sachem, 100
IRASECOTT: Indian Sachem, 52
IRASECUT: Indian Sachem, 53
IRASECUTT: Indian Sachem, 53
IRASEEKE: Indian Sachem, 49
IRESONES: John, 82

INDEX

IUKRAIN: Thomas, 59

J

JACKSON: Elizabeth, 116; Frances, 63; Francis, 33, 34, 38, 64, 73, 88, 102, 105, 115, 116, 123; Mary, 116; William, 115
JACOBS: Thomas, 110
JAMES: Richard, 61, 94, 97, 132; William, 6; Wm., 6
JAMISON: David, 123
JANATAN: Indian Sachem, 53
JAY: Hanah, 114; Hannah, 121; John, 8, 9, 10
JEFERIES: Francis, 20
JEFFRES: Francis, 82
JEFFREYS: Francis, 82
JEFFRIES: Francis, 41, 42
JENCKIN: Job., 91
JENCKIUS: Job, 96
JENING: John, 4
JENKINS: Jno., 6; Job, 94, 115; John, 4, 6
JENNINGS: John, 61
JOB: Geo., 38; George, 24, 25, 42, 86, 87; John, 39, 46, 59
JOB: John, 87
JOBE: John, 130
JOBES: George, 61; John, 21
JOBS: George, 44, 87; John, 87
JOHNES: Robt., 73
JOHNSON: John, 42, 43, 44, 53, 54
JOHNSTON: David, 132, 135, 136; James, 41, 66, 94, 128; John, 41, 44, 55, 58, 60, 61, 62, 63, 64, 65, 102
JOHNSTON, ESQR.: John, 102, 131
JOHNSTONE: Benjamin, 137; Doctor, 130; James, 110; John, 95
JONATAN: Indian Sachem, 53; Indian Scahem, 55
JONATHAN: Indian Sachem, 52
JUGELO: Richard, 95

K

KEETH: George, 72
KEITH: George, 69, 73, 97, 99, 111, 126, 127, 136
KEMBLE: Samuell, 110
KERR: James, 95; Walter, 95
KICK: Benjamin, 61; Joseph, 60
KILMASTER: Sarah, 104
KILMISTER: William, 59
KING: John, 29, 31, 132

L

LAFETRA: Edmind, 124; Edmond, 37, 40, 66, 77, 128, 129, 136; Edmund, 17, 18, 20, 21, 22, 23, 29, 38, 48, 58, 137; Frances, 58; Sarah, 58
LAFFETRA: Edmond, 76, 87, 92, 114; Edmund, 80, 107; Edward, 107
LAING: John, 126; William, 100, 107, 123
LAKE: Richard, 10
LANE: Gilbert, 121
LAPHETRA: Edmund, 14, 15, 16
LAPHITRA: Edmund, 6, 7
LAURIE: James, 137
LAWRANS: Will, 42
LAWRENCE: Ben, 121; Benjamin, 113; Elisah, 132, 133; Elisha, 63, 74, 85, 98, 99, 119, 120, 132, 134, 135, 136, 137; James, 83, 84, 113, 121; Job, 88; John, 83, 84, 132, 133, 136; Joseph, 84, 88, 119, 132; Lucy, 134; Ruth, 98; Sarah, 90, 119; Thomas, 47; William, 21, 41, 49, 69, 75, 76, 77, 79, 83, 84, 93, 98, 99, 121, 133, 134, 135; Wm., 1, 7
LAWRENCE, JR.: William, 60
LAWRENCE, JUN.: William, 30
LAWRENCE, JUNIOR: William, 83, 98, 127, 134; Wm., 136

INDEX

LAWRENCE, JUNIR: William, 99
LAWRENCE, JUNR.: William, 32, 37, 48, 50, 85
LAWRENCE, SENIOR: William, 119
LAWRENCE, SENR.: William, 53, 83, 84, 85
LAWRENCE: William, 132
LAWRIE: G., 86; Gawen, Governr., 35; Gawin, 91, 99
LAWRY: Garvin, 123; Isabella, 123; James, 123; Rebecca, 123
LAYTON: Samuel, 129, 131; Thomas, 73; William, 17, 28, 47, 48, 57, 64, 69, 97, 101; Willm., 131; Wm., 7
LAYTON, JUNIR: William, 97
LAYTOR: William, 37
LE MASTER: Francis, 16, 18, 20
LE MESTER: Fra., 22; Francis, 16, 17
LEACOCK: Robert, 59, 95
LEADS: Margaret, 43, 44; Tho., 43; William, 43, 44, 49
LEEDS: Daniel, 93, 113; Daniell, 92; Jonathan, 60; Margaret, 113; Thomas, 30, 113, 124; William, 29, 30, 38, 41, 42, 43, 48, 49, 56, 60, 61, 66, 69, 100; Willm., 40
LEEDS, JUNIOR: William, 60, 92; Wm., 136
LEEDS, SENIOR: William, 92
LEEDS, SENIR: William, 92
LEFATRA: Edman, 24
LEFETRA: Edmund, 25
LEMASTER: Francis, 24, 25, 71
LEMESTER: Fra., 23; Francis, 23
LEMNARD: Samuell, 25
LENARD: John, 43, 44; Samll., 40
LENORD: John, 43, 44, 45; Samll., 43, 44
LEOANRD: Henery, 83
LEONARD: Hanah, 85; Henery, 14, 22; Henry, 48, 120, 133, 136, 137; James, 7; John, 28, 48, 71, 76, 77, 89, 120, 132, 133; John, Capt., 137; Mary, 48; Mr., 137; Nathaniel, 80; Nathaniell, 46, 85, 88; Sam, 23; Saml., 42, 81, 130; Samll., 39, 44, 104, 105; Samll.., 45; Samuel, 22, 29, 33, 37, 59, 116; Samuell, 29, 40, 46, 48, 60, 61, 64, 66, 75, 83, 109; Samuell, Capt., 129; Samull., 76; Sarah, 48; Thomas, 39, 83, 119, 120, 132
LEONARD'S SAW MILL, 69, 71, 89: Henry, 135
LEONARD, ESQUIRE: Henry, 125
LEONARD, SENR.: Henry, 35
LEOND.: Samll., 40
LESLEY: Richard, 71
LEWIS: Gawen, 39
LIMING: John, 35, 39, 133; Prudence, 104
LIMMING: John, 28, 30; Prudence, 104
LINDLEY: H., 129
LINDLY: Henry, 128
LING: Mathew, 110
LIP'CT: Moses, 133, 134
LIPENCOTT: Richard, 6
LIPINCOT: Rd., 2
LIPINCOTT: Remembrance, 114; Richard, 3
LIPITT: Manthaniel, 15
LIPPINCOTT: Abigail, 111, 114, 118; Bartho., 7; Hannah, 81; Jacob, 111, 126; John, 38, 101, 112, 113, 114, 115, 117, 122, 127; Margarett, 96, 114; Postore, 31; Rd., 5; Remberance, 82, 97; Rembrance, 66, 93, 98; Rememberance, 96, 101; Remembrance, 36, 74, 79, 84, 111, 113, 117, 118, 119, 122, 125; Reserve, 133; Restere, 73; Restore, 30, 48, 81, 93, 97, 108, 110, 131; Richard, 4, 5, 6, 8, 96, 115; Robert, 124; Rostere, 72; Rostore, 38
LIPPINCOTT, JUNIOR: John, 61, 106, 115
LIPPINCOTT, SEN.: John, 128
LIPPINCOTT, SENIOR: John, 106, 114

INDEX

LIPPINCOTT, SENR.: John, 124
LIPPINGCOOT: John, 44
LIVINSTONE: Robt., 110
LOCKISON: John, 135
LONGSTREET: Stofell, 121; Stoffill, 122; Stophel, 137
LONNGSTREET: Stoffel, 122
LORD: William, 60
LUCER: Mark, 6
LUCOR: Mark, 6
LUETT: George, 70
LUNSDALE: Gilbert, 43
LURIES: Garvin, 128

M
MACHAYIS: Indian Sachem, 52
MADDOCK: Lewis, 74
MALLSON: Daniell, 54
MARCH: Henry, 41
MARKES: Christian, 37
MARKS: Christian, 36
MARLIN: John, 54
MARLON: John, 54
MAROLE: Edward, 51
MARSH: Hener-, 97; Henery, 21, 64, 65, 75; Henry, 28, 52, 53, 56; Jonathan, 109
MARSSH: Henry, 56, 57
MARYSON: Jonathan, 94
MASS: Michael, 9
MASTERS: Clame, 44; Clement, 63, 103, 107; Clemment, 61, 76, 89; Fra., 7, 16; Francis, 6, 14, 16, 76, 79; Mary, 76
MATISON: Arra, 132
MATTAGE: Thomas, 132
MATTIS: Lewis, 12
MATTIX: Lewis, 11, 65, 66
MATTOCK: Lewis, 113
MC DERMOTT: Joseph, 25, 67, 102, 137
MEIKLE: Alexr., 91
MENINVEIN: Indian Sachem, 47

METSHATT: Indian Sachem, 100
MIDGLEY: Tho., 110
MILLER: James, 86, 91, 123
MILWGRD: Rob., 123
MOLLISON: John, 86
MOOR: Richard, 7; Samuel, 22; Thomas, 5
MOORE: Samll., 49, 50, 54; Samuel, 16; Samuell, 49, 50
MOORE, SENIOR: Thomas, 13
MORFORD: John, 30; Thomas, 48, 69, 134
MORLIN: James, 74
MORRIS, 132: Coll., 66; Isabella, 71; L., 71, 72, 76, 88, 89, 91, 92, 94, 95, 101, 103, 105, 118, 119, 136; Lewis, 28, 30, 31, 32, 35, 39, 40, 41, 42, 44, 45, 50, 51, 54, 56, 57, 58, 60, 61, 62, 63, 64, 65, 66, 71, 73, 74, 77, 78, 81, 82, 88, 89, 99, 101, 102, 104; Lewis, Coll., 30, 35, 39, 59, 67; Lewis, Collo., 39, 50, 51
MORRIS, ESQR.: Lewis, 89, 118
MORRIS, JUN.: Lewis, 43
MORRIS, JUNIOR: Lewis, 23
MORRIS, JUNNO.: Lewis, 42
MORRIS, JUNOR.: Lewis, 44
MORRIS, SEN.: Lewis, 42
MOSEHOPPE: Indian Sachem, 55
MOTT: Gershom, 93, 96, 116
MOUNT: Catherine, 101; Georg, 6; George, 6, 15, 17, 21, 62, 101; Mathias, 64; Rebecca, 44; Rich., 44; Richard, 37, 44, 101
MYAWICKE: Indian Sachem, 52

N
NAPESON: Indian Sachem, 47
NAUGHTY: William, 95
NESTOA: Indian Sachem, 100
NEUMAN: John, 45; William, 45
NEWMAN: John, 96; Mary, 96

INDEX

NICHOLS: Richard, Collonoll, 4
NICOLLS: Mathias, 25
NOCHTOHA: Indian Sachem, 49
NORTH: William, 96

O

O'KESON: Samuel, 136
OKISON: John, 134
OKISSON: John, 117
OLIPHANT: William, 95
OLLIVE: Tho., 113
ONG: Isaac, 22, 34; Isaak, 23; Isack, 113; Mary, 33, 34
ONG, SENIOR: Isaac, 113
OUNG: Isaac, 27

P

PAGE: Antho., 7; Anthony, 47
PALMER: John, 39
PANDAM: Indian Sachem, 52
PAPPAMORA: Indian Sachem, 5
PARDON: Mr., 20; William, 19
PARKE: Joseph, 32
PARKER: George, 91, 106, 115; Joseph, 13, 14,15, 16, 17, 20, 21, 22, 25, 27, 28, 30, 31, 32, 33, 50, 51, 59, 71, 74, 83, 91, 105, 114, 115, 117, 121, 122, 124, 125, 136, 137; Nathaniel, 128; Peter, 12, 14, 15, 21, 22, 61, 71, 74, 124, 126; Petter, 1; Robert, 89; Sarah, 14, 91; Thomas, 89, 120; William, 91
PARKER, ESQR.: Joseph, 83
PATRIDGE: Thomas, 96
PATTISON: Edward, 1, 5, 6, 7, 89; Mary, 89
PATTISSON: Edward, 6, 9; Faith, 9
PEACE: William, 117
PEARCE: John, 43, 64, 75, 136
PEDLOR: Mary, 69
PEIRCE: John, 35, 40
PEMHOOSE: Indian Sachem, 52

PENHOOSE: Indian Sachem, 52
PERCEY: Henerey, 7; Henry, 8; James, 15; Kathern, 11
PERCY: Cathern, 11; Henry, 1, 2; Kathern, 2
PERORACK: Indian Sachem, 52
PERROPA: Indian Sachem, 48
PERUPPO: Indian Sachem, 52
PHILLIPSE: Rombout, 53
PINHORN: William, 136
PINTARD, 137: A., 101, 111, 114; Anthony, 74, 112, 136, 137
PLUMSTED: Clement, 127, 129
PLUMSTEEDS: Clemment, 99
POLLHEMUS: Johanes, 133
POMFRET: Walter, 45
POOR: Richard, 10
POORE: Rich, 10
PORORE: Indian Sachem, 55
PORORO: Indian Sachem, 55
PORRUPPO: Indian Sachem, 52
POTROAS: Indian Sachem, 100
POTTER: Ann, 9; Anna, 95; Ephraim, 40, 60, 61, 118, 120; Sarah, 110; Thomas, 6, 9, 11, 15, 44, 60, 63, 71, 72, 81, 82, 90, 94, 95, 103, 104, 105, 107, 108, 109, 110, 111, 114, 118, 125, 126
POUND: Rack, 132
POURAAS: Indian Sachem, 100
POWELL: Thomas, 95
POWRAAS: Indian Sachem, 49
POWROPA: Indian Sachem, 48
PRESTON: William, 137
PUMPHREY: Walter, 70
PUROPA: Indian Sachem, 100

Q

QUAHICKE: Indian Sachem, 52

INDEX

R

RACHAN: John, 55
RACKMAN: John, 98
RANDOLPH: F., 61
RAPER: Thomas, 110
RAY: Robert, 124; Robt., 123
READ: John, 63
REAP: Sarah, 69; Sarah, Mrs., 113; William, 125; Willm., 4; Wm., 6
REAPE: Sarah, 70, 74, 76, 81, 87, 93, 112, 121, 130, 135; Sarah, Mrs., 113; Willa, 7; William, 74, 120; Wm., 5, 6, 7
REEAP: Sarah, 125
REED: John, 98, 120
REES: Johannes, 133
REID: George, 91, 92, 127; Ja., 91; James, 91, 126, 128; John, 69, 73, 74, 83, 85, 86, 90, 93, 98, 99, 103, 104, 105, 120, 122, 124, 125, 126, 128; John, 129; John, 131, 132, 133, 135; John, 135; John, 136, 137; Jonh., 135; Mr., 137
RENSHALL: Tho., 34; Thomas, 36
RICHARDSON: John, 50; Rd., 2, 3, 5, 7, 8, 9, 11, 12; Richard, 1, 6, 7, 8, 23, 42, 43; Wm., 4
ROBENS: Moses, 120
ROBERTS: Thomas, 60, 83, 84, 121
ROBINSON: James, 75; John, 39
ROGERS: William, 10
ROGGERS: Benjamin, 82
RORIE: George, 117
RORUY: George, 117
ROUSELL: Thomas, 53
ROUSLE: Thomas, 43
RUCKMAN: John, 3, 6, 43, 135; Jonathan, 132; Samll., 135; Thomas, 130
RUCKMAN, JUNIOR: John, 74
RUCKMAN, JUNIR: John, 75
RUCKMAN, SENIR: John, 74, 75
RUSKMAN: Jno., 7; John, 3, 6

RUTMAN: John, 69
RYLEGH: James, 9

S

SADLER: Jane, 87, 90, 100, 108; Richard, 7, 14, 15, 17, 20, 22, 23, 25, 30, 31, 32, 34, 36, 38, 39, 42, 43, 46, 50, 53, 87, 88, 90, 108; Richd., 37
SALTER: Richard, 97, 124, 125, 127, 130, 134; Richard, Capt., 127
SALTON [SALTER?]: John, 98
SANDFORD: William, Atto., 18
SANFFORD: John, 12
SANFORD: Wm, Attourney, 19; Wm., Capt., 20
SARRA: Nicholas, 118
SATTON: John, 77
SCHUYLER: Brand, 110
SCOTT: James, 86; John, 131; Will, 45; William, 41, 49, 53, 59, 60, 64, 74, 96, 97, 103, 106, 107, 114, 131; Willm., 40, 131
SEABROOK: Daniell, 75
SEAHOPPA: Indian Sachem, 49
SECOES: Indian Sachem, 100
SECPHA: Indian Sachem, 100
SHACKERLY: William, 10; Wm., 9
SHADDOCK: Am., 5; William, 4, 6, 10, 29; Wm., 5, 6, 7
SHAKERLEY: Wm., 6
SHAKERLY: Wm., 6
SHATTOCK: William, 36, 59, 81, 82, 101, 102, 108, 127, 128
SHATTOCK, JUNR.: Samuell, 51
SHATTOCK, SENR.: Samuell, 51
SHATTOCKE: Willm., 34
SHEARMAN: Thomas, 40
SHENATAPO: Indian Sachem, 52
SHENOLAPE: Indian Sachem, 55
SHENOTAPE: Indian Sachem, 55

INDEX

SHENOTOPE: Indian Sachem, 52
SHERIFE: Caleb, 123
SHOAN: John, 76, 77
SHOUGHAM: Indian Sachem, 100, 101
SHREEFE: Calleb, 43
SHREEVE: Caleb, 115, 126
SHREIVE: Caleb, 30, 31, 32; Calieb, 64, 91
SHREVE: Caleb, 106; Sarah, 106
SHRIMPTON: Mr., 18, 22; Samuel, 16
SHRIVE: Caleib, 74; Calieb, 61
SIER: Henerey, 14
SILLVESTER: Natha., 5, 6
SIMMANS: Peter, 96
SIMPSON: William, 27, 39; Wm., 27
SISSOLL: Richard, 6
SKELTON: Alce, 103; Alie, 103; Robert, 103
SLOCKIN: John, 45
SLOCUM, 29: John, 10, 23, 27, 29, 31, 32, 33, 34, 37, 38, 39, 40, 43, 51, 59, 60, 74, 79, 101, 113, 118, 131; John, Capt., 38, 65; Meribah, 74; Nathaniel, 47, 127, 131; Nathaniell, 27, 30; Nathll., 31
SLOCUM, SENIOR: Gyles, 10
SLOCUME: Gyles, 10
SLUCUM: John, 59
SMITH: Abraham, 64, 65; Barnard, 11; Chr., 50; Dirrick, 5; Edward, 2, 3, 6, 47, 52, 57; Jno., 7; John, 6, 15, 17, 22, 47, 52, 53, 54, 55, 65, 100, 101; Mary, 65, 127; Peleg, 120; Phillip, 44, 51; Shuball, 79; Smith, 11; Tho., 135; Thomas, 127; Wm., 12
SMYTON: Wm., 12
SNASSELF: Thomas, 22
SNAWSELL: Thomas, 23, 28, 29, 35, 36, 38, 39, 49, 50
SNAWSELL, SENR.: Thomas, 46
SNAWSELL, THE ELDER: Thomas, 46
SNEAD: William, 44
SNELL: Heugh, 42; Hugh, 33
SNOSELL: Thomas, 23, 43, 54, 55, 56

SNOWSELL: Tho., 48; Thomas, 22
SNOZELL: Thomas, 25
SOHOPPO: Indian Sachem, 53
SONMAN, 126
SOUMANS: Peter, 99
SPEERE: Benjamin, 6
SPICER: Samll., 57; Samuel, 2, 3, 6, 7, 121; Samuell, 69
SQUIRE: Edward, 50, 51
STANLEY: Richard, 131
STANNARD: Anna, 107
STARKE: John, 59
STARKEE: John, 95, 96; Mary, 96
STARKEY: John, 103, 104, 105, 108; Mary M., 105
STATHAM: Thomas, 54
STEENWICKE: Corn., 46; Cornelius, 46
STEENWYCK: Margarett, 39
STELL: John James, 120
STELLE: Gabrial, 136; Pouncett, 77
STEPHENS: John, 103
STEWARD: Elizabeth, 119; John, 119, 126
STEWART: Elizabeth, 119; John, 119, 135, 136; Samuel, 136
STICK: Benjamin, 60
STIEFFE: Stephen, 79
STILLWELL: Jeremiah, 121, 125, 128, 136; Peter, 92; Rebecka, 103; Thomas, 134
STILLWELL, ESQR.: John, 103
STOENWICKE: Cornelius, 29
STORY: Robart, 10; Robert, 6, 7, 8
STOUT: Amos, 134; Benjamin, 127, 135; David, 127, 132; James, 48, 63; John, 20, 21, 25, 34, 36, 37, 41, 47, 48, 49, 50, 52, 53, 54, 62, 63, 69, 87, 94, 97, 98, 104, 108, 127, 133; Jonathan, 60, 127; Penelope, 46, 47, 55; Peter, 127; Rich., 44; Richard, 3, 15, 47, 52, 55, 64, 65, 92, 94, 125, 127; Richard, Capt., 137;

INDEX

Robert, 125, 132
STOUT, JUNIOR: Richard, 100
STOUT, JUNIR: Richard, 97
STOUT, JUNOR.: Richard, 43
STOUT, SENIOR: Richard, 56, 124
STOUT, SENR.: Richard, 21, 35, 46
STOUT, SENYOR.: Richard, 54
STOUT, THE YOUNGER: Richard, 69
STOUT, YE ELDER.: Richard, 21
STOUTT: Jo., 17; John, 7, 14, 15, 65, 88, 90, 96; Rich, 7; Richard, 2, 3, 4, 5, 6, 7, 8, 17, 22; Richd., 5
STRAKE: John, 95
STTENWYCK: Mr., 39
STUART: Elizabeth, 118; John, 113, 118
SUNNANS: Peter, 109
SUTTON: John, 77; Mary, 61, 63, 94
SWINEY: John, 84, 85; Mary, 15; Thorlagh, 48; Thorlogh, 15; Thurley, 85; Thurlough, 85
SWINTON: I. S., 53
SWINY: Thorlagh, 48; Thurley, 84
SWYNY: Fenwicke Thorlagh, 47; Thurlagh, 11

T

TALINQUANECAN: Indian Sachem, 97
TART: Edward, 75, 88, 94
TARTT: Edward, 6, 7
TASCALAWAY: Indian Sachem, 97
TATHAM: John, 91
TAYLOR: Edward, 134; Robert, 6, 10; Thomas, 11
TAYLOR, JUNR.: Edward, 129
THOGMORTON: John, 36
THROCKMORTON: Alce, 103; Alie, 103; Freegift, 3; Jo., 17; Job, 7, 21, 22, 25, 32, 43, 61, 69, 109, 130; Job., 53; John, 6, 22, 25, 33, 37, 38, 39, 40, 42, 43, 44, 47, 49, 50, 51, 52, 53, 54, 55, 59, 60, 62, 64, 94, 103, 119, 130, 134; Joseph, 65, 129; Rebecka, 103
THROCKMORTON, JUNIOR: John, 3
THROCKMORTON, SENIOR: John, 3
THROGMORTON: Job, 48; John, 27, 28, 32, 33, 35, 36, 41, 48
THROKMORTON: Joseph, 57
THROPP: Mary, 74; Samuell, 72, 90, 94
THURSTON: Edward, 6, 32, 73
TILLTON: John, 5; Peter, 14
TILTON, 135: Daniel, 132; John, 2, 3, 5, 6, 76, 77, 81, 89; Peter, 4, 10, 13, 27, 28, 29, 30, 31, 32, 33, 35, 36, 37, 38, 39, 40, 41, 43, 47, 48, 49, 50, 51, 52, 53, 54, 56, 58, 59, 60, 61, 62, 63, 64, 65, 67, 69, 74, 77, 79, 80, 81, 84, 85, 93, 96, 97, 98, 100, 101, 105, 113, 114, 117, 130; Petter, 42, 44, 45, 54, 55, 56, 57; Rebecca, 48
TILTON'S MILL, 132
TILTON, JUNIOR: Peter, 117
TILTON, SENIOR: Peter, 117
TIMISSON: Derrick, 12
TIPPITES: Henery, 6
TIPPOTTS: Henery, 6
TOM: [Black slave, Widow Grover's], 92
TOMKINS: Bathl., 6
TOMMASON, 60
TOMSON: Jno., 7
TONASON: Derick, 25
TONKINS: Nathaniel, 6
TONOSSON: Derick, 24, 25
TOWNSEND: Jno., 6; John, 6
TREDWELL: John, 117
TREUAX: Jacob, 53
TROKMORTON: John, 56
TRUAX: Philip, 119
TRUWAXE: Jacob, 100
TUCKER: John, 45, 63, 72, 82, 89, 97; Ruth, 97
TUNISON: Derick, 9, 23; Dericke, 53

(153)

INDEX

TUNISSEN: Derrick, 39
TUNISSON: Derick, 22; Derrick, 22; Direck, 29; Dirick, 40
TUNMISON: Derick, 12
TUNNISON: Derick, 15, 60
TURNER: Robert, 95

U

ULMESH: Jonathan, 7
URSINTONE: Frances, 53
URYS: Peter, 10
USSELTON: Providence, 78

V

VACHAN: John, 57
VACHON: John, 98
VAN CORTLAND: S., 110
VAN HOOK: Lawrence, 137
VAN NORWICK: Simon, 137
VAN-HOOK: Lawrence, 136
VANDERVENTER: Peter, 133
VAUGHN: John, 37, 38, 40
VAUHAN: John, 57
VICARS: Thomas, 63
VICKARS: Thomas, 101, 109, 112, 117
VICKERS: Thomas, 79
VILANTS: David, 92
VINSENTT: John, 110
VN. COURTLAND: Stephanis, 103

W

WAINERIGHT: Nicholas, 129
WAINEWRIGHT: Thomas, 63, 66
WAINRIGHT: Nicholas, 129
WAINWRIGHT: Alce, 104; Alce A., 104; Elizabeth, 80; Mary, 120, 131; Nicholas, 104, 107, 120, 130, 131; Thomas, 61, 63, 104, 105, 130
WALL: Garret, 42, 60, 75; Garrett, 73, 75, 94; Gerard, 37, 48; Gerrat, 42; Great, 44; Jaret, 122; Jerat, 117; John, 135, 136; Rebecca, 44; Walter, 6, 7, 22, 23, 48, 65, 117
WALL, JUNIOR: Walter, 115, 116
WALTERS: Anthony, 13
WAMATAM: Indian Sachem, 53
WAMUTON: Indian Sachem, 53
WARD: Marmaduke, 7; Thomas, 52
WARDEL: Joseph, 136
WARDELL: Efiakim, 23; Eliakim, 2, 4, 5, 6, 7, 20, 22, 23, 36, 41, 59, 66, 79, 80, 108, 118, 125; Elliakim, 42; Joseph, 111, 118, 121, 122, 125, 135; Joseph, 136, 137; Lydia, 58, 59, 79
WARDILL: Eliakim, 1
WARN: Tho., 97; Thomas, 64, 99
WARNE: Tho., 90, 117; Thomas, 64, 65, 85, 86, 99, 128; Thos., 118
WARTE: Thomas, 13
WATSON: John, 122
WAWAPA: Indian Sachem, 48
WAYANOCAN: Indian Sachem, 64
WAYMOTO: Indian Sachem, 55
WEBB: George, 6; Samll., 110; Samuel, 124; Samuell, 110
WEBLEY: Andria, 96, 104; Audrey, 67; Edward, 100, 101; John, 35; L., 105; T., 104; Tho., 51, 59, 64, 66, 70, 73, 74, 75, 76, 77, 78, 80, 81, 82, 83, 85, 87, 88, 89, 91, 92, 93, 95, 96, 98, 102, 103, 104, 105, 107, 108, 109, 111, 112, 114, 136; Thomas, 40, 45, 50, 58, 59, 70, 71, 73, 77, 80, 89, 101, 105, 112, 119, 121; Thos., 62
WEBLY: Tho., 45
WELLS: Daniel, 113
WERRILL: Christo, 113
WEST: Bartho., 1, 5, 6; Bartholomew, 6, 7, 32; Ephraim John, 63; John, 45, 46,

INDEX

58, 61, 63, 66, 78, 80, 88, 92, 102, 103, 105, 118, 128, 131, 135; Joseph, 45, 60, 63, 66, 77, 79, 84, 87, 88, 112, 113, 114, 124, 128; Margarett, 88, 90; Mary, 124; Nichaoll, 92; Robert, 6, 45, 66, 70, 74, 77, 81, 87, 88, 114; Sarah, 89; Stephen, 45, 66, 67, 70, 87; Steven, 25; William, 66, 70, 76, 81, 88, 89, 90, 91, 102, 103, 121; Willm., 126
WEST, SENIR.: Joseph, 87
WESTGATE: John, 106
WESTON, 55
WEVER: Thomas, 120
WHARTON: Edward, 3, 6, 51, 61, 122; Edwd., 5; George, 51, 61
WHIT: Jon, 43
WHITE: John, 59, 60; Peter, 34, 35, 36, 41, 55, 71, 72, 82, 91, 94, 97, 108, 109, 114, 115, 117; Petter, 42, 44, 45; Saml., 40; Samll., 39, 40; Samuel, 20; Samuell, 40, 88, 102; Thomas, 39, 40, 45, 71, 82, 90, 93, 95, 134; Willm., 21
WHITELOCK: John, 73, 76, 88; Thomas, 73, 90; William, 73, 75, 90
WHITELOCK, SEN.: Thomas, 75
WHITELOCK, SENIR.: Thomas, 73
WHITLOCK: John, 20, 29, 38, 44, 76; Thomas, 6, 38, 69, 76, 88; William, 38, 39, 75, 76, 96; Willm., 28, 37; Wm., 29, 39
WHITTLOCK: John, 20; Tho., 7; William, 20
WIKOFF: Peter, 135
WILDE: John, 61
WILIAMS: John, 25
WILLCOT: Samuel, 21
WILLET: Samuell, 23
WILLETT: Samuell, 64
WILLIAMS: Edward, 46, 58, 61, 64, 66, 67, 70, 76, 80, 101, 102, 105, 111, 124, 126; Elizabeth, 125; John, 30, 42, 44, 45, 58, 60, 64, 66, 72, 76, 79, 105, 113, 119, 125, 134; Mary, 110; Robart, 10; Thomas, 24
WILLIAMS, JUNR.: John, 125
WILLIAMSON: John, 62
WILLIT: Sam, 24
WILLOCK: George, 98
WILLOCKS: George, 104, 126
WILLOKS: Geo., 102
WILLSON: John, 4, 6, 7, 14, 33, 45, 137
WILLSON, JUNIOR: John, 61
WILLSON, JUNOR.: John, 43, 44
WILLSON, SENIOR: John, 64
WILSON: Alexander, 116; Andrew, 135; James, 128, 136; John, 127, 136; Mr., 137; Peter, 93, 128, 135, 136; Petrer, 137
WILSON, JUNIR: John, 74
WINDER: Samuel, 41
WINDERS: Mr., 39
WING: Joseph, 119, 135, 136
WINTERTON: Tho., 5, 6, 7; Thomas, 5, 9, 125
WINWRIGHT: Thomas, 102
WOLLCOTT: Nathaniell, 67; Samuell, 81
WOOD: Jno., 7; John, 6, 32
WOODMANSY: Thomas, 121; William, 73
WOODWARD: Anthony, 132, 134
WOOLEY, 137
WOOLLCOTT: Nathaniell, 66; Samuell, 33, 67, 70, 105
WOOLLEY: Ann, 93; Edward, 70, 72, 76, 97, 99, 120, 121, 124; Emmanuel, 5, 6; George, 63; John, 48, 71, 78, 81, 82, 90, 107, 108, 111, 118, 119, 120, 132, 133; Lydia, 124; Walter, 17, 18; William, 58, 66, 70, 71, 79, 89, 93, 107
WOOLLYE: Edward, 124; Lydia, 124
WOORTHLY: John, 44
WORLEY: John, 116
WORTH: Morris, 122, 126; William, 64,

INDEX

82, 127
WORTHLEY: Elizabeth, 116, 126; John, 21, 22, 61, 71, 72, 79, 94, 109, 111, 112, 116, 126
WRIGHT: Sarah, 108; Susannah, 59, 65; Thomas, 10, 17, 65; Walter, 73; William, 108
WROMASUNG: Indian Sachem, 52

www.ingramcontent.com/pod-product-compliance
Lightning Source LLC
Chambersburg PA
CBHW080436230426
43662CB00015B/2286